Implementing Japanese AI Techniques

Turning the Tables for a Winning Strategy

Other McGraw-Hill Books of Interest

Sheldon	*Introduction to PC and MS DOS*
Girard et al.	*Building Expert Systems Using PC Shells*
Hart	*Knowledge Acquisition for Expert Systems*
Levine, Drang	*A Comprehensive Guide to AI Expert Systems*
Levine, Drang	*Neural Networks: The 2nd AI Generation*
Rolston	*Principles of AI and Expert Systems Development*
Dickinson	*Developing Quality Systems*
Modell	*A Professional's Guide to Systems Analysis*
Hwang, DeGroot	*Parallel Processing for Supercomputing and Artificial Intelligence*
Brule, Blount	*Knowledge Acquisition*
Murray, Murray	*Expert Systems in Data Processing: A Professional's Guide*
Baker	*AI with ADA*

Implementing Japanese AI Techniques

Turning the Tables for a Winning Strategy

Richard Greene

McGraw-Hill Publishing Company

New York St. Louis San Francisco Auckland Bogotá
Hamburg London Madrid Mexico Milan Montreal
New Delhi Panama Paris São Paolo
Singapore Sydney Tokyo Toronto

HF
5548.2
G6718
1990

Library of Congress Cataloging-in-Publication Data

Greene, Richard (Richard Tabor)
  Turning the tables.

  1. Business—Data processing. 2. Artificial intelligence. 3. Expert
systems (Computer science)—United States. 4. Expert systems
(Computer science)—Japan. 5. Electronic data processing—
United States. 6. Electronic data processing—Japan. I. Title.
HF5548.2.G6718 1989   650'.028'563   89-12260
ISBN 0-07-024327-1

1 2 3 4 5 6 7 8 9 0 DOCDOC 9 8 7 6 5 4 3 2 1 0

ISBN 0-07-024327-1

The editor for this book was Theron Shreve; the production supervisor was Suzanne W. Babeuf; it was set in Times Roman on the
Ventura desktop publishing system.

Printed and bound by the R. R. Donnelley & Sons Company.

For more information about other McGraw-Hill materials, call
1-800-2-MCGRAW in the United States. In other countries, call
your nearest McGraw-Hill office.

This book is dedicated to my wife
Ritsuko Watanabe Greene,
whose love it is, and to
Richard Donald Greene,
my father, whose dream it is.

Contents

Preface   xv

Part 1   **The "Engine of Automation" in Japanese
                Firms**   1

Chapter 1   **The Fundamentals**   3

                The Successful AI Program   3
                How to Measure AI Application Success   5
                The Enemy of Effective AI Application in Industry   8
                Impressions upon Returning from Japan   10
                The Concept of Competitive AI   11

Chapter 2   **The Role of Management**   15

                The Causes of "Clone" AI Programs   15
                The Meta-Cognitive Organization Theory   19
                    Socio-Technical Systems Theory   20
                    Participatory Management Theory   22
                    Primal Community Theory   22
                    Strategic Work Force Theory   23
                    Uniform Structure Community Theory   23
                    Skyblue-Collar Worker Theory   24
                    Management by Contradiction Resolution
                       Theory   25
                    Monastic Management Theory   25
                    Learning Conscious Organization Theory   26
                    Management by Events Theory   26
                    Management of Cognition Theory   28

Chapter 3 The Objectives   **29**

Learning from Japan   29
An Argument that May Doom AI in U.S.
   Companies   32
The Objectives of a Japanese-Style AI
   Application Program   37
      The Paramount Objective   37
      The Master Objectives   37
      The Competitive Objectives 37
      The Enabling Objectives   38

Chapter 4 The Japanese Way   **41**

Rational AI Implementation   41
Typical Japanese AI Projects   42
      The Robot Maintenance Campaign   42
      "No-Man" Factory Construction   42
      "No-Man" Engineering in Software Factories 43
      A New Factory Standard for AI   43
      Automobile Vending Machines   43
      The Cure for Drunk Driving in America   43
The Protestant Ethic and the Spirit of Japan   44
Implementing AI as an Organization   47
Timing Corporate Life by Companywide
   Engineering Campaigns   52
Minimizing Technology in Production   54
Disseminating Design Processes throughout a
   Work Force   56

Part 2 AI Applications and the Corporation   **61**

Chapter 5 Explaining AI to a Corporation   **63**

Initial Roles for AI in Corporations   65
      Capture of Expertise   65
      Performance Stabilization 66
      Intelligent Documentation 66
      Diagnostic Recovery   67
      Program Enhancement   67
      Cognitive Load-Lifter   68
      Knowledge Portability   68
Some Advantages Inherent with AI   69

	Simulation and Estimation	70
	AI Process Control	71
	One Data Model of the Part	72
	Process Planning	73
	Diagnosis and Recovery Procedure Design	73

Chapter 6	**Some Practical Applications**	**75**
	Preventing AI from Becoming Isolated	75
	Initial AI Application Projects	76
	Design for Assembly	77
	Simultaneous Engineering	77
	Variational Engineering	78
	Dimensional Simulation	79
	Kanban	80
	Process Inspection	80
	Generic Documentation	80
	Supplier-User Co-Design of Process/Product	81
	One Mathematical Model of the Product	81
	What AI Offers Design	82
	Enhancements to Variational Engineering	83
	Design Process Backtrack Facility	83
	Construction of Solid Models	83
	Automatic Dimensioning of Parts	84
	Self-Modifying Database	84
	Self-Tutoring Environment	85
	Shared Knowledgebase Network	85
	Evolutionary Programming	85
	Semantic Geometry: A Step Toward Intelligent Geometry	86
	Beyond Manufacturing	87
	The Business Intelligence Function	88
	Retail AI	90
	Office Work	91
	Office Networks	92

Part 3	**The AI Software Revolution**	**95**

Chapter 7	**AI and Exploratory Programming**	**97**
	Disciplined and Error-Free AI	97
	When Will Ordinary Programming Be as Exploratory as AI?	99
	AI as Defined for Businesspeople	101

Chapter 8   Goals for Artificial Intelligence   105

Artificial Intelligence and Fulfilling Expectation   105
One: The Non-Deterministic Programming
  Potential   106
Two: The Specification Programming Potential   108
Three: The Heuristic Programming Potential   108
Four: The Transparent Programming Goal   109
Five: The Level of Abstraction Programming
  Ambition   111
Six: The Machine Learning Programming Goal   113
Seven: The Logic Programming Goal   114
Eight: The Modularity Programming Goal   115
Nine: The Automated Expertise Extraction
  Programming Goal   116
Ten: The Modeling The Mind Programming Goal   117
Eleven: The User Expertise Programming Goal   119

Chapter 9   Revolutions in Programming   121

Evolutionary Programming   122
Shared Knowledgebase Networks   124
Simulation Style Program Building   125
Mental Protocol Modeling Way of
  Constructing Programs   126
Automatic Program Construction   126
Programming by Differences   127
How Corporations Can Benefit from the AI
  Revolution   127
The Genealogy of Artificial Intelligence   128
Kanban Coding   133

Chapter 10   Making AI a Reality   137

Seven Strategies for AI   137
  One: The Cognitive Strategy   137
  Two: The Software Revolution Strategy   138
  Three: The Integration Strategy   139
  Four: The Automation Strategy   139
  Five: The Reliability Strategy   141
  Six: The Electronic Manuals Strategy   141
  Seven: The Knowledge Compilation Strategy   143
AI Versus Ordinary Software   144

Relating AI to Ordinary Software in Seven Stages 147
    Stage One: Potpourri of Old Programs   147
    Stage Two: Parametric Programming   147
    Stage Three: AI Object Taxonomy Built of
      the Parametric Model   147
    Stage Four: AI Capture of Heuristic Rules   148
    Stage Five: AI as Manager of Old Programs   148
    Stage Six: AI as an Object-Oriented
      Database   148
    Stage Seven: Automatic Construction of
      New Programs   148
Overcoming Barriers   149
Standards and Dynamic Technologies   154

Part 4   **A Tri-Level Approach to AI Implementation** 159

Chapter 11   **The Aggressive AI Program**   **161**

The Seven Components of a New Technology
    Delivery System   161
The Three Sizes of Development Platforms for AI 165
Tri-Level Training Systems for New Technologies 168
Three Sources of AI Projects   170

Chapter 12   **Program Development and Corporate Polity** 175

A Three Part Development Rhythm   175
The New Authority—Meta-Polity   182

Part 5   **Computer-Integrated Manufacturing and AI** 187

Chapter 13   **New Social Systems**   **189**

Effects of Learning Properties   189
Incremental Implementation of Technologies   194
The Eight Levels of Future CIM Systems   198

Chapter 14   **Competition and Societies of Industry**   **205**

The Polis Principle   205
A Japanese Alternative for
    Computer-Integrated-Manufacturing   207

How CIM and CASTS Reshape Artificial
Intelligence   216

Part 6   Intelligent Platforms   219

Chapter 15   Establishing Platforms   221

              Types of Platforms   221
                  The Expert Dealer Sale Platform   222
                  The Expert Dealer Service Platform   222
                  The Expert Customer Product Design
                      Platform   222
                  The Expert Business Intelligence Platform   222
                  The Expert System Corporate "Spec"
                      Publisher Platform   223
                  The Expert Finance Platform   223
                  The Intelligent Document Platform   223
                  The Intelligent Text Platform   223
                  The Expert Electronic Social System
                      Platform   223
                  The Intelligent Graphics Platform   223
                  The Intelligent Software Development
                      Platform   224
                  The Intelligent Facilities Simulation
                      Platform   224
                  The Expert Real Time Process Control
                      Platform   224
                  The Expert Product Simulation Platform   224
                  The Expert Production Process Simulation
                      Platform   224
                  The Expert Training Platform   224
                  The Intelligent Interface Platform   225
              The Minimal Criteria of Platform Performance   225
              Detailed Components Lists of Some Key
                  Platforms   229
              How Platforms Affect AI Delivery   232
              How Platforms Should Be Used   233
              The Competitive Use of Platforms   234

Part 7   **Setting Up a First-Rate AI Delivery System**   **235**

Chapter 16   **The Social Delivery Vehicle**   **237**

The Three Aspects of Delivery   237
Components of a Vehicle   238
    The AI Auxiliary   239
    Application Qualification Tours   239
    AI Application Workshop Fairs   240
    Pilot Projects   242
    Tool Courses   243
    Structured Group Readings in AI   243
    Group Structured Coding Sessions   244
    AI Circles   245
    Problem Solving Events   246
    The AI Meta-Applications Group   247
    AI Application Generator Conferences   248
    Vendor Education Seminars   248
    Cognition Improvement Training   249

Chapter 17   **A New Outlook**   **251**

AI Circles Programs   251
Setting Up an AI Program   255
Theories of AI Delivery   256
An Agrarian View of Industry   259
Structural Reading   261
Change of the Cognitive Technologies   264
    Computer-Supported Cooperative Work   264
    Cognitive Measurement of Work   265
    A Neutral Cognitive Currency Across
      Disciplines   265
    Socio-Technics of Distributed Computing   265
    Cognitive Augmentation of Work   265
    Technology Transfer   266

PREFACE

This book discusses the technology of Artificial Intelligence (AI) from a business-use perspective. It explores in depth the contrasting methods that American and Japanese firms use to introduce and implement AI in the workplace.

Though the subject matter of this text is artificial intelligence, the Japanese methodologies used to introduce and implement AI can be equally applied to any new technology. These methods, which provide a consistent, thorough, competitive, and quality-conscious delivery vehicle for new technologies, are the main thrust of the book. This book, however, is not a summary of AI activities in Japan, nor is it an update on the Japanese fifth and sixth generation computer projects. Rather, it simply explains the methods which the Japanese use to promote and deliver new technologies. As American business is already aware, Japanese methodology often leads to cheaper and more thoroughly implemented technologies.

This text explains how U.S. business can best enhance and use these methods to exploit fully the business strengths unique to the West. By doing so, European and American firms have the opportunity to "out Japan" the Japanese with respect to delivering AI and thus put themselves in a better position to react quickly to any Japanese moves in the AI field.

It is easier to understand the ways the Japanese implement artificial intelligence when you consider how they introduced "kanban," Policy Deployment, Just-in-Time inventory, and quality circle disciplines into their manufacturing environment. The Japanese implemented American quality control methods (of Mssrs. Juran and Deming) years ago. American industry is finally employing these same methods with considerable success. However, Americans and Europeans consistently copy particular Japanese quality practices themselves instead of the generators of these practices. The key here is that the Americans don't distinguish "what" generated particular Japanese methods from the methods themselves. Because Americans fail to make this distinction, the Japanese continue to hold a strong market share in consumer electronics, automobiles, steel, and other industries. Copying, if it is not to be suicidal, must be accompanied by the process of copying not only particular Japanese practices, but copying the methods that generate such practices as well.

So, how does AI fare when it is exposed to Japanese methodology for introducing and implementing new technology? What is the rationale behind this system? Where did these methods originate?

What benefit can American and European firms receive by learning these Japanese techniques and theories? What new forms of artificial intelligence are Japanese methodologies discovering? Toward what ultimate roles for AI are Japanese firms gravitating? All of these questions will be answered in this book.

An ironic situation has developed. The Japanese methodology for applying artificial intelligence is surprisingly different from U.S. techniques and, oddly enough, that difference is based upon the Japanese following U.S. and European business insights for delivering new technology. In other words, the Japanese defeat their Occidental competitors by paying closer attention to American-European ideas than the Americans and Europeans do themselves. This "cognitive" dimension to Japanese competitive advantage does not occur by accident; it is planned. A fundamentally more cognitive image of a nation and a nation's industry is evolving in Japan. Japanese theorists, Swedish theorists, and some American theorists are beginning to talk of Japan as a Meta-Cognitive Nation. (The prefix "meta" denotes beyond. In this book, it refers to a turning back on oneself reflectively from a distant vantage point.) It turns out that artificial intelligence will play a major role in the achievement of Meta-Cognitive Nationhood. On a smaller scale, Meta-Cognitive Firms are now being discussed in Japan. Here, firms will participatorily manage their own psychological protocols for doing work. Just as any cognitive scientist knows, memory is essential to learning. So too, according to William Ouchi, a Professor at UCLA's Graduate School of Management, social memory is essential to societal learning. The Japanese social memory capacity of late has exceeded that of the U.S. and Europe and is a fundamental determinant in the development of the Japanese economy as a whole. So technology delivery, whether on the level of a small business or a large nation, is governed by cognitive factors of the organization performing the task delivery. This book presents the beginning of a theory of organizational cognition and illustrates how it determines the effectiveness of delivering technology. It also presents the particular constructs and tools that push organizational cognitive properties toward even more effective technology delivery.

In spite of the Japanese effectiveness, however, the West does have an advantage in implementing the Meta-Cognitive Nation and Meta-Cognitive Firm. Western Academe combines the cognitive sciences and AI, and then aligns these principles with human factors of industry. This drives Western firms rapidly toward the Meta-Cognitive Firm concept. This is occurring well before a true theory of Meta-Cognitive business performance is available. The implementation of AI itself on a businesswide scale further accelerates this trend. The possibility exists for the West to attain competitive advantage in product after product, and market after market, by accelerating these trends and fully realizing their potential for new business. This book will show how Meta-Cognition ideals generate competitive advantages from a bottom-line perspective.

Perhaps the most profound topic being debated in the world's major industrial economies is the issue of learning to benefit from technological application rather than being destroyed or distracted by it. For example, in many firms management is placing personal computers on the desks of their staff only to find later that this "new" technology is being underutilized, if utilized at all! At the same time, many companies are buying system integration services that enable more and more pieces of hardware and software to "talk" to one another. Also, recently major players in the computer market have been emphasizing computer services at the expense of computer products. It is as if the era of computer products were over and a new era of computer services had begun. How artificial intelligence will be perceived in a world where systems integration is the constraint can only be speculated. Very few companies are planning to use AI in distributed processing networks. This book discusses these issues and examines the capabilities of this new constraint set upon AI and the properties of AI and AI systems that result from applying such constraints to AI.

Independent of this integration issue, companies face heightened competition from Japan, Korea, and Taiwan. Everywhere within management staffs the same factional split is occurring: those who seek to compete by adopting lean Japanese minimalist technology tactics in conflict with those who seek to compete by "out-automating" the Japanese. So, in addition to restating the function of AI from a distributed computing network perspective, the role of AI must be rearticulated from a lean Japanese-style business perspective. Which methods of AI implementation and which application phases are consistent with lean production and design systems? This book will give a detailed portrait of this type of role for AI which spares it from becoming a victim of the escalating argument between the "leans" and the "automates" in firms confronted with Oriental competition.

This book does not define Artificial Intelligence. There are numerous articles in the popular business press and excellent introductory books like David King's *EXPERT SYSTEMS* and Rex Maus' *EXPERT SYSTEMS APPLICATIONS AND TOOLS* available to the reader. Rather, this book demonstrates how to implement the new technology. Since AI is a Cognitive Technology, it may be applied everywhere expertise and other computer programs are found. AI is an intimate technology that "mines the minds" of people in an organization and, as a result, it is more difficult to grasp than some other recent technologies (such as machine vision). Moreover, because work around the world is becoming more intellectually intense, AI's ultimate role and importance is vastly underestimated while at the same time its difficulty is overestimated. Indeed, most American firms are designing their AI implementation systems based on information appearing in the media. Hundreds of firms are spending millions of dollars to copy what others have already done and none of them gain the least competitive advantage. The Japanese find this "copy cat" mentality of American management laughable and counterproductive, for they build in competitive advantage from the very inception of their AI programs. This book shows how the Japanese achieve this ability to compete from the outset.

This book also explores how AI fits into the overall strategic posture of the firm, as well as the ways its applications must be shaped to enable the firm to respond successfully to new challenges and situations. An AI delivery vehicle that can be subsequently used with minimal modification for the delivery of other new technologies is described. A firm can achieve greater efficiency and effectiveness when successive technologies are delivered by a consistent delivery vehicle over a period of time. This way, the firm can learn through experience the effectiveness of its delivery techniques and find ways to improve and enhance the delivery of other technologies in general. A few major American firms are attempting this efficient delivery of technology which amounts to an automation of the automation process itself. This process creates formal structures at every level of the firm that transform present technologies into future ones. Present social systems that surround and support current technologies are then shaped into new social constructs to support the new technologies. Management itself splits into two distinct entities: maintenance management, dedicated to the optimization of learning and gaining experience with existing technical commitments, and transition management, dedicated to incremental evolution into new technical systems.

Finally, there are those who so blindly believe in the inevitability of Yankee ingenuity that they deny any indication that the ultimate direction of economic and technical creativity might be drifting across the Pacific. These technical fundamentalists, hoping and praying that innovation will save the pre-eminence of the U.S. economy, forget one thing: it takes money to innovate. As the money streams to the Orient to take advantage of the favorable business conditions (thereby creating profits for Japan, Korea, Singapore, Taiwan, and Hong Kong), innovation follows. If the American and European economies hope to innovate, they will need money.

The Origin Of This Book

This book originated through anxiety, opportunity and experimentation, and observation. After spending nearly a decade in Japan, I experienced anxiety during my first few months back in the States. In Japan I worked for several of the largest and most profitable firms. Once back in America, I observed many firms attempting to copy Japanese ways. However, these firms were implementing Japanese methods just as inefficiently as they had implemented the ones being replaced. The U.S. firms were headed in the right direction, but they failed to understand fully those aspects of Japanese businesses they sought to duplicate. This in turn led to superficial, poorly implemented technologies which in no way would give these firms any competitive edge whatsoever. American technology was becoming mired in lost opportunity: the failure to implement efficiently U.S. systems and the failure to implement correctly Japanese systems.

Strangely, amidst these double failures, I sensed a change in the most fundamental requisite of competitive advantage — the desire for victory. Before my stay in Japan, every person I had known in the United States had made improving his personal lifestyle his number one objective. But upon returning, I could sense a new undercurrent: people were motivated by something more than the acquisition of possessions. There was a recognition of the need for a national rather than individual effort. It was precisely this kind of effort that launched Japan on her journey to economic development. This less egocentric outlook can have far greater impact than any new method or technique, and it is a very encouraging sign for the United States.

Finally, I had the opportunity to conduct an experiment at General Motors Electronic Data Systems (GM/EDS) where I was able to test Japanese systems of delivering new technology in a U.S. industrial environment. It was my job to deliver artificial intelligence. After making certain modifications for use in the United States corporate environment, I implemented Japanese delivery tactics. The GM/EDS workplace was an ideal testing ground for implementing the Japanese theories of technology delivery which I had learned and used in some of Japan's very best firms. For instance, there were six groups competing for AI application projects when I was hired. When I finished, there were only two, and their applications were ultimately welded into one detailed and well-articulated corporate AI strategy. During this time I saw how well my Japanese-derived implementation strategies worked relative to real and serious tactics of competitor groups. Since then, I have consulted with several American and Canadian firms on AI projects, and in most of these firms I have conducted other small scale experiments. Some of these experiments rapidly evolved along more aggressive lines than my work at GM. This book summarizes these experiences too, since the same Japanese delivery tactics were used in each instance.

An Edge-Of-Field Bias To The Book's Content

Before writing this book, I had to decide how to handle the proprietary information about the AI programs in which I had been involved. In Japan I had designed initial AI programs, and in the U.S. and Canada I had consulted or managed AI programs. Preliminary phone calls to the companies involved revealed no "permission to publish" would be forthcoming for anything except the imitative and non-innovative aspects of their programs. Anything unique to the firm and, hence, most of my contributions, would be denied publishing rights. That left me to publish an authoritative book on the aspects of AI applications which everyone in America was already doing, or I could publish an edge-of-field book heavily encumbered with deliberate disguise to safeguard corporate secrets. As the lesser of two evils, I chose the latter. I hope readers will concur with my choice. I have made every effort to conceal the origin and place of use of each AI application technique discussed, and my remarks have been cross-checked with what has already been published. Most of the charts and diagrams used in the book combine entities from several companies into one overall coherent model. As a result, the portrait of AI that emerges is probably of a more comprehensive and aggressive magnitude than any single example. This approach provides one integrated picture of a general, coherent implementation strategy for any new technology.

Inherent Difficulties Finding The Edge-Of-Field In Japan

In Japan, modesty is almost always used as a political tactic — it is a "Lao-tsu" vacuum tactic. That is, by denigrating yourself excessively, you can provoke the other person into praising you, the way that a vacuum, with no power of its own, draws things its way with its own nothingness. Unfortunately, many Westerners in Japan, unattuned to the cultural differences, can't realize that modest statements about Japanese AI technology don't even begin to tell the whole story.

It takes a good six or seven years to penetrate deeply into Japan's best firms to learn how they generate successive winning systems such as Just in Time and Policy Deployment. Because AI is a newer technology, it is hard to pinpoint the origin of a firm's strategic decisions about its use. Furthermore, Japan is not a society given to abstract theorizing about its actions. Hence, I had to translate nontheoretical commitments to certain practices into terms, new both in Japan and in the United States, that nevertheless accurately capture new forms of handling technology in Japan. As a result, this book may surprise and astonish Japanese readers who have been employing most of the methods described in this book, but who may have lacked the terminology to articulate precisely what it is they were doing.

The Western Phenomenon Of Ignoring Japanese Competition

An unfortunate phenomenon occurs when Westerners travel to Japan. Instead of appreciating the unique aspects of Oriental culture, many express a wish for Westernization to overtake the country. Frankly, many Westerners are scared by the prospect of another way to do things. They stubbornly cling to the notion that their way is best, although Western academic theories are far from infallible. In fact, some of these theories do not fare well in the face of contradicting Japanese data. For example, many Westerners feel threatened by the Japanese lifetime employment system and almost hope that it dies. The academics in the West research the minor difficulties of the system and make dire predictions. These predictions have appeared with monotonous regularity for the past forty years. Like any system, the lifetime employment system has faced difficulties, but it has not conveniently disappeared, nor is it expected to soon.

Some Westerners take another approach. They point out that the lifetime employment system covers up the fact that the Japanese labor force is composed of part-timers and subcontractors crushed under the heel of industrial domination. They make the unique aspects of Japan's industrial system into an elite anomaly in a basically oppressive social substratum. Those who come up with this clever argument certainly deserve an "A" for effort.

While lifetime employment may be legally enforced in the big Japanese firms, it is socially enforced as a norm and an ethic in all other Japanese businesses. To illustrate, the owner of the tiniest sushi shop in Japan, when forced by declining business to lay off a cook, spends months phoning every person he knows to find his cook another position. As soon as his business picks up, he will rehire his cook. He will even go so far as to arrange for his relatives to give his displaced worker discounts and other in-kind services. Westerners confuse the legally guaranteed practice with Japan's standard social practices and thereby exhibit their own societal neuroses.

Therefore, while I was in Japan, I was determined to use Japanese conceptual axes of explanation and suppress Western ways of thinking. I hope to capture not just overt Japanese techniques, but the mental underpinnings that gave birth to their techniques. I wanted access to the minds of upper middle management that produced these Japanese post-War business methods. I found a number of major differences in conceptual axes almost immediately. For example, everything I had read stated that the major difference between Japanese and American unions was that the Americans had industrial unions whereas the Japanese had company unions. The "major difference" was something else entirely. Japanese union leaders pointed out that their unions contained both white- and blue-collar workers. The combined talents of these two groups provided superior resources for research, education, and technical training which are, for the most part, completely unavailable to American unions at any price.

Perspectives On Technology Delivery

My background furnished me with four helpful screens for viewing and understanding Japanese phenomena. First, almost twenty years ago I graduated from MIT, concentrating on writing computer programs in LISP that counted and named the main points in passages of text. That meant that upon arriving in Japan, I knew enough of the origins of AI first hand to see the difference between contemporary applications and the revolutionary aims of AI. Also, building AI expert systems in Japan, it turned out, was an excellent way to model Japanese minds.

Second, I spent eight years in a management consulting company staffed entirely by a religious order — the Institute of Cultural Affairs (ICA) and the Ecumenical Institute (EI) in Chiago. The disciplines and methods of that monastic order were excellent preparation for dealing with Japanese industrial management styles and intents. Conversely, Japanese management styles were excellent remedies for major flaws in ICA and EI theory and practice. The ICA and EI were the most participatory organizations I could find anywhere, but their tactics led to one of the common failings of participation programs. They were so engrossed in their own tactical system implementation theories that they failed to put these theories in action. Somehow this conceptual cop-out was all too typical of American society and I went to Japan to find the solution — and it was there. It turned out that the methods used by religious orders to manage people and their behavior were analogous to the Japanese methods. Further, my job at ICA was to manage the psychological protocols of all 2,000 members of the order. This, combined with protocol analysis from AI, gave me methods for transcribing Japanese protocols of meeting, deciding, and designing.

Third, I spent some time setting up participatory management programs in America just before leaving for Japan. Upon arriving in Japan, I found my U.S. credentials did not translate well. It was up to me to develop new credentials in Japan. To do this, I applied American management-participation methods to over a dozen Japanese towns, businesses, and government offices. What an amazing learning experience! The American methods produced very peculiar results in Japan. For example, in a town meeting workshop where ordinary citizens design various urban programs, people in the United States would eagerly support their own positions so that the workshop leader got a variety of ideas by going from person to person. In the same workshop in Japan, the first person asked to express an opinion whispered to the person next to him and a whole stream of whispering ensued until finally, the oldest person seated cleared his throat and announced some basic feeling about the issue. The person originally asked then parroted what the elder had just said and each Japanese in turn said essentially the same thing. Instead of fifty different answers from fifty different people as in America, there was one answer from all fifty people.

I was invited to design workshop procedures for an eight hundred person Venture Business Valley Development Consult in an area of Japan undergoing industrial re-entrenchment. My efforts produced fourteen business plans, six of which became viable businesses in later years. These and other activities produced Japanese press coverage that became my Japanese credentials and brought me to the attention of some of the leading firms. This enabled me to observe how democracy, participation, autonomy, and similar concepts were implemented differently in Japan.

Applying AI In Different Types Of Firms

To gather data on AI application in Japan, I needed wide exposure to business and industry. Through a leading brain surgeon, I was introduced to the directors of the Sekisui Chemical Company, Japan's leading plastic producer. This company, representing an old, mature industry, was an amazing showcase of Japanese creativity and innovation. Among other things, Sekisui Chemical had two subsidiaries, Sekisui Heim and Sekisui House, that were pioneering the mass production of custom houses based on a modular construction concept. This allows a housewife, tired of her old living room wall, to order a new one and get it delivered and installed the same afternoon. These mature industries are eagerly transforming themselves into new industries and provided a good place to start learning about Japanese methods, their origins, and their implications for using AI.

Also, I managed to get hired by a "sunrise" industry, Matsushita Electric Industrial Co. Ltd's Wireless Research Lab. At the time I was hired, that lab had six hundred of the most productive human beings on the planet. They excelled in sales per employee as well as net revenue per unit equity per employee. It is not an overstatement to say that three of my product innovations are directly attributed to the routine, everyday culture of that lab. It changed my life. The intense daily innovative chatter of the lab surpassed anything I had known in comparable labs in the United States.

Both Sekisui and Matsushita are immense firms employing hundreds of thousands. Taiyo Kogyo, with its five hundred employees, a much smaller firm in comparison, makes giant tents, artificial mountains, and artificial undersea reefs — all of fabric. Small as it is, it has a world class research and development operation. On the Taiyo Kogyo chairman's office wall is a photo and description of every single employee in the firm. As employees are moved or promoted, the chairman switches their pictures accordingly. The chairman's outlook symbolizes the concern company management has for its people.

I arrived in Japan with the notion that it was not an innovative country, that it mostly copied other countries' inventions. But this notion just did not agree with what I was actually experiencing: intense daily innovation, invention, product design, and marketing tactic trials. In the public sector I worked with the staff of Osaka Medical School, Japan's leading medical school. Typically it admits many of the top twenty students in all of Japan each year. In cramped old quarters, doctors who spend a full day taking care of patients devote an additional six hours to research at night. Much of this research is on the cutting edge of medicine. Many of the doctors I worked with spent seven days a week there. One of my students won the Mayo Clinic's prize for best research during his stay there. It is too simple to throw up your hands and ask why clever methods are needed when there are people willing to work that hard. But people with this attitude miss the point. Hard-working people are central to the issue. The book is not about clever methods or techniques. It is, however, about getting people to work hard. It is about how to motivate people to work for something more intangible but no less important than their individual self-betterment. It is about making each structure in a company push its people beyond their own lifestyle absorption. And, most importantly, it is about doing all this fairly and not merely as a ploy to make senior management look good. There is an essential requirement for competitive implementation of a new technology: once that new technology is in place, the people who implemented it work just as hard as those Japanese doctors. There is simply no way for a firm to be competitive without total employee commitment. A firm cannot compete "worklessly."

Efforts Toward a Motivated High Tech Delivery

The willingness to work comes through motivation. Americans often compete by demoralizing and destroying one another in their quest to attain personal success (sometimes at the expense of the projects on which they worked). The connection between motivating people and delivering artificial intelligence may appear remote at the moment. The connection will become clearer in later chapters where it will be shown how AI proceeds along a distinctive path in Japan because the people who deliver it are motivated differently than their American counterparts.

While setting up AI programs under Japanese management, I observed a new form of AI evolving. Using Japanese methods to deliver AI to the United States (and later, Canada), I discovered amplifications of Japanese methods in new, more innovative Western management directions. The resulting hybrid fuses elements from Japan and the West. This book presents the fusion of American and Japanese techniques for developing AI programs and delivering them (as well as other new technologies) to the workplace. In this case, the whole is greater than the sum of its individual parts and promises to improve industry everywhere.

Implementing Japanese AI Techniques

Turning the Tables for a Winning Strategy

1

The "Engine of Automation" in Japanese Firms

"Priore and Sabel (1984) have recently argued that the "crisis" in U.S. manufacturing stems from industry in this country having grown too wedded to rigid mass-production technologies, while other countries—Japan, in particular—have developed systems of "flexible specialization" that do not tie product design, marketing strategy, and organizational form so closely to the dictates of technology. A historical reason for this tendency may be the greater legacy in U.S. job and organizational designs of the Scientific Management movement, which pressed for maximal fit between the social organization of the factory and the rhythms and flows of its technical operations (Cole,1979)."

Lincoln, J. H.; Hanada, M.; McBride, K.; "Organizational Structures in Japanese and U.S. Manufacturing;" *Administrative Science Quarterly*, vol. 31; no. 3/338-508; September 1986; p. 362.

New technologies are delivered to the workplace in Japan differently than in the United States. The delivery of artificial intelligence is no exception. The who, what, where, when, why, and how of Japanese AI delivery are simply performed in other ways. Yet, in spite of these dissimilarities, the Japanese principles of delivering technology can be applied just as successfully in the United States. Indeed, many delivery techniques have already been applied in at least one major corporate AI program. The results of these applications are pretty impressive from both cost-benefit and strategic advantage perspectives.

The chapters that follow explain differences in delivery techniques and how America can gain competitive advantage by following Japanese methodologies. In particular, a general machinery which Japanese firms use to deliver successive new technologies, including AI, will be illustrated completely.

1

The Fundamentals

The Successful AI Program

What does a successful AI program look like? The answer depends upon initial expectations. Within a year of implementation, an evaluation of its performance should be made based on actual performance in contrast with initial expectations. The accomplishments would naturally take a position alongside certain trade-off dimensions: social versus technical implementation, conservative versus venturesome implementation, and elite versus participatory implementations. The inclusion or exclusion of specific poles and axes would indicate the scope of the imagination with which one entered the initial AI program.

Why portray an example of a successful AI program at all? Artificial intelligence has uncovered the immense importance of the human ability to make estimates and how this behavior ultimately relates to design, decision and optimal work. Estimating is the kind of heuristic, qualitative reasoning that gets you near an answer and tells you enough about an outcome to let you know whether you want to pursue it to its conclusion. The image a firm has of "successful AI programs" and adequate "first year accomplishments in AI application" will almost entirely determine what is actually accomplished. Furthermore, cultures and nations have their own images of what constitutes a successful AI program. When some nations have higher expectations for AI, the presence of differing images becomes a live issue. When some business cultures maintain profound and challenging images of program success, foreign competitors lose heart and the will to win. These vague, undefined images of shared success in individuals, in workgroups, in firms and in national economies often determine the outcome of overall AI implementation.

Peruse, then, the following mandate of first year accomplishments for an American AI program and see if these accomplishments and ideals are in keeping with your own expectations.

1. Creating an AI development environment using 386PC and Sun workstations for AI application. (This approach is accomplished at one-tenth the cost of programs using more costly hardware and software yet performs 80% of the work of these more expensive machines.)
2. Defining 46 expert systems projects in six divisions of a corporation, prompting the consideration of using current divisional funding in a quarter of the projects defined.
3. Implementing a nine course knowledge engineer training program (including instruction for the training faculty).
4. Obtaining a $5 million government contract for advanced AI text platform construction on engineering workstations.
5. Establishing AI consultations for five companies outside the current company of hire.
6. Negotiating contracts for $4.5 million to be used for eleven expert system projects.
7. Designing and implementing a "self-compiling" expertise strategy constructed to train ordinary engineers in AI and thereby eliminate expensive knowledge engineers.
8. Establishing a pilot division and a pilot AI function at that division with $5 million written into an annual budget (at $1 million per year) for AI CAD applications at that division.
9. Establishing a fourteen component "Social Delivery Vehicle" to automate the delivery of AI and successive technologies.
10. Applying software integration to AI so that an expert platform results allowing a shared knowledgebase network among several sites to replace what otherwise would be scattered, separate expert systems. This amounts to computer supported cooperative work forms of AI.
11. Implementing a "Meta-Application Center" for early commercialization of AI (before such tools are made expensive by venture businesses getting hold of them) by applying cognitive modeling tools of university psychology departments. This center also replicates small AI project victories into dozens of similar applications projects within weeks.

12. Defining corporate strategy for AI implementation and securing approval from all divisions of the corporation.
13. Using AI as a "Cognitive Delivery Vehicle" for other technologies through experiments in publishing engineering specifications in AI rule form.
14. Organizing AI workshops for 750 managers and over 55 AI vendors.
15. Funding "Intelligent Geometry AI platforms"—These applications use workstations that are network connected.
16. Creating AI application groups.
17. Completing one AI project within four months of start.
18. Developing an advanced variational engineering AI graphics platform.

This is an impressive mandate indeed. Let's say that to accomplish all the above the resources at your disposal were the following:

1. One person with 23 years of AI experience.
2. Three very bright recent college graduates with little AI knowledge or expertise.
3. An overall budget of absolutely zero (except for free travel within the organization), a single microcomputer and limited general office services.

Considering the paucity of resources, fulfilling the mandate would be truly impressive. This scenario actually occurred in a U.S. firm where credit for success goes to the firm itself, its astute, visionary management and its devoted development team. Credit also goes to the methods employed to promote and deliver AI to the corporation. As you continue reading, you will learn how these accomplishments were achieved using certain Japanese principles and constructs for delivering new technologies.

How to Measure AI Application Success

There are several ways to gauge the success of an AI program. A successful program helps a firm resist the onslaught of Japanese competition. On a national scale, it diminishes the trade imbalance that now exists between Japan and the United States. Additionally, AI contributes to the firm's bottom line. The extent of AI's contribution to the profit picture depends upon the manner in which it was implemented. Instead of these robust criteria of success, many firms default to savings. The savings that AI brings to the organization can be measured. This category, savings, needs elaboration. Corporations labor under the misconception that new technologies and methods justify themselves solely because of the (supposed) savings they generate. Projects are approved or shelved based on estimated savings. But decision making practices are often flawed for several reasons:

1. Those performing the estimates are those who want funding for the project. They obviously possess a biased point of view.
2. Usually only the literal project costs are estimated. (Omitted are the transition costs of switching from the old system to the new; the costs of training workers to handle the new technology; the social costs of doing things by impersonal equipment and systems rather than by social arrangements of human beings; the costs of monitoring the new technology and bringing it to a high level of excellence; and the costs of getting the technology and other relevant new programs and changes in the workplace to mutually support each other. New technology and other changes must co-evolve so that incompatibility and other system troubles do not appear later.)
3. Seldom are studies conducted to determine if the projected savings will be large enough to help the firm compete effectively.
4. Absent is an accounting system to indicate whether the implemented technology realized its potential to save the firm money based on the preliminary estimates.

There are unhappy results when these flaws are present: No one manages and disciplines the technology once it is in place to insure it performs year after year in a way that it contributes most fully to the overall competitiveness of the firm. (In Japanese companies, during the final stages of implementing a new technology, the committee that designed the technology is formed again to guarantee that the projected revenue earnings and savings will be realized. In addition to this Meta-Application group, there are other corporate constituencies involved in the design of technology implementation. They enforce the constraints and purposes of technology delivery system decisions.)

Two flaws have significant importance. First is the failure to measure AI application success against the firm's overall competitive situation. And second is the general lack of an enforcement mechanism to make sure that the projected "savings" which justified undertaking the project in the first place are actually realized upon project completion. To Americans, this sounds like an inflexible attitude that hinders innovation, but that is precisely the point. Japan closely scrutinizes all new technologies and as a result gets leaner and more productive implementations. American firms, on the other hand, leave technologies untouched far too long and adopt a wait-and-see posture rather than plunging right in.

The Japanese exploit this difference; their firms formulate and plan new technology introduction with far more work force participation than U.S. and European firms. With a large percentage of workers involved in new technology introduction, major constituencies are created around particular design and delivery decisions. These supporters remain in place years after project implementation. T y remember why particular design and delivery decisions were made in the beginning and they enforce these values and alternatives. (These values later have significant bearing when the technology matures.) This constitutes a "social memory" property of the organization which is essential to insure that the organization enforces the values created in the formulative stages of new technology introduction. This analysis represents an evaluation of new technology application from the viewpoint of a firm's needs. There is another dimension of the evaluation of new technology implementations that often is confused with the preceding example. The other dimension concerns categories of functioning that are necessary for the effective delivery of the new technology.

The economics, politics, culture, and foundation of the new technology delivery system must be examined. The economics include the resources necessary for its delivery, the mechanisms needed for its production, the system for its distribution and application, and its productivity contribution to the firm. The politics are the orderly principles for handling the technology, a system of just participation and procedures for making decisions, a clearly delineated opportunity space for the new technology to operate in without being asked to do things only mature technologies can do, and an anticipation system that adjusts the technology to reflect future developments. The culture section includes the development of the actual skills for delivering and working with the technology, the styles developed in the program, the symbolic meaning the program and its people take on within the organization, and the plurality of tactics and understandings about the technology fostered by the program. Finally the foundation of the technology liberates the firm from old techniques and involves parts of the firm in venturesome activity. With the new technology, the workers cause historic change and witness the beginning of new and unexpected technological accomplishments for the firm. What is more, they have the satisfaction of having worked hard.

The Enemy of Effective AI Application in Industry

Current methods of AI application in U.S. industry stem from its origins in the Defense Advanced Research Projects Agency (DARPA). This agency of the Department of Defense funds edge-of-field research that might be of value to the military. Briefly, the AI that emerged from DARPA laboratories featured expensive, incompatible, and inflexible systems. This style of technology application is highly inappropriate for use in industry, but unfortunately, the DARPA legacy lives on. (This is not to say that DARPA is not good at innovation—it is—but it does not socialize what it invents to productive values.)

I surveyed sixteen American companies implementing AI and all of them followed the "Naive AI Scenario" described here. A company decides to implement AI and hires a bright, young college graduate with an advanced degree in computer science/AI. Soon after, a manager approaches the new employee and says, "You need something to work on, don't you? Make me a list of the hardware and software you want us to order for you." The juvenile "AI Einstein" asks for a Symbolics 3600 machine ($95,000 per single user workstation) and KEE software (over $60,000 per single user license). This totals to more than $150,000 per workstation and the manager can't help but wonder how this prohibitively expensive technology will ever spread throughout the company. The new employee, of course, does not wonder. After all, while in college, research was performed using KEE software running on a Symbolics machine; why waste all that training and experience learning how to use new software and hardware? The young novice, however, does not understand certain aspects of business accounting policy—in particular how these systems are financed. Vendors donate hardware and software to colleges, but they are not quite so generous to companies. Moreover, the luxury of working on AI environments and tools vastly more complex than the problems to be solved cannot be tolerated in industry. In reality, vast AI environments and tools generate more error per line of written code than COBOL, previously the most error prone computer production language. And, since it takes so long to learn vast AI environments and tools, companies could be faced with years of mistake-laden programming from their AI development teams. These people could, for all intents and purposes, be lost in an elaborate AI jungle which they unfailingly believe is the only way to implement AI techniques. The argument is made that an expensive development system creates the software which then runs on cheap workstations. However, one of AI's important benefits is its capability of permitting end users to modify software. Therefore, end users need code development capability. Also, 80386 hardware and Sun 4's are so fast that development work can easily be done on PC's instead of expensive LISP machines.

In America, hundreds of companies today follow this very scenario. Because there is no one in the firm who has a practical working knowledge of AI, it is assumed that the young and inexperienced student will lead the way. The situation is totally different in Japan where new employees are first socialized in the firm's values and strategies in intense initiate training programs. So, too, Japanese firms adapt new technologies to their values, tactics and strategies. A typical Japanese firm stresses that every person can use AI, that all programs in the firm can benefit from AI and that AI can be developed and delivered for less than $10,000 per workstation. This philosophy enhances the application and implementation of AI across the Japanese corporation. Conversely, American and European firms turn to AI "professionals" to provide their management with fundamental assumptions about AI technology and its delivery potential. This relinquishment of management input and control to the naive AI professionals weakens the economic and competitive effectiveness of the new technology and gives decision making responsibility to persons who are generally ignorant of the needs of the firm.

The best firms in both Japan and America hire the same intelligent graduates, but in Japan, instead of giving these individuals a carte blanche for ordering machinery, firms provide these new developers with systems appropriate to the task. For example, the new employee might end up with OPS2000 ($250) talking with PROGENESIS ($1,000) and running this enhanced software on a 80286PC ($2,000). Both OPS2000 and PROGENESIS are latest generation "embedded AI" languages. AI features are imbedded in ordinary language syntax, all written in C running under UNIX 5.3. For $5,250 retail, the Japanese have a development environment achieving 80% of what some American firms achieve for a $150,000 investment. In addition, they get enormous benefits beyond the mere AI features available. Competitive rivals who unwisely develop applications on a platform cost ratio of $150,000 : $5,250 (a negative 30-fold disadvantage) can be put out of business in short order. Once U.S.

firms realize that bigger does not necessarily imply better, they will be ready to wisely implement AI systems that are genuinely suited to their needs.

Impressions upon Returning from Japan

The first thing I noticed was the imitative nature of AI application programs in the United States. I found hundreds of firms, each of them spending millions of dollars, and not one of them is gaining any competitive advantage. Next, I was surprised to find that technology in this country is controlled by professionals and not firms. Again and again, young and inexperienced employees were put in charge of major technology application decisions. I found that American managers had little knowledge of the new technology. In the belief that "a manager can manage anything," they had participated in a few AI seminars and then set about delivering AI—often with sad results. Finally, I discovered that the people working on hardware and software were more interested in esoteric research than trying to find suitable industrial applications for AI.

In this country, the overall consensus was that AI could be applied to anything, no matter how poor, counterproductive or misguided the application. While this enthusiasm is fine, an overall trivialization of quality causes companies to lower their technological sights. This in turn produces a generation of people with unambitious and unstrategic assumptions about AI technology. U.S. firms proudly announce trivial AI applications as major breakthroughs. Ph.D's report on easy AI projects that high school educated blue-collar workers have already accomplished in Japan. As a result, a competence gap emerges between university level AI applications and trivial business AI applications.

The exclusiveness of AI application in the U.S. overwhelmed me. A firm creates an AI group and gives it a budget. Soon this group produces various projects. Articles describing the projects are written and reported upon at conferences for AI developers. Suddenly there is a whole AI subworld created within the firm possessing political strength, budget clout, and its own lingo and mores. This technological fiefdom is guarded by project professionals who prevent the technology from becoming part of the mainstream corporate strategy.

I was amazed by the inability of firms to understand the major cost, competitive and product-feature benefits that AI could achieve for them. I heard people say things like, "AI is a new technology; it is good. New technology helps the firm. Most uses of new technology are probably powerful. New technologies are still untested so it can't be known which applications are best. New software will be better than old software." These shibboleths were believed unquestioningly—without evidence, study or detective work. Somehow, no one performed the hardthinking essentials necessary to build a good business case. Blind faith was operative here—or perhaps sheer laziness on the part of middle management. There is a religion in U.S. firms whose god is "Progress" and anything new is regarded as "Progress." No matter how many times new hardware had been delivered only to make things more expensive and more liable to error, nobody bothered to analyze the new technology to see which of its infinite profitable and competitive uses could actually help meet real needs of the firm today. The exclusive nature of AI program implementation in the U.S. today discourages this bottom line analysis.

Like other new technologies, AI application in America is enmeshed in careerism. Although Japanese employees are every bit as competitive as their Western counterparts (perhaps even more so), the nature of Japanese organizations mitigates career aspirations and produces objectivity about new technology's overall contribution to the business. This type of cooperation is not seen in American firms where factions fight to control AI application. Managers who have been assigned boring, mundane tasks might be "given" AI as compensation. Therefore, any AI projects, no matter how trivial, are reported in academic papers so that AI staffers can pad their credentials and embellish their resumes. Budding AI groups actively discourage the firm from hiring people truly competent in AI who might show them up. Compared to Japanese firms, American firms employ very few checks on individual career ambitions which are often at odds with the good of the company.

The Concept of Competitive AI

Competitive factors are an integral part of all AI programs. From their inception, aggressive AI programs have built-in tactics that not only imitate but defeat the programs of competitors. Most firms just beginning their AI application programs generously allow themselves to go through an initial learning phase with the technology. During this period, they break no new ground and merely duplicate other people's work. They delude themselves by thinking that at some later point the learning phase will be over and then competitive advantage can be sought. In reality, if competitive advantage is not pursued in the early start-up years, the very thought of a competitive and profitable program becomes a threat to those who wish unconstrained forgiving play with the technology. They end up defending their learning-phase style AI from competitiveness itself! These people shield themselves from the realities of the business world by presenting the same tiresome, invalid argument that AI is "new." The fact is, American and European industry cannot afford to wait.

There is even a more important point to be made about AI. If, as in Japan's best firms, there is a long-term, consistent delivery vehicle for implementing new technologies, then the quality with which AI is delivered can be compared to the quality of delivery of other technologies like machine vision, robots, and automatic guided vehicles. This basis of comparison can make AI competitive in a new sense. No longer will AI be examined solely for content but also for the quality of implementation and delivery.

In contrast with Japanese methods, American firms delegate creation of new projects to plant managers which in turn leads to each manager completing individual projects and agenda. Ultimately, there is almost no way to directly compare performances. In Japanese firms, there is a consensus at the top: all managers across the firm follow the same plan. Because the projects are fixed and virtually the same for all plant managers, the major criterion considered for promotion is the competency with which a manager implements an assignment. Not surprisingly, Japanese firms excel at implementing new ideas. AI, like other new and unfamiliar technologies, will languish in European and American firms for years as a vague, undefined entity with no clear cut consensus for its implementation. Eventually, an internal interest group will form around AI to actually discourage its implementation because of the threat innovative AI poses to the present and safe order. This group may impede its delivery in order to monopolize expertise. However, if the firm has a tradition of comparing various implementations of high technologies, AI is spared from mishandling. Its implementation is closely scrutinized.

A kind of "schizophrenic" AI implementation is needed to achieve competitiveness. Dividing implementation tactics into two distinct sets is required from the outset of the application program. The first set of tactics is conservative. It is conceded that the firm does not fully understand the new technology and that the technology itself is not yet mature. The firm imitates the best examples available and takes small, incremental steps as the technology becomes more familiar. The second set of tactics pursues an aggressive course. The firm is aware that merely copying others will never lead to any kind of competitive advantage. Therefore, everything copied is in some small way modified in directions of possible improvement. There are experiments with these modifications to locate avenues of advantage. A library of work, sole property of the firm, is compiled for publication only after attaining several generations of successful improvements. Too often each inconsequential increment is publicized for no other reason than beefing up the resumes of the AI staff.

A split cognition approach corresponds to this split implementation approach. If a firm is content to let knowledge of AI reside in the profession—journals and seminars—rather than in the firm itself, then it develops no intellectual capital in the new technology. By settling for the lowest common industrial denominator of AI expectations, attempted applications never rise above the industrial norm. If, however, the firm encourages and develops its own imaginative AI resources beyond what is available from seminars and the press, then intellectual and competitive advantage can and will evolve.

Of course, a company must have confidence to set as its goal the surpassing of norms in a technological field. Many American (as well as some Japanese) companies have a stagnant, corporate culture that says, "Industry norm is the best we can obtain." Such firms, while not dead, are certainly moribund. Anything more than a small accident or financial loss will knock them out of the competition. Along similar lines, newly hired AI people will resist when asked to exceed the accepted norms of their field. They may resort to talking to management in technical and obscure jargon and rely upon the "mystery" of their science to prevent their performance from being judged by competitive AI criteria. Companies, then, are faced with socializing new employees into this "schizophrenic" implementation system.

2

The Role of Management

The Causes of "Clone" AI Programs

This "clone" syndrome is not just a phenomenon of AI; it pervades the American technological scene. It has led to a decline in the ways the U.S. utilizes its technology. To remain (or even become) competitive it is imperative that industry be aware of the problem.

"Clone" AI programs share several detrimental characteristics:

1. Delayed innovation—Only after a feature is in general usage does the firm incorporate it into its own technology programs.
2. Lowest common denominator—Entire industries decide what is acceptable performance for new technology (generally what is the most simple and least controversial) rather than what is best.
3. Lost competitive advantage—Copying competitors never leads to innovation needed for gaining a competitive edge.
4. Uncritically evaluated implementation—The indiscriminate copying of competitors includes borrowing the bad ideas along with the good.

The cause of the "clone" syndrome in U.S. firms is purely psychological. There is an inherent timidity in management styles which is easily seen by examining the way major corporations manage AI. The conventional program utilizes the following criteria:

1. First, appoint a generalist manager with no background in AI as project leader.
2. Send that manager to executive seminars on AI.
3. Give that manager an in-house training budget for all of the development staff and end users.
4. Develop the AI program with the "newly-acquired" knowledge combined with generalist management capabilities.

The myth that a manager, despite a total lack of knowledge of a new technology, can himself train to do anything in ten easy lessons, dies hard in America. We confidently blunder ahead and hope for the best. On the other hand, some European countries (who outperform Americans in per capita income, wealth, and exports) develop managers with an in-depth understanding of the technology in the fields they manage. The Japanese carry this even further by developing the entire work force into tens of thousands of engineers, each of whom has the responsibility to experiment with the new technology as part of his daily job. In both of these instances, the myth that "a manager can teach himself anything" does not operate. The Japanese are famous for their generalist managers who, unlike their U.S. equivalents, rely heavily on lower level technical people for information. The U.S. manager, after a few seminars, thinks his knowledge matches or even surpasses that of his technical people and rarely solicits their advice.

The belief that "a manager can teach himself anything" results in insecurity. Managers who are forced to pretend that they have an indepth understanding of thirty years of AI work after only a superficial introduction have no choice but to minimize the sophistication of the AI projects they initiate. All projects performed are at the managers' limited level of technical understanding. They cautiously select projects to implement and then move at a tortoise-like pace into the various areas of AI. This lackluster style of implementation permeates the firm's entire AI program. Major AI paybacks, attained only when a much bolder course is taken, are largely ignored.

The unfortunate results of this insecurity are readily evident in the daily routines and conversations of these undertrained managers and their staffs. They constantly try to equate the information given them by their technical people to what was said at the latest executive seminar (which in all likelihood was led by someone with little competence in the field). New projects and distinct efforts are inevitably turned down on the grounds that "AI is not going in that direction" or "other companies are not doing that." In other words, because these managers have such a poor grasp of the fundamentals they minimize the technology and its potential. They adopt a conservative approach to protect their careers. The technology is never used to its fullest and the firm, therefore, never rises above mediocrity.

In comparison, all Japanese workers become involved in new technologies—even their lunchtime conversations can be an exciting technical experience. Blue-collar workers who design complex production equipment for outside suppliers of the firm (as well as build expert systems in blue-collar AI Circles Programs) eagerly propose new AI initiatives knowing that upper middle management will listen and rely on them for technical content. Each year, the company hires a new crop of AI majors from the best universities: these graduates mix with the highly technical blue-and-white collar workers to design the AI strategy for the company. Conversely, the American approach relies on the mind of one person or a very few persons, instead of many, to design the AI program. U.S. corporations depend on outside pseudo-repositories of expertise in the form of executive seminars or consultants; the Japanese rely on university-trained experts. The American system results in an overly cautious approach toward implementing new technology programs while the Japanese methods instill increasing boldness and positive desire from the project beginnings. This aggressive attitude serves to make local AI programs distinct from any competitor programs.

Since American management relies so heavily on executive AI seminars, such seminars should be examined in greater detail. They can be fairly characterized by the following:

1. Famous names are hired (mainly as decoration) to give "beginner" and "evaluative" speeches which describe the potential of the technology.
2. Company AI seminars are organized by newcomers to AI. The best AI researchers almost never set up these seminars because they have better things to do.
3. Proprietary information is not released. Most edge-of-field AI research and application work is proprietary, so many of the true advances in the field go unmentioned.
4. Seminars with the "what everybody else is already doing" mindset replace a solid understanding of AI with general surveys. These generalizations overwhelm initiative to change or advance the direction of AI.

In a typical example, a manager of a new AI program is sent to an executive seminar to hear topics selected by amateurs in the field.

Famous names (famous for AI work done a couple of generations back) deliver speeches whose content has been simplified beyond usefulness and dwells mainly on outlining yesterday's news. No wonder, then, when these managers return to their firms, they are uncertain how to proceed. Achieving competitive advantage is the last thing on their minds.

What, constitutes the ideal—an AI program set up by an expert? First, the program identifies the edge-of-field areas key to future competitive advantage and implements them as a hardware and software platform that all AI projects can be built upon. Second, instead of "famous names," the program hires young, business-oriented and up-to-date researchers who are pioneering competitive advantage right now. Third, the program (as well as the program's management) understands AI's ultimate roles and only implements AI accordingly. For example, AI has a revolutionary impact on all software development. From the beginning of the program, the firm trains its entire software group to use AI technology. It seeks to add AI to virtually all existing software in the firm, not in some grandiose impractical project, but rather in an incremental long-range program. Fourth, the program operates with the future economics of AI software tools and hardware platforms—that is, tools and platforms which will dominate three to five years from now are used now, not today's most widespread tools. Present tools, perfected with a past vision of AI needs, are at least five years out-of-date.

Why do American firms appoint unknowledgeable managers to lead their high technology programs? In a word, politics. In American business, control of a new technology is viewed as a perk. It confers status and compensates for monotonous work assignments. When I consulted for sixteen U.S. firms, I was amazed to discover the number of AI programs being managed by people who had been given the program as an employment perk. Some major corporations had established "advanced technology sections" which, in reality, amounted to little more than ego-boosters. These companies erroneously believed that it was cheaper to reward a manager with a new toy to play with rather than raising his salary or his intellectual level.

In this kind of firm, one political faction automatically monopolizes all the prestigious work assignments. Naturally, this causes harmful repercussions. The rest of the firm is demoralized because everyone has to follow new technology directives formulated by an ignorant central political faction. The high technologies become mired in misunderstanding and ignorance before they can even be introduced. And while the "advanced technical section" busily works up the appearance of competence, the implementation of new technologies is delayed. Finally, because the "advanced technical section" is devoid of experts, the firm is subject to the arrogance and whims of outside vendors who reap hefty commissions by taking advantage the situation.

The Meta-Cognitive Organization Theory

Obsolete management theories are not easily identified, because the companies that practice them generally go out of business. International trade has so completely brought the world's major economies into inter-dependence that one nation's successful manufacturing and marketing techniques are readily apparent to others. Japanese business, which has recently gained worldwide recognition, is not an overnight sensation. It earned that recognition gradually as it competed in the world marketplace. Those who look upon Japan as a model are ridding themselves of passe management practices as fast as shrinking revenues and sales permit them. Indeed, management theory is in a state flux both in Europe and the United States. It could well be called the "Japanization" of management theory were there not other important factors also at play. These modern theories are leading to a new model that conceptualizes enterprise and national economy management. This Meta-Cognitive Organization Theory is described below.

Five major bodies of management study contributed to the birth of this theory. Scandinavian work in the early 1950's on socio-technical systems (which just recently reached the pages of leading U.S. management journals) influenced post-War American and Japanese management philosophy. The American human relations and company culture schools of theorizing absorbed the systematic insight of the Scandinavians without regard for the democratic methods behind it. Japanese post-War management theory borrowed heavily from pre-War theory, especially the fundamental "otherworldliness of the firm" assumptions of pre-War "Protestant" ethic Japanese behavior. Recently, the work force has become more professionalized as new technologies are introduced. This Cognitive Economy Theory in conjunction with post-War Japanese theory created the Meta-Cognitive Organization Theory as illustrated in Figure 2-1 on p. 21.

Eleven sub-theories of the Meta-Cognitive Organization Theory can be distinguished. Each of these pushes AI application in a unique direction. Depending on which of these sub-theories a firm chooses to practice, an outcome can be predicted. Since firms in

America, Europe and Japan are all examining and adopting these eleven sub-theories, they are becoming increasingly important predictors of an organization's behavior.

AI, as a key component of the Cognitive Economy Theory, plays an active role in the emergence of Meta-Cognitive Organizations. AI gives companies the power to encapsulate bodies of expertise within the firm itself. It, therefore, can map and monitor the growth, distribution and effectiveness of various kinds of expertise that previously had been isolated and not easily distributed on a mass basis. (This is because each body of expertise was formerly encapsulated in a particular human personality and body.) This, in turn, leads firms and their people to learn how expertise influences events and vice versa. It makes expertise portable and distributable in ways unimagined before; a firm can focus on participatory management and enhancement of its expertise capital. Since learning produces expertise, a learning-conscious organization starts to develop. AI has an explicit role to play as a tutoring system in this learning process, but something more beyond technical learning is involved. As the firm discovers more and more that its ultimate well-being rests on the appropriate generation and management of expertise, the people within the firm base career images on these ideals as well. This creates a "learning conscious organization" not only in the technocratic sense, but in a sense where each employee manages himself as a learning worker.

The Meta-Cognitive Organization Theory and its eleven subtheories influence a company's implementation of AI. Firms able to envision the interplay of these forces will design AI programs that improve profitability and enhance employee expertise. Firms not understanding this interplay will merely duplicate the work of others. And for all the millions they invest in new Cognitive Technologies, their bottom line will remain unaffected. The eleven sub-theories and their impact on AI programs are presented here.

Socio-Technical System Theory

This theory states that for each new increment in technological development, there is a corresponding increment to the social system to handle it and vice versa. Autonomous work groups that design and manage their own work discipline and content are the outcome of actual experiments launched by this theory. There is another offshoot of this theory. Workers participate in research, not as mere

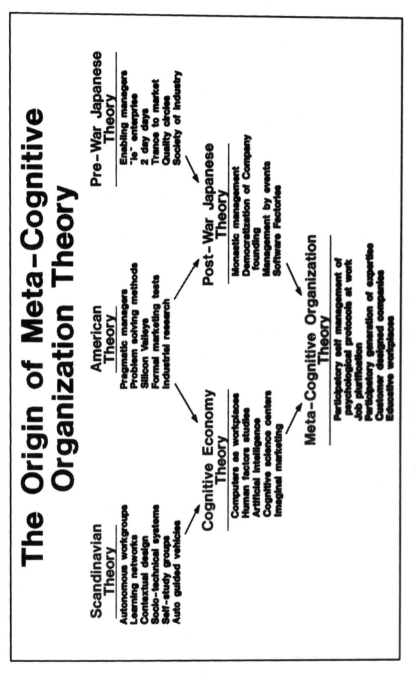

Figure 2-1 The origin of Meta-Cognitive Theory.

apprentices, but as full-fledged co-researchers in theory development. Each project member contributes research, design, control, and interpretation of project results. The Socio-Technical System Theory permits any interested work group in the firm to develop AI expert systems. These people have AI staff experts available to them for assistance and have enough confidence and drive to improve themselves by learning and implementing a new technology as an ordinary part of their work routine. AI assistants, who act as a repository of work group lore and technical knowledge, characteristically develop when this theory is put into use.

Participatory Management Theory

This theory envisions managers not as order-givers but as people who facilitate employee involvement in all aspects of work. The workers possess an untapped reservoir of knowledge which in many cases has not found its way into company work process design. Many firms in Europe and the U.S. experimented with this theory in the 1960s and 1970s and got mixed results. Workers quickly found that once they learned formal group analysis procedures for improving their own work processes, there were still many variables controlling work processes that were determined by systemic variables acting across many work groups. Seldom were participation programs extended to include workers tampering with these systemic variables. Participation programs, generally a bottom-up effort, can lead to key work groups developing their own expert systems in tandem with a joint campaign across the entire work force. For example, various types of machine tools need diagnostic AI advisors and the expertise for this comes from the machine tool operator and the mechanic that services them. Participation programs, if they envision the work force as intelligent and capable, can create pilot work groups that make their own expert systems, relying on outside resources for initial training and techniques.

Primal Community Theory

This theory sees the work group as a type of village—a complete social entity with a study life, a spiritual life, an acting-through-words life, and an acting-through-deeds life, all held together by a work group defined corporate discipline. This theory rejects the notion that the workplace is a small segment of society in a trade-off relationship with the rest of society. It resists the ideas that work is "bad, unhealthy and unpleasant" and money is paid to "compensate" for work intruding on the rest of life. A primal community work group accepts new technologies through its study life. As an individual work group, it pilots the application of AI through its acting-through-deeds life.

Strategic Work Force Theory

This theory states that the key prerequisite to business effectiveness is the degree to which each work group in the firm knows the relative quality and cost/benefit of its work compared to the work done in parallel work groups in competing firms. All work groups in a firm need access to an information system that allows them to calculate the productivity of competing work groups performing the same function. All actions are accompanied by a 50% component that achieves competitive advantage beyond what the competitors do in the same area. This theory yields AI implementation that is split into two sets of tactics. One tactical system calls for the imitative approach, that is, it follows the typical beginning steps for learning AI as a new technology. The second tactical system builds special strategies into each. step of the first tactical system. These special tactics are unique to the firm and unlike anything competitors are attempting at that stage of development. The second tactical system achieves permanent competitive advantage in AI. Famous total quality methods such as Quality Function Deployment, Kansei Analysis, and Policy Deployment are aspects of this theory in Japan, and each offers a new quality method of specifying software systems—including AI software.

Uniform Structure Community Theory

This theory holds that whole societies are organized in such a way that the general structure of the largest segments of society is identical to that of the smallest segments. That is, national entities have their distinct counterparts on the regional and local levels. This applies to entire industries which share the same basic social structure as firms and the work groups within the firms. The same pattern is repeated at each level of society. This uniformity of structure across size scales results in a vast copying system. Actions on the national scale are immediately responded to and copied by every single work group in the nation. The technical term for this is "Fractal Society Theory," based on Dr. Mandelbrot's fractal mathematics. (Japan has achieved actual implementation of this particular theory. When the energy crisis occurred, millions of Japanese work groups responded with the world's fastest, most complete, most participatory, and most economically effective energy savings program.) An overall national economy map of AI applications becomes embedded in the particular tactics of each industry, firm and work group. If the national economy categories of AI expert system are neuronal modeling and the verbal reasoning machine, as Japan's fifth and sixth generation computing projects are, then we can expect individual work groups across major industries to study and work out associative memory representations of shop floor systems. They can also be expected to develop verbal-dialog driven manufacturing and design operations as part of work group projects and circles.

Skyblue-Collar Worker Theory

This theory states that four historical perspectives determine the work group's environment today. First, traditional white-collar workers are acquiring blue-collar responsibility for line operation success. Second, blue-collar workers are given more former white-collar responsibilities. Third, all workers are assigned to find ways to automate their jobs. Fourth, it classifies all work units in the firm into sixteen different types of mini-venture businesses. Work groups in this case imagine themselves as nascent venture businesses and view their accumulated expertise as a possible product. They use AI as a way to market their own expertise and sell it initially within their firm to co-worker "customers" and later as an actual product to customers outside the firm. Furthermore, AI becomes a shared network where blue- and white-collar people tap into the same knowledgebases. This theory also holds that all work groups participate in events, circles, evolution/devolution, and valley dynamics of the firm. (This will be more fully explained later.) Circles programs form the basis of companywide campaigns wherein all work groups develop an expert system simultaneously over an eighteen month period. Circle conferences monitor progress and expert advice is directed to improving actual prototype systems developed by work group circles.

Management by Contradiction Resolution Theory

This states that although organizations face myriads of issues, the firm needs to address only one critical issue at a time. Companies use a formal analysis procedure to filter out key issues from those that are superficial or merely symptomatic. The critical issues, once identified, are then socially and semantically analyzed to determine where underlying creative blockage exists within the firm. "Contradiction" is the term used for whatever prolongs the creative blockage and workers devise tactics to overcome the contradiction. Presumedly, if the contradiction is overcome, forces within the firm will be released to address the critical issues. This is a form of management in which local issues are played off a global focus of key issues. It rapidly uncovers the immense implications of new cognitive technologies for the life and work of the firm. Having made this discovery, management develops an overall global plan to respond to the cognitive technologies, including a structured, formal AI application component. AI, then, would be merely one component along with the other cognitive technologies. The systematic interrelations of these technologies would be used to focus and enrich the overall AI application.

Monastic Management Theory

This theory envisions the firm as fundamentally a religious order. Most firms take on the culture, discipline and mores from the society in which they are embedded, a basic violation of this particular theory of company operation. Instead, effectiveness is found by enhancing and intensifying key aspects of the embedded culture with a perpetually revised set of rules and customs. The firm works to achieve a concentrated attentiveness to its market, responding decisively to any minor discrepancies in product design in conflict with market needs. Issues are avoided within the firm and a guaranteed path of evolution is the norm. This means performance differences do not determine who gets the prestigious assignments, but instead determine whose opinions are listened to from whatever position the individual is normally allotted. The Monastic Management Theory leads to minimalist AI. The market penetrates so intimately and deeply into all internal company criteria, moods and decisions, that only AI that can be justified by its contribution to market is implemented. The company reduces AI applications to the absolute minimum and makes a long-term commitment to this lean form of AI. There is no desire to come up with imitative and unnecessary uses for AI just for the sake of appearance.

Learning Conscious Organization Theory

This management theory holds that the nature of jobs is changing as the work force becomes increasingly professional, as computers become workplaces and as economies evolve from an industrial base to a service base. Management is effective only when it leads to rapid worker learning. This requires that managers become educators rather than order givers. Similarly, jobs viewed as unpleasant segments of the overall process are replaced by intellectually, emotionally, and socially balanced jobs that make the work group into a miniature business venture. AI becomes one stage in the process of learning enhancement when this theory is put in practice. AI has a role as tutor and transmitter of knowledge. In general, the Cognitive Technologies are applied to work group functions; to the invention of new workshop, group consideration and meeting procedures; and technological realizations of those new cognitive means and functions.

Management by Events Theory

This theory establishes a way for one organization to be two or more organizations simultaneously and to evolve as needs dictate. This theory supposes events (planning, product design, market testing, accounting, personnel assignments, pilot production, production systems design, packaging, and delivery) in which a majority of the work force participates on an occasional basis. These events, therefore, fulfill all the dynamics of a venture business—a venture business that exists only a few hours each week. In this way, wholly new methods and opportunities can be tested by a majority of the work force in free training sessions without anyone realizing that, in effect, a full company was brought into existence during those biweekly or monthly events. When this theory is in effect, entire work forces experiment with AI application techniques during biweekly meetings. Indeed, various types of AI as well as other new technologies can be turned into different product lines of the firm. The successful venture businesses receive formal organizational status and are promoted to actual business entities.

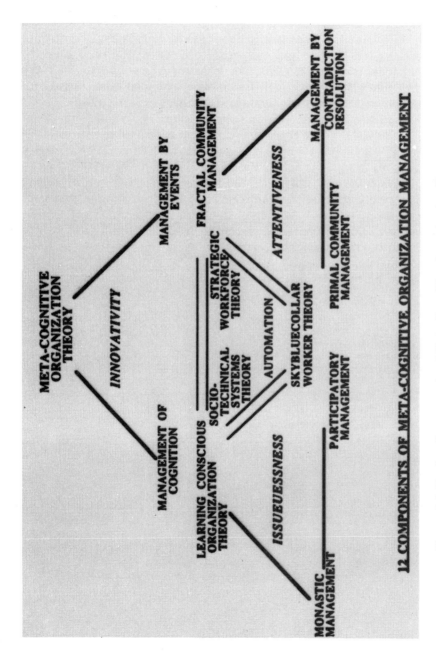

Figure 2-2 Twelve Components of Meta-Cognitive Organization Management.

Management of Cognition Theory

A firm, through its use of Cognitive Technologies, can objectify its expertise and gradually bring into being the management of this expertise. Because the expertise is disseminated, management control is usually participatory and each work unit is requested to catalog and enhance its expertise. This theory makes AI a fundamental part of every job within the organization. For example, each secretary builds and maintains an individual secretarial expert advisor. Each janitor builds a personal cleaning agent expert advisor. All jobs are assigned to maintain a representation of themselves in expert system form. The sum total of all these sub-theories is the Meta-Cognitive Organization. It is the radical interplay of social systems with technical software. It turns organizations into active and creative brains. It converts careerism into contemplative meditation on company mission. It turns lives into amplifications of themselves, enhanced in Cognitive Technology form. Refer to Figure 2-2 on p. 27 for a summary of the eleven sub-theories of management.

3

The Objectives

Learning from Japan

The main objective of American companies is to survive Japanese competition. To do so, they will have to understand Japanese methods and tactics for delivering new technologies. Ultimately, the survival of Japanese competition will require a total transformation of the firm. A simple readjustment of old styles, methods and values will not suffice. (The companies that survive will not succumb to the "reaction syndrome." That is, Japanese industry attacks a foreign competitor's key market or product and it suffers losses. It then scrambles to lower costs and improve quality but finds it hard to do so. The firm frantically studies how its Japanese rivals achieve these improvements.) Hasty reaction to any sudden attack does not produce desired results. Perhaps a better understanding of the problem can be obtained by seeing how the leading firms in Japan counter each other's competitive moves. The following illustration, Figure 3-1 explains how Japanese firms apply a commonsense approach to overcome competitor tactics.

There are four phases leading to successful competition:

1. Copy competitor tactics.
2. Package those tactics in special ways to compensate for differences in the business environment.
3. Improve on what is thus copied and packaged.
4. Build national or regional strategic advantages into those improvements.

29

THE "SURPASS" DIMENSION IN COMPETING WITH JAPAN

	TWO DIMENSIONS: AUTOMATION VERSUS COMPETITION			
	DIE	SURVIVE	CATCH UP	SURPASS
METHOD APPROACH	copy Japan	package tactics for copyings	improve on Japanese techniques that are copied	US competitive advantages built in as improvements on Japanese techniques
SOCIAL APPROACH Toyota	copy what in Japan invented kanban for example	package tactics for copying what invented kanban	improve on what invented Japanese techniques such as kanban	US competitive advantages built into improvements on what invented kanban
AUTOMATION APPROACH Honda	automate what invented Japanese techniques	automate packaging tactics for what invented Japanese techniques	automate improving what invented Japanese techniques	automate using US competitive advantages as improvements on what invented Japanese techniques
KNOWLEDGE AUTOMATION APPROACH	AUTOMATE AUTOMATION			

Figure 3-1 The "Surpass" Dimension.

These four phases represent level one. At this most superficial level of competition, a firm simply copies other's highly noticeable techniques. Of course, by the time a competitor's technique is visible to outsiders, it is generally fully enough developed to constitute a considerable time-to-develop advantage. That is, if your competitor has fully implemented AI Circles, it is possible that by the time you notice and respond by copying, this competitor may very well have adopted some new tactic not yet visible. Firms that do no more than copy other people's visible tactics condemn themselves to perpetual mediocrity. And, unfortunately, many American firms are guilty of this second rate behavior.

Level two applies these same four phases not to the competitor's visible methods or tactics but, rather to the generator of these methods and tactics. First, the competitor's generator is copied. Second, the copying of that generator is packaged. Third, the packaged generator is improved. Fourth, natural strategic strengths are built into these improvements.

Level three is deeper still. It applies these four phases to automation of the generator that creates the competitor's best techniques and methods. First, a company automates the copying of the generator; second, it automates the packaging of the copied generator; third, it automates improving the packaged generator. Finally, strategic strengths are automated into the improvements made in the packaged generator of a competitor's best methods and techniques. To achieve this degree of automation, both social and technological systems must be considered. All that can possibly be done by social means alone must be performed first. Technology is then given the responsibility of handling only what cannot be achieved by social means.

Level four—the most profound level of all—is automating automation itself. It requires the building of a consistent delivery vehicle to deliver new technologies throughout the company. This vehicle must also deliver a succession of new technologies until its use leads to the mastery of the automation process and becomes an overall skill of the organization.

Kanban is a useful illustration of the above. Most U.S. manufacturers are committed to kanban for inventory reduction. They omit the customer-pull aspect of kanban and instead copy the surface technique which lets them cost justify it by inventory savings. The cognitive dimension of kanban, the meditative trance quality which causes the whole organization to respond to the tiniest fluctuations in the market, is omitted as too vague to have any value in the American business environment. (Kanban is, of course, based on one of Japan's strategic advantages, its small geographical size. The Japanese are amused at the U.S. for attempting to copy a system not designed for a large country. Kanban is, after all, inherently easier to apply to a national economy situated on compact islands.)

Strangely enough, when Japanese people are asked about inherent American business strengths, most will cite without hesitation the English language. Japanese businessmen and scientists consider our language to be one of our key competitive advantages. English is precise with an immense specificity of reference and a huge vocabulary. Japanese grammar, on the other hand, has a tendency for ambiguity which inhibits precise expression. In leading Japanese laboratories, researchers begin the discussion of a scientific topic in Japanese, but when the issue really heats up, they start speaking in English. Ironically, it is easier for them to argue and compare precise points in English rather than in Japanese, even though their English speaking skills are far below their Japanese skills. English gets things done through words and verbal expression that in Japan can only be accomplished by physically putting people together. To a certain extent, computer systems help the U.S. overcome its geographic size, but only when they enable precise expression in English. However, the fact that Americans exchange concepts whereas Japanese exchange affect and commitment causes Americans to fail at implementing the brilliant ideas they generate. This means computer systems may delay Americans from correcting their weakness at implementing things. Indeed, Japanese carefully minimize certain roles for computers.

Many people agree that the Japanese are not leaders in the AI field and there is no need to copy their systems. The fifth and sixth generation computer projects are clearly derivative copies of earlier U.S. and European attempts to model mind on machine. The Japanese have the scale and scope to lead the way, but they have added no new goals or methods until recently with the invention of unrestricted Horn clauses. However, there is one facet of Japanese AI programs that competitors would do well to emulate and that is the way the Japanese deliver AI to the workplace.

An Argument that May Doom AI in U.S. Companies

Today the managements of many major American firms are increasingly split into two opposing camps: the "leans" and the "automates." Each of these factions has a fundamentalist core group surrounded by a more reflective and conservative element. It is the fundamentalist core in both of these factions that endanger (or even oppose) the implementation of AI.

After spending nearly a decade in Japan, I was amazed by the behavior of American managers who were seeking information about AI programs. These managers summoned their staffs to AI presentations and then proceeded to sabotage the meetings. They expressed doubt that AI even existed and, if it did, it probably did not live up to all the claims being made. At times, some managers stopped the presentation and demanded to be shown how AI differed from ordinary software. When shown the differences, they stubbornly refused to see them. In short, they revealed to me an argumentative and close-minded attitude about the new technology. They demanded that it measure up immediately and prove its right to exist. This attitude represents industrial suicide in its purest form; the future must prove itself only to absolute fools. Perhaps underlying this hostility is a desire not to implement AI for no other reason than others have already done it. Perhaps deeper still, remain scars from the implementation of previous technologies that resulted in the workplace being more expensive, more complex and more error-prone. Indeed, because of bad experiences, there exists in every American firm a powerful constituency against automation altogether. This faction supports its view by pointing out Japanese success. I call these people the "leans."

This is their argument:

1. Japan outproduces the United States.
2. Japan uses little blue pieces of cardboard for factory scheduling and bypasses technology altogether.
3. Japan minimizes computer use.
4. Let's copy this minimized technology aspect of Japan.
5. Let's reward managers for how well they implement uniform, companywide programs of minimal technology.

Another constituency in the firm, the "automates," presents this argument:

1. Copying today the systems that Japan fully implemented three years ago will give the U.S. no competitive advantage.
2. U.S. ability to innovate, an inherent strength, must be utilized.
3. The U.S. can gain competitive advantage over Japan by automating more than the Japanese.

These two constituencies influence many individual, isolated little decisions about AI and possible projects. A manager may listen to part of an argument in support of AI and then announce, "Japanese firms do that without any computers at all for one-fifth the cost." This manager represents the "lean" point of view. Another conversation with a manager might evoke this comment: "We've never solved this lightpipe raytracing problem before. Perhaps AI can help us." This is an example of an "automate." The "leans" lose any competitive advantage they might have had by their refusal to automate. They argue that a system must be competitive on paper before automation is added to the design. They have no use for AI at all. The "automates" go to the other extreme and assign every unsolved problem in the firm to AI. Figure 3-2 summarizes the "leans" versus "automates" debate. And it must be remembered that AI does not solve impossible problems; it does not even solve all solvable problems. Eventually, all AI application groups in all companies will face these issues:

1. What kind of "lean" role can AI adopt as a technology minimizer?
2. What types of problems can AI be realistically expected to solve?

With very few exceptions, AI programs in the U.S. have not addressed these issues. Few firms have attempted to find a "lean" role for AI. And while some have made an effort to identify the types of problems for their AI programs to handle, this effort is, at best, incomplete. Everyone in the organization must be aware of corporate strategies and weaknesses to better identify the appropriate applications for AI. Instead, small AI groups of a dozen or so persons try to do this thinking with their twelve minds rather than harnessing the power of the ten thousand minds of the entire work force. The following items outline the bare fundamentals of implementing a new technology. Subsequent chapters will delve into greater detail.

1. A sizable majority of the work force must make an incremental self-implementation of successive new technology campaigns.
2. Systems designed on paper must be fully competitive before automation is added to the design.
3. A socio-technical system approach must be adopted where "lean" social systems and "lean" technology are designed by those who actually implement them.

THE LEANS VERSUS THE AUTOMATES

A Controversy About Technology's Role in Achieving Competitiveness

THE LEANS
1. **Japan beats** the U.S.
2. Japan uses little blue **cardboard cards** for factory scheduling
3. Japan **minimizes** computer use
4. This technology minimization strategy achieves **lower cost** and greater **reliability** for the Japanese
5. **Let's copy** this aspect of Japan
6. Let's reward managers **not for what** they do **but for how** well they implement uniform corporate programs of minimal technology

THE AUTOMATES
1. Copying today systems Japan fully implemented 3+ years ago will give the U.S. **no competitive advantage**
2. Inherent U.S. strength in **inventivity** must be harnessed
3. Let us **automate more than** Japan automates to gain advantage

THE RESOLUTION OF THIS CONTROVERSY:
A. An **incremental self** implementation by sizeable segments of the entire workforce of successive new technology campaigns
B. A system designed on paper to be fully **competitive before new automation** systems are added to the system definition
C. A **socio-technical systems approach** where lean human systems design and lean technology design by those who would end up using the technology supplant elite staff design of technology
D. **Automation of automation** by building a **social delivery vehicle** and **cognitive delivery vehicle** that can be used to deliver successive technologies

Figure 3-2 The Leans Versus the Automates.

4. The automating of automation must come about by the building of social and cognitive delivery vehicles that can be used for the delivery of successive technologies.

5. A delivery and development environment for AI (that runs on the same engineering workstation type hardware for one-tenth the cost of present AI vendor hardware and software systems) must be invented.

6. The style and mode of AI delivery must not be done in the manner of DARPA.

7. Scattered, isolated expert systems must be removed from AI programs in favor of shared knowledgebase networks that support a team of users using AI together in real time.

Currently, the "automates" are losing ground to the "leans." In the recent past, firms have used automation as a quick fix solution which only served to exacerbate their problems. The work forces were not trained thoroughly enough to make the transition to new automation systems that some "automate" managements attempted. The "automates" now desperately seek some conceptual clue that will guide them to defeating Japanese competition. Without this clue, the morale of management plummets. Meanwhile, the "leans" are driven to a desperate anti-automation stand by the same Japanese pressure. They believe, in absence of a conceptual principle for defeating the Japanese, that copying is the only workable approach. Both groups have a piece of the puzzle. We need the "leans" who encourage us to maintain lower costs and make use of human systems in lieu of technological systems. We also need the "automates" who urge us to go beyond copying to find a way to true competitiveness. Progressive firms are making gradual attempts to unite the two factions in the hope of achieving a more balanced technology program.

And while the debate between the "leans" and the "automates" heats up, the professional staffs who "own" the technologies in most American companies remain oblivious. Because they do not set overall policy, they ignore the turmoil around them and concentrate on their work. They are paid to use technology and don't think in terms of competitiveness, even though a majority of managers see this as a suicidal approach. It is equally alarming when the technologists have the ascendancy and promote technology as the sole road to competitive advantage over the Japanese. In both cases, the technical staffs are the problem. They can't visualize the purposes, the delivery means, and competitive business constraints that the new technology must embody. This dooms them to overutilize or underutilize the technology. Unfortunately, traditional American managers, ignorant of technology when compared to their European and Japanese counterparts, capitulate to their technical staffs in the automation debate. Of course, there are some exceptions. These managers are found in the firms responding best to the Japanese challenge.

The Objectives of a Japanese-Style AI Application Program

The main points of this book have been strung across a number of chapters. These points, however, are fairly difficult to grasp and are so inter-related that they need to be seen together in a number of different configurations. One such configuration is depicted in the following "goals for an AI application program" compiled from several Japanese and two American companies.

The Paramount Objective:

To automate the automation process of the firm.

The Master Objectives:

To develop a Social Delivery Vehicle for one technology, artificial intelligence, and apply it to successive new technologies.

To develop the role of artificial intelligence as a Cognitive Delivery Vehicle of successive other new technologies.

The Competitive Objectives:

To use completed projects to define a role for AI lean enough to survive Japanese competition.

To use completed projects to define an AI network of shared knowledgebases that strips AI of its overindividualistic assumptions and origins.

To overcome the styles and habits of AI's origin in Defense Department funded DARPA research that are inappropriate for business.

To accompany with improvements every bit of AI copied from competitors so as to give strategic advantage from the very beginning of the AI program.

The Enabling Objectives:

To accomplish mass development of AI by every single work group of the firm through implementation of an AI Circles program wherein all ordinary workers develop their own expert systems.

To accomplish elite quality enhancements to AI by establishing a core group that commercializes AI capability still untried in the industry.

To achieve a Self-Training Work Force in AI by implementing constructs that allow the entire work force to teach itself about AI without the delay and expense of hiring competent outside instructors.

To implement from the beginning AI enhancements to all software whatsoever in the firm thereby preventing AI professionals from "owning" the technology.

To implement the Meta-Cognitive Organization by disseminating new workshop and participatory research procedures throughout the AI project and circle networks so that the work force can be trained to participate in the management of their own psychological protocols at work while using AI to enhance their cognitive work performance.

To establish credibility for AI technology by initiating projects that will lead to a large bottom line payback.

To protect the ultimate roles of AI from more trivial implementations forced by short-term profit orientations of the firm through management support of "strategic roles for AI" experiments.

To mobilize the curiosity that exists about AI and propel it toward the creation of useful projects. Too often that initial curiosity is sqandered on inane course work, unrealizable project objectives, purist AI projects, squabbles among AI suppliers, or the purchase of incompatible and overpriced nonstandardized AI tools.

To invent and prove out as rapidly as possible a software development rhythm for AI that implements the best of what is known about mass production of ordinary software. To strip AI quickly of the excuse that its newness and unfamiliarity entitle it to slower and more error-prone development and permit it other undisciplined excesses inherited from its origins in Defense Department funded R&D.

To avoid naive overapplication of AI to problems that could be solved just as well, if not better, by other technologies. To avoid giving in to those who resist AI because their career plans, expertise, and repute are threatened by a new software technology.

This brief list of objectives represents a minimal disposition toward effective AI. Much is omitted in order to focus on certain core principles and accomplishments. As can be seen, there are a number of polarities in the above list: short-term versus long-term paybacks, elite versus everyman implementation, and generation of enthusiasm versus constructive channeling of that enthusiasm. The aforementioned list makes implicit that the entire organization implements the new technology. This puzzles European and American executives trained to create another organization chart box every time a new phenomenon appears. To them, it is inefficient to ask the whole organization to do something that could very easily be made the exclusive domain of a few experts. The Japanese, keenly aware of efficiency, see the effectiveness of everyone in the organization participating in the new technology. From the immense consultation systems that enmesh Japanese firms to the after-hours parties that salve bureaucracy-wounded egos, the Japanese work force is totally involved. For them, "participatory" takes on an ontological quality of the essence of the organization itself as it embraces a new technology and fills it with the lore and aims of the firm. Necessarily, this "cosmic mother" approach begins gradually and moves by almost imperceptible steps. Yet, because it teaches everyone in the organization about the new technology and builds a corporate imagination of what that technology portends, and because, in short, it tailors the new technology to people's needs, there is enormous cooperation with its implementation. Elitists are prevented from "owning" it and building up their market value above others in the firm. It becomes "our" not "their" technology and all benefit perceptibly from its improved and widespread use. The bottom line payback reveals the difference between cooperation and greed. New technology implementation performed on a shared-basis makes everyone proud to be a contributor. When these tasks are performed solely for the benefit of a selected few, the majority becomes envious of the new technology and resents those who use it for career building purposes.

European and American firms consider these objectives to be major stumbling blocks. Many have no idea how to achieve them, although all would know how to build credibility by getting initial paybacks. This credibility issue needs elaboration. Credibility, in its shallow sense, means persuading people to trust a new technology and allow it to be used in their particular area of the firm. Credibility, in its rarely used serious sense, means implementing a new technology in such a fashion that everyone can see how it forces the firm to overcome competitors in the market. When managers demand "credibility" for the initial projects of a new technology, they ignore competition and the fate of the company and devote their energies to minor victories in a lost war. After all, it is for these minor victories that they are promoted and paid. In other words, incentives for the long-range form of credibility must be built into AI programs to ensure their ultimate success. This means that AI must be implemented rationally.

4

The Japanese Way

Rational AI Implementation

Researchers have long known that rational behavior defeats intelligent behavior, that is, when "rational" is defined as following procedures that actually succeed in attaining goals. Therefore, it pays to be rational rather than intelligent. But what is rational behavior for a company? Books like *In Search of Excellence*, by Tom Peters and Robert H. Waterman, Jr., suggest that bureaucratic rationality is in fact irrational and counterproductive. The authors note that rationality is in a trade-off relationship with scope. If rationality is increased, it is done only by decreasing to near meaninglessness the scope of data to which the rational concepts relate. Clearly, then, it is best to implement an AI program rational in a way that expands the scope of data handled. A model of rationality has been built by Japanese engineers which serves as a guide to AI programs that achieve their goals.

There are four main sections to this model which break down into two polarities: human limitations versus human creativity and indicative grouping of data versus mathematization of data. Being rational, then, means (1) accounting for human limitations, such as lies, theft, dereliction; (2) grouping data indicatively rather than imposing ready-made deductive theories or category sets; (3) achieving cognitive efficiency of representation through transmitting the data into symbol systems (mathematization); and (4) checking the model against human creativity. Attention to the phenomenon of interest must be balanced by powerful expression of the results achieved from analyzing that phenomenon. An AI program that accounts for human limitations, derives its structures and processes from the data, achieves powerful cogent expressiveness of models, and allows for and invites human creativity beyond anyone's expectations, will be rational and accomplish its goals.

There is nothing radical or new in these guidelines. Japanese rationality seems to have familiar constituents, yet the emphasis is subtly different because the priorities are new. Rational thinking in Japan's best enterprises assumes that humans will not behave as told and that human nature will intrude on the AI delivery system. It assumes that program structures and processes must be indicatively created in response to the data that emerges from implementing AI rather than trying to follow some inflexible "right" way of delivering it. It assumes AI programs must have great cogent intensity. Finally, it assumes that human creativity will occasionally intrude into the program with results far more beneficial than expected. Humans are curious animals: they are less than we plan for and more than we allow them room to be.

Typical Japanese AI Projects

We can see how the rational approach to AI has fared in Japan by examining the types of projects on the drawing board. In the following paragraphs I have listed some of the AI programs being considered in Japan.

The Robot Maintenance Campaign

Several companies have achieved almost everything in the field of robotics that the current generation of robot technology will handle cost-effectively. Therefore, they have begun making robots to disassemble other robots for calibration, lubrication, and parts replacement.

"No-Man" Factory Construction

Japanese construction companies have demonstrated that land can be cleared and surveyed and that building foundations can be laid all without human intervention.

"No-Man" Engineering in Software Factories

AI use represents up to 25% of all code lines written in these new institutions that mass produce software. One-fourth of the programmers in software factories survey the programming work of the other 75%. They then develop tools written in AI languages that automate what that 75% does.

A New Factory Standard for AI

Standardizing features and capabilities for AI is currently out of the question because AI is changing so quickly that it cannot be predicted which future enhancements will be available next year. So, for now, AI must pursue a connectivity standard rather than a feature standard. By building expert system components into each expert system component, that is, each inference engine contains a mini-knowledgebase, a population of components can be maintained with new features wrapped in a connectivity package. This allows new AI capabilities which appear every year on the market to be immediately added to that population of components for use in a company's expert systems.

Automobile Vending Machines

According to the Japanese, the customer should be the ultimate designer of a car. Hence, Computer-Aided-Design (CAD) needs to evolve toward Customer-Aided-Design where the customer sits in front of a computer and plays with video game type controls to design a car on the screen. After capturing the initial design, the customer-designer takes the design drawing through simulated riding conditions. He then deposits 25,000 quarters into the machine and presses the "order" button. That afternoon, the custom-designed car is delivered to his driveway.

The Cure for Drunk Driving in America

AI can automate car navigation by using artificial barriers put along highways. These barriers detect pedestrians and hazards and guide cars automatically. Those who have had more than one drink simply let technology take over. They are automatically chauffeured down the road to a central car lot and from there take a taxi home. For the price of a short cab ride, those who have over-indulged arrive home safely.

Although none of these are direct AI application projects, they each symbolize AI's vast potential. Most impressive, however, is the wide range of the product domains they express. The future of AI in Japan is being molded by a profound imaginative environment that is asking many technologies and product families to reach beyond conventional limits. American and European firms, recently devastated by overseas competition, must deal with psychological loss. But if they focus too strongly on survival, they lose an overall optimism about their industry, market, and product. They become discouraged to the point where they cease moving forward imaginatively. They adopt a "let's survive" mentality. Fundamentally new value-added improvements to industry, market and product are just not invented. By concentrating on kanban, circles, cost, quality and import restrictions, they become distracted. They forget what can be done with contemporary methods and technology. It is this impoverishment of the imagination that precedes the destruction of national economies. AI, as exciting as it is in itself, becomes even more so when it is part of a visionary scenario of general industrial fulfillment.

The Protestant Ethic and the Spirit of Japan

The Japanese technical press these days speaks of four kanbans. The entire Just-in-Time inventory system is predicated on a flow vision that customer behavior dictates the schedule of all actions in the firm. It is a very Buddhist-like image of the firm. The firm, with its legs crossed as for zazen and heart utterly stilled, has workers with guaranteed promotions who are totally undistracted by careerism. In this manner, the firm quiets its soul and attends solely to its market. In that spiritual stillness of being, even the smallest deviations from the norm are seen as magnificent dramas. Here, customer wants and/or frustrations with the firm's product are given overwhelming attention and response. Actions, so as not to break the meditative intensity of effort, are rapid and decisive. In Japan, AI is being introduced into this divine image of the firm. And the tone is not one of excitement caused by a new technology, nor is it one of curiosity. It is utter concentration on the market, undistracted even for a second with any ancillary (illusory) charms of technology. AI implemented in firms this way differs profoundly from AI implemented by professionals whose lives are wrapped up in the glamour of the technology.

American and European firms are currently implementing only one of the four kanbans already fully implemented in Japan. For some reason, the other three are not even discussed in the English language press. Yet much more than physical inventories in firms need to be scaled down. All four of the kanbans are listed in Figure 4-1. The inventories they eliminate are described below.

The first kanban deals with unmet customer needs and unanswered customer complaints upon receiving the first shipment of a product. That is, the firm designs products so that certain problems with market acceptance (impossible to predict ahead of actual market use) can be dealt with quickly because alternatives were built within the design and manufacture process. This allows for adjustment of product characteristics, as well as adjustment of corresponding manufacturing characteristics needed for efficient manufacture of the new product features within weeks of the first shipments.

The second kanban reduces design alterations. The design process of medium-complexity products is so lengthy these days that changes of assumption may occur halfway through the process and ultimately modify the entire design. Due to the length of the design process,

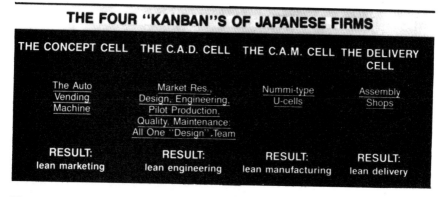

Figure 4-1 The Four "Kanbans" of Japanese Firms.

data gathered in the later stages of the process change earlier specifications. In both these cases, even more time is tacked on to the design process as new data are incorporated into the design. Designs that are correct from the outset eliminate the inventory of design repetition.

The third kanban is the most familiar to Americans. Products or parts in the plant are stored only short periods of time before being shipped to customers. In fact, the parts or products do not exist until the customer orders them. Only then are the products assembled and shipped. Therefore, the company does not pay for the storage of parts or partially completed products.

The fourth kanban reduces the inventory of the assembly function itself. A current experiment in Japan creates retail shops in which ordinary citizens, under the guidance of an expert engineer, buy home appliances and assemble them at neighborhood retail shops. This can reduce the purchase price by one-third.

AI has a serious role to play in minimizing and modernizing design and manufacture worldwide. AI design assistants help achieve the first two kanbans. For example, artwork and finite element analysis by AI design assistants show how the product can be manufactured and at what cost. They shorten the design process from weeks to typically under thirty minutes. AI schedule and assembly assistants achieve kanbans three and four.

Beyond this superficial analysis, however, lies a more profound role for AI as a minimizer of design and manufacturing tasks. AI can be implemented in such a way that it eliminates (or greatly reduces) the use of more expensive technologies. Computer-Aided-Design (CAD) provides a good example. Many firms are interested in the solid modeling of parts and use static finite element analysis. For this, a firm has an engineer create a mesh of finite elements encompassing the part. The analysis program then considers all properties and characteristics of the mesh testing compatibility. When problems are encountered the engineer must then re-enmesh and redesign the problem component to eliminate the excess values displayed. Every part of this process can be achieved using AI, even by utilizing AI techniques in practice nearly a decade ago. Industry does not need expensive human beings who peer at an even more expensive graphic display terminal and, because they see too many little red elements, make the decision to change material or thickness to solve a particular problem. Instead an expert system can "see" the excess redness and follow design rules to eliminate the red. This means a firm can reduce the total number of CAD workstations involved in the project to about thirty percent of what is forecasted for use without AI. That is, AI can easily handle seventy percent of routine industrial design problems. AI used for design will cost the firm about one-third as much as conventional methods. However, few firms understand this and instead invest in expensive new generation CAD workstations while relegating AI to the sidelines as a mere curiosity.

This is but one of a number of proven examples. Simply put, AI replaces other more costly technologies. Indeed, common sense dictates that a firm make a list of all the expensive technology it is planning to implement in the near future to see if perhaps AI can help reduce or eliminate some of the items on the list.

Implementing AI as an Organization

In most firms it is customary to assign specific groups the responsibility of applying new technologies. This practice is followed almost universally without much thought. Those who perform the initial application of AI in most companies are:

1. A small group,
2. of highly educated people,
3. a little more progressive than most in the firm,
4. gaining a lot of attention as the vanguard of new technology,
5. pretty uninterested in the mundane matters of profit and loss,
6. likely to make things more complex rather than simpler.

These AI implementors probably envision the following scenario as the normal progression of events:

1. Initial expense training of themselves in AI.
2. Initial evaluation of vendor systems.
3. Selection of easy pilot projects.
4. Focus on the bottom line payback of a successful pilot project to show management.
5. Gradual build up of a little AI subworld.
6. Attend academic conferences to present papers.
7. Receive better salary offers elsewhere and have the opportunity to move on.
8. Launch an AI program within the firm.
9. Familiarize management with AI potential.
10. Eventual creation of an annual AI budget and appointment of an AI group manager.

Both of these lists should be well known to all. They represent the standard and unimaginative AI programs found everywhere in the United States. And most companies are firmly committed to these lists. The fact is, this "business as usual" attitude has permitted foreign competitors to wreak havoc upon American markets. Not even this, however, influences companies to mend their ways. Underlying this approach to AI delivery is the unshakable belief that only a small segment of the work force implements any new technology. The Japanese believe just the opposite: the entire organization implements a new technology.

In this respect, Japan is consistent. In 1871, the Iwakura Mission, consisting of the Prime Minister and the majority of his cabinet, left Japan for an eleven month tour of industrial facilities in Europe and the United States. When was the last time a U.S. President systematically toured foreign industrial facilities? From the beginning of her modernization, Japan borrowed selectively from Western industry. When a Japanese firm confronts a new technology, it figures out how all the complex structures and events of the firm can participate in absorbing and digesting it. Moreover, the Japanese share a model of the historical forces which act on and influence the international workplace. This model demonstrates in detail how all parts of the firm support new technology implementation. This is an indicative model of the work group and the forces acting upon it. It portrays not how things should be, but how they inevitably are. It traces not ideas but historical trends beyond any one firm's power to resist. It does not represent the humane treatment of people by people but rather the humaneness of all in an organization that acknowledges the future and refuses to resist it unnecessarily. This model is presented in Figure 4-2.

Two sets of polar forces are operating on work groups worldwide. In the first set, the boundary line separating the white- and blue-collar functions is becoming blurred. Until recently, the white-collar and blue-collar workers were on opposite ends of the spectrum, but this polarity is now disappearing. Firms are thinning their middle management ranks and training their managers to be participative enablers rather than order-givers. In addition, staffs are now at the beck and call of line needs rather than vice versa. Special privileges, uniforms, and executive parking are disappearing. Whatever is done in support of white-collar staff is also done in full measure for all blue-collar workers. For example, white- and blue-collar workers are sent to conferences to present papers in equal numbers. Both sets of workers are asked to design the same things. Quality circles, just-in-time, simultaneous engineering, and other major movements within

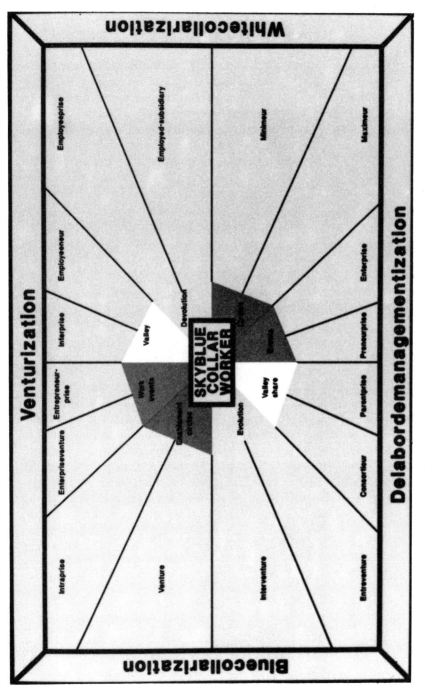

Figure 4-2 The Greene Model of Participatory Management.

manufacturing practice during the past twenty years, have all moved the firm in the direction of upgrading its work force. The two forces—labor and management—that used to exist in every firm are now merging into one entity. The Japanese refer to this new style employee whose job entails both white-and-blue collar functions as a "Skyblue-collar worker." "Gray-collar," a term used in the academic literature of the West, is considered too dingy a color for this very positive phenomenon.

The second polar pair is job automation and venturization. Historically, industry has always moved away from direct labor toward automation and the invention of comfort. In Japanese firms, job automation is a significant part of any worker's job. That is, each person hired, whether in labor or management, is assigned to find ways to eliminate his own job through automation. (Modern cognitive technologies offer more likelihood of replacing white-collar staff organizations than blue-collar work organizations.) Company promotion systems, incentive systems, pay systems and merit conferences, and awards are designed to enforce this policy of eliminating one's own job. Measures are established throughout the bureaucracy of the organization as performance indicators. A certain increment of each manager's job performance is transfered down to a lower level of the organization chart each month. Giant measures are shunned in favor of an overall drift toward the self-automating of jobs.

With workers striving to eliminate their own jobs, how are people to stay employed? The answer is venturization. Since the 1930's, all major Japanese firms have surrounded themselves with subsidiaries. For example, Hitachi has over five hundred subsidiaries and Matsushita nearly four hundred. The officers and directors of these subsidiaries are former employees of the parent company. Automation eliminates jobs in exact proportion to the creation of jobs by venturization. In effect, automation is a form of shared unemployment; its partner, venturization, is a form of democratizing company founding. The parent company serves as a training ground for running a subsidiary company later on. Of course, those in charge of the new venture firms have it easy. When they go to the bank to secure a loan for the new start up company, someone from the parent firm accompanies them. Because the parent firm has tens of millions of dollars on deposit, few bankers would consider denying the loan. And those who did would find themselves in trouble.

These four major forces, white-collar workers taking on blue-collar functions, blue-collar workers acquiring white-collar responsibilities, job automation, and venturization—are historical. They are not company policy or even necessarily good ideas. They merely are the way that history is moving. Together these forces define a one-culture company with a uniform kind of employee. Companies that fight or resist these forces cling to an illusory image of current events. There is little option but to submit.

At the center of the model is a circle divided into two halves of four corresponding sections each. Valley, Evolution, Circles and Events—all of which support the blue-collar worker taking on white-collar responsibilities—correspond respectively to Valley Share, Devolution, Enablement Circles, and Work Events (all of which support the white-collar worker taking on blue-collar functions). The valley axis connects each person in the firm with both the customers and the suppliers of the firm. All jobs require contact in these two directions. The devolution axis has blue-collar groups taking on tasks formerly performed by management, and white-collar groups taking on some of the tasks that used to be done by blue-collar workers. The circles axis deals with successive technology circles. Every work group in the firm takes part in campaigns that last six to eighteen months. Each campaign promotes one new technology across the whole firm. The white-collar Enablement Circles support blue-collar circles on a one-to-one basis. The event axis includes work events wherein hundreds of people in the firm complete a task in a short time that otherwise would have taken a handful of people weeks to do. Usually, the most distasteful and boring jobs are treated this way so that no one gets stuck with the bad assignments for a long period of time.

These eight central weekly/monthly activities form an engine of response to the outer historical trends. Between activities and historical trends, there are sixteen forms of venture business. But these venture business types are not firms outside the parent company but instead ways to organize the work within the parent as business ventures. Each business unit specifies its market inside and outside the firm, devises its own customer support, has its own product development, and keeps track of its profit figures. After years of practice in the parent as a small venture business, workers and managers are well prepared to launch real ventures on the outside. Artificial Intelligence is made to fit this overall model of work group. AI accelerates the trends of merging white- and blue-collar roles, job automation, and venturization. AI has obvious merit for removing human labor from the loop of many routine tasks of analysis and interpretation throughout the firm. Expert systems can be built by blue-collar groups thereby upgrading their technical level. Similarly, white-collar work groups can distill their expertise into expert system advisors that are made available to blue-collar groups.

The eight inner dynamics most powerfully effect AI implementation in Japanese firms. AI can be delivered through companywide circles campaigns in which nearly every work group develops its own expert system. Additionally, work events can be held in which hundreds learn how to build expert systems. Devolution and evolution can take on expert system building forms. Valley dimension work can capture in expert system form outside expertise as well as the knowledge needs of a company's suppliers and buyers. Again, Japanese firms implement AI that is shaped to meet overall strategic thrusts. This causes their AI programs to take on unpredictable and unique features not seen in the West.

Timing Corporate Life by Companywide Engineering Campaigns

Ask a worker in a leading Japanese firm when he met his wife and you are liable to hear something like "during the gate array period" or "during the inspection automation campaign." All workers in that firm will know exactly the time period to which he is referring. Companywide campaigns that deliver new technologies are major participatory events in Japanese firms. In weekly or biweekly circle meetings, both blue- and white-collar workers gather to train themselves in the new technology, study its appropriate applications, and develop pilot projects. Conferences every two months assemble all those involved, and leading circles report on their successes.

Before a technology can be delivered to the circles, it must be down-sized into small, easily learned increments. The technology must be accompanied by self-training materials specially prepared by the firm so that all ordinary workers can understand the principles behind the new technology without having to consult an expert. Additionally, the firm must already have in place the tradition of worker self-study so that employees have the confidence to learn the new technologies on their own. Finally, the management of the firm must be committed to mass dissemination of the new technology instead of permitting selected people to hoard it. If these conditions are present, then any technology whatsoever, if implemented slowly and thoroughly, can be learned by an entire work force. Figure 4-3 illustrates one hundred such technologies that have actually been delivered in three Japanese firms by following these principles.

Note the small and almost trivial nature of the technologies involved. Station automation engineering, for example, involves each worker, whether line or staff, in automating key functions of his own workstation. Inspection automation engineering, as another example,

SOCIETY INVENTION ENGINEERING	VARIATION ELIMINATION ENGINEERING	JOB CONSTRUCTION ENGINEERING	STATION AUTOMATION ENGINEERING	TOOL INVENTION ENGINEERING	INSPECTION AUTOMATION ENGINEERING	PRODUCEABLE PRODUCT ENGINEERING	ROBOT INVENTION ENGINEERING	SOFTWARE INVENTION ENGINEERING	KNOWLEDGE INVENTION ENGINEERING
Little Full Society Inclusions	Statistical Process Charts	Deindividualization of Work & Jobs	Kanban - Debuffering	Multi-tool Single Handle Tools	Make Inspection Criteria Visual Devices	Tandem Product and Production Process Pair	Parts Recognition	Structured Software Design	State Representation
Whole Management Group Design	Cause-Effect Detection	Democratization of Styles Methods & Values	Kanban - Buffering	Automated Positioning Tools	Electronic Recognition of Fault Patterns	Feature Trade-off Charting	Voice Control Systems	Group Form of Programming	Self Learning Programs
Strategic Business Development	Self Environment Analysis	Vertical & Horizontal Task Integration	Human Size-ation	Automated Force Application Tools	Electronic Feedback Control for Faults	Product Family Production Lines Design	Hand Control Systems	Programmer's Assistant Tutor program	Family AI Production Programs
Circle Establishment with Circle Inclusion	Refiguring Tool Design	Workplace Sky-humanization	Video feedback Audio control Helmet workplaces	Tool Change Speed Up	Automated Fault Cause Diagnosis Circuitry	Market Research and Business Plan Building	Operator Specific Languages for Control	Software Factories	Associative Memories
Committeeization	Self Maintenance	Event Jobs Invention	Process Energy Recycling	Tool Palmetco Design	Pre-fault warning automation and inspection automation	Competition Response & Technology Building	Grasp Technology	Application Generalization	Semantic Nets
Cognitive Balance Establishment	Automated Preventative Maintenance	Co-work groups, units, unions, inference, teams	Multi-complementary process by 1 worker	Signal Tool & Material Placement Automation	Pre-fault Fault cause Correction Devices	Workgroup Parent Support Task Force	Tactile Sense Feedback System Skins	Analogical Program Building	Meta Knowledge Production System
Total Resource Parent Establishment	Reliability Redesign of Product	Cognitive Physical Balance Analysis	Tactile & Visual Forming	Specification Excess Elimination	Criteria Scale Promotion & Technology Invention	Tool Producitization	Product Embedded Broadcast of Instruction to the robot	Real Time Control Microprocessor Techniques	LISP & PROLOGUE
Time & Money: Tactics for Attention	Interpretation and Intelligent Conveyor	Resource Workplace Rehumanization	Other worker Feedback Display & Signal System	Excess Tolerance Products & Markets Identification	Inspection While Transferring Devices	Reverse From Tool Range to Market Product Design	Robot self Preventative Maintenance Automation	Machine Machine Interface Interactions	Logic Semi Prover
Human Feeling Tactics & Assignments	Human Attention Ergonomics	Multi-company Job Weeks	Modularly Moving Station Systems	New generation Tool Specs Design	Station Coalescence Fault Detection	Down Time Station Products Design	Fault Recovery Automation	Whole Workforce Tagged Tutor Routine of Advice	Syntax Interfaces
COGNITIVE BODY ENGINEERING	MAINTENANCE AUTOMATION ENGINEERING	WORKFORCE WORKGROUP ENGINEERING	VIDEO MANUFACTURING ENGINEERING	CAD-PROCESS PLAN ENGINEERING	VISION & CONTROL ENGINEERING	COST REDUCTION TECHNOLOGY ENGINEERING	SENSORATIVE WORKFACE ENGINEERING	WORKPLACE CLARIZATION ENGINEERING	FACTORY CONSTRUCT ENGINEERING

Figure 4-3 The 100 Engineerings of the Participatory Company.

has each work group automating the inspection of its work quality. Variation elimination engineering, done about ten years ago at most leading Japanese firms, uses statistical process charts and other techniques to eliminate factors that cause variation in the work process of each group. It didn't matter if these variation factors were the coffee breaks in white-collar clerical groups or machine lubrication irregularities in machine tool stations among blue-collar groups. Notice that knowledge automation engineering is included as a whole work force campaign by these three companies.

Minimizing Technology in Production

There is an apparent paradox in Japanese high tech companies. Their products are clearly state of the art but their means of manufacturing them are something less—or so it appears. The question is: why would companies with such great technical capability underutilize new technology as a means of production? The truth is, it only appears that Japan does not use new technologies to the fullest. But, if we dig deeper, we find that new technology is inevitably present, only it is being implemented in smaller increments and on a smaller scale than would be found in the West. Moreover, ordinary workers are responsible for the gradual implementation of the technology instead of elite professional staffs. Japanese robots provide a typical example. For years, the American press reported that the Japanese had more production robots than the U.S. only if the simple pick-and-place robots were included in the total. But that misses the point. The Japanese deliberately avoided the highly technical and complex robots prevalent in U.S. companies in favor of incrementally simpler worker-designed robots.

I observed two companies in Japan that had disbanded their robotics teams and transformed them into teams to automate the maintenance of robots. These firms had reached the limit of cost-beneficial robotization and had decided the next frontier was the maintenance of robots by other robots. It was a fairly simple procedure to construct robots to maintain the relatively uncomplex pick-and-place robots that were already in place. On the other hand, if the initial robots are the complex, anthropomorphic kind, even humans have a hard time putting them back together.

I found that Japanese companies were taking a similar approach to expert systems. They deliberately minimized the technical complexity of the expert systems they implemented in favor of immense, widespread and technically simple systems. For example, instead of building highly sophisticated, isolated single machine diagnostic expert systems, firms introduced campaigns that allowed large numbers of worker-staffed AI Circles to construct their own systems. These campaigns stressed that workers consider the ultimate objective of the project rather than a display of flashy technology. The workers used AI to produce a long-term and definitive form of system documentation. Instead of confusing, hard to understand paper manuals, AI knowledgebase documentation of the system explained every single complex piece of hardware and software. This allowed users of the equipment to index all information about the system in understandable terms. In fact, this knowledgebase documentation system was much simpler than the full tutor systems and full AI diagnostic systems found in the United States. This Japanese-style system, a new form of publishing technological information, has had a profound effect on company efficiency.

An amusing incident occurred (my first major mistake in Japan) when I attempted to implement my first AI project in a Japanese company. I presented a proposal to management for an AI diagnostic system for machine tools. It was a trial expert system project to establish the payback, cost, and credibility of AI technology. The management quietly endured my presentation, and, after I finished, the room remained still. I thought they perhaps had not understood my imperfect Japanese. Finally, a senior member of the group nodded to a junior member who said, "Mr. Greene, in our firm, machine tools never break down, so we have little need of diagnostic AI systems." Indeed, in this company, preventative maintenance, carried on by ordinary operators at each machining station, was so thorough that machine breakdown was a rare, once a year kind of event.

There are several lessons to be learned from this. First, in U.S. firms, AI diagnostic systems threaten to "automate the problem" rather than prevent it. These systems make it easier for preventative maintenance to fail and, paradoxically, lead to breakdowns by diagnosing them while they occur. Second, this example shows how automation for the sake of automation can easily infest American AI programs. On paper, it makes perfect sense to promote AI diagnostic systems. But the Japanese find it cheaper to encourage human operators to train themselves to maintain their machines so AI diagnosis becomes unnecessary. Substituting complex technology for effective social systems of human beings is an economically fatal mistake in a world where human minds significantly outperform machines over a broad range of problems. The human mind is simply more efficient and economical than many machines. Third, this example reveals a profound and long-term vision of AI. Artificial intelligence, instead of replacing the human mind of the expert operators, eliminates the paper documentation systems that frustrate human operators who have to continually learn and adjust complex generations of equipment in the workplace.

The ways decisions are made about AI can also "automate" a problem. When I persuaded one Japanese manager to sponsor an AI plant capacity advisor, he looked at me at the end of our discussion and asked, "What about commitment?" He was referring to commitment by the social organization and other managers of the firm to the advisor's recommendations. He lectured me about Westerners and their obsession with the "right" answer. "You Westerners sometimes think the work stops when the right answer is found. But you have to realize, that, once the right answer is found, people must be persuaded that it is, indeed, the right answer. The process of finding the right answer must be followed up by convincing people to support the solution." For AI planning advisors, this meant the existing Japanese management system was based on maximally integrating consideration processes and answer development. Right answers were always found in a tandem form as right-and-believed-in answers. Hence, my intention to establish an AI planning advisor system was modified into something not often seen in American AI programs. A team of managers organized the creation of an expert advisor for a number of planning problems. Each group of managers designed and built its own planning advisor so that belief in the system accompanied the "right answer" AI system.

AI used in a documentation system role reduces the role of AI but expands its importance. It minimizes the technical sophistication demanded of any one AI project but increases the areas in the company that require AI expert systems advisors knowledgeable in hardware, software and the social system of the firm. It minimizes the use of high technology to maximize high technology output. It is typical of the ways the Japanese tailor AI to meet their needs.

Disseminating Design Processes throughout a Work Force

There is a fundamental difference between U.S. and Japanese firms that can be seen by examining the ways they design systems. In Japan, the ordinary blue-collar workers design the equipment they work on. They specify the system features and even go so far as to engineer some of the features that the next generation of equipment will need. This role of designer transforms the blue-collar worker's overall relation to the workplace. In the United States, skilled engineers do all such designing with little input from those who will actually use the machines. Employees become disempowered with this split of design and implementation functions. More than that, in recent competitions, when groups of people joined together in the design and implementation, they fared better than groups who had divided the tasks. In purely economic terms—product quality, efficiency of production process, and responsiveness to the market—the firms that join people together come out ahead on both humanitarian and economic grounds. The involvement of entire work forces in the design of systems they work with pays off handsomely. Firms that significantly extend the design function to a majority of the workers put themselves in a position to reap greater financial rewards.

This kind of program is most effective if it has been built up incrementally over a long period of time. The Japanese have involved workers in the design process for seventy years. In part, this was made possible by active labor initiatives which encouraged companies to respect (an Oriental axis of value) the intelligence of the average worker. Additionally, major changes resulted from a severe shortage of skilled workers in the 1960s that forced companies to redesign the workplace to keep highly educated workers interested in their work. Because workers were involved in the design of the systems they worked on, even ordinary work tasks became intellectually challenging enough to satisfy the well-educated workers of post-War Japan.

There is evidence that decades long efforts supported by strong labor initiatives and encouraged by severe labor shortages were sufficient to bring about work force participation in the design process. It is not clear how other countries, faced with different circumstances, will implement this Japanese system. In the United States, there does not exist a concentrated effort to extend involvement in design processes to the actual users. There have been sporadic campaigns in this area, but they were not as far-reaching as their Japanese counterparts. In any case, the needed change of direction is perfectly clear.

Design involvement enhances the workplace in several ways. First, jobs are split into active and reflective components. The active component is the actual performance of work on the work system, while the reflective component is the worker's thoughts on how to bring about possible improvements in the design of the work system. Second, design involvement alters the nature of the relationship between the skilled professionals and the ordinary workers. Instead of being an inaccessible repository of knowledge, the skilled professionals serve as a resource for worker learning. Systems exist in Japan to facilitate this knowledge exchange. For instance, in major firms, newly hired college graduates (even Ph.D's) are told that there is little likelihood that their work in the firm will directly involve their area of expertise. However, these graduates will be asked to answer questions in their field and tutor workers on specific projects. The new employee is treated more as a person with general mental training rather than a specialist. This is but one example of the powerful systems that transform skilled professional workers from a monopoly of expert knowledge into a resource for worker learning. Third, worker involvement in design adds new dimensions (such as research, experiment, and discovery) to otherwise dull, routine jobs. In some firms, the workers are told that their task is not only to perform the job but also to automate it out of existence. (This does not cause undue concern because of the lifetime employ system that operates in Japan.) Fourth, workers involved in design processes are more likely to update their knowledge on all aspects of ordinary jobs because well-designed systems require current knowledge of all technical job functions. A skilled work force in this sense is a work force whose knowledge is current.

In these four areas of worker design involvement, there is a momentum established. A worker progresses from learning aspects of the individual job to learning aspects of the entire work force's technical context. The systems through which the work is performed undergo constant technical improvement and updating. It is fitting, then, that work itself be acknowledged as the continual learning process that it is. And in the world's most economically successful companies, this trend can be seen. Having workers design the systems that affect them directly is the first step toward worker design of the larger systems within which particular jobs are embedded. When design is extended to these larger systems, it is important that the design and implementation functions should not be separated once again. Many participatory management programs extended worker design to these larger systems, but left implementation to ordinary company systems. This reinstituted the designer/implementor split and led to the failure of the systems implementation altogether. Whether the workers or skilled staff design the systems, separation of designers and implementors yields poor results.

How does AI fit into all this? As already mentioned, Japanese and American firms differ fundamentally in new technology design and delivery. In the United States, it is accomplished by elite staffs; in Japan, it is done by literally tens of thousands of workers. It is perpetually hard for people in the U.S. to believe this. This democratization of the intellectual content of the work process by someone other than the United States or a European country irritates something in the Western character. Historically, it is quite marvelous; economically, it is a fearsome powerhouse; emotionally, it is hard to admit. But it has happened. It is not going to go away. And it is probably something other nations will have to learn in order to achieve full economic competitiveness with Japan. In the U.S. and Europe, AI is an elite technology that is nurtured by elite colleges. It is then disseminated through elite government defense R&D contracts and finally captured by elite groups within companies. As such, it is already competitively dead. The only way to compete with Japan is to make AI accessible to a wide range of people. The entire system of high technology delivery in the U.S. must be democratized. AI projects established for personal career advantage will have to give way to projects using AI for national competitive survival. And this type of implementation requires a role for AI unlike anything being done in the United States at present.

Part

2

AI Applications and the Corporation

"As an example, there is a potential for coordination systems to reduce the need for rigid work schedules. Much of the temporal structure of what goes on in organizations is driven by the need to be able to anticipate completion. If the manager knows that a certain task will be done every Friday, then he or she can make a commitment to do something that uses its results on the following Monday. For many routine tasks, this is the best way to guarantee effective coordination. But it can also be an inflexible straitjacket that reduces the space of possibilities open to workers in organizing their activities. If effective coordination on a conversation-by-conversation basis could be regularized [through Expert Electronic Social System facilities like Coordinator software], then the rigidity could be relaxed, altering the conversational structure to make the workers more productive."

Winograd; Flores; *Understanding Computers And Cognition*, Ablex, New Jersey; 1986, page 170. (Insert by Richard Greene.)

This part of the book discusses the reasons why a corporation should consider an AI program—especially an aggressive and imaginative program rather than the safe, "follow-other-companies" type. In particular, the impact AI has on design, manufacturing, office work, and marketing is fully examined.

It is generally pretty difficult to explain AI to corporate managers who are already skeptical of new technology. Because of AI's cognitive nature (it captures certain types of mental processes in computer code form), it is harder to explain than most other new technologies. This portion of the book makes the hard business-case arguments for AI that have convinced middle management in major firms to start AI programs. These arguments do not deal with the nature or purpose of AI. They treat the bottom line by explaining AI's impact on a business under competitive pressure.

5

Explaining AI to a Corporation

Artificial intelligence has two important functions: 1) it captures the human ability to estimate which until recently had been too vague and qualitative to put into computer systems, and 2) it makes this captured knowledge portable. This makes it possible for the corporation to use the knowledge whenever it is needed without resorting to bringing in outside experts.

Knowledge integration can be understood in a chronological context of stages. First, in the 1950s, huge databases were built, and these served to integrate firms in many ways. But gradually, each database became an empire unto itself, and the firm's organization chart repeated itself in database form. Databases became a mirror image of the organization chart of the firm.

Second, Japanese competition forced American firms to develop co-designing and co-planning relationships with their customers and suppliers. A network of suppliers and customers developed subsequently, first in human contact form and later in computer system tie-in form. This integrated the firm by putting all parts of the company in contact with the buyers and suppliers.

Third, leading Japanese firms devised systems for simultaneous engineering wherein the product design people and the manufacturing design people were in constant contact with one another. This enabled all aspects of design to be optimized at once. Product characteristics for the market and product characteristics for manufacturing were established concurrently as part of a single process. Physically putting people together is the next step after integrating the computer systems they use.

Fourth, data integration firms (Electronic Data Systems, for example) pioneered a "one data model of each part" system in which the entire firm shares and updates one model of any product or part. This one mathematical model supports every function from styling and artwork to process planning and machine vision inspection using captured Computer-Aided Design (CAD) data. This represents a profound step that drives systems integration overall.

Finally, knowledge engineering integrates firms by capturing heuristic rules and estimating schema from every division of the firm. These rules and schema are made available much earlier in the design process and the decision-to-produce process. So designers have available to them, for example, process planning rules, parts maintenance rules, design rules for quality assembly, and right-the-first-time design rules. This places heavier constraints on the designer. But since an AI advisor enforces these constraints automatically, the designer still feels as though there is an infinite design space of possibilities. There is only one major change: each of those infinite design possibilities is now effectively producible whereas, in the past, most were good ideas, but impractical to produce. AI makes knowledge portable, objectively examinable, and more manageable. Figure 5-1 illustrates this case.

Integrate By:	Approach	Style	Issue
Building Databanks	Pre-Japan Computerization Approach	Automate What's There	Data Bureaucracy
Networking Suppliers and Buyers	The Method Approach	Copy Japan	Copy What Invented Kanban
Physically Putting People Together	The Social Approach	Circles For All Technologies	How to Achieve No-Man Production
Sharing One Data Model	The Data-Driven System Approach	From Data Derive the Firm	Flexible Mfg.'s Flexibility and Creativity: Standards without Rigidity
Automating Human Experience	The Knowledge Automation Approach	From Knowledge Derive the Firm; Standards without Rigidity	Automating Learning and Innovativity

Figure 5-1 Five Methods of Integrating AI Companies.

To be competitive, firms need to utilize all five of these methods of integration; it is not a matter of choosing among them. Together they define the evolving methodology of corporate form much better than all the leadership and "quick fix" management books around. Some firms, for historical reasons, will find themselves already integrated in the networking of buyers and suppliers. Perhaps they will then introduce the one data model of parts. They might follow this by adding knowledge automation. No matter which route a firm follows, it must eventually utilize all five types of integration. Firms that build hundreds of expert systems without understanding AI's capacity to integrate the company end up with "salt and pepper" AI. As the name suggests, these companies have isolated, elite expert systems sprinkled throughout the firm; this is a strategic error. Firms avoiding this pitfall develop companywide shared knowledgebases that many departments update and use together. It is important to notice that the five methods of integration have both social and technical aspects and illustrate the sociotechnical systems (STS) approach to organizational change.

Think back to the Automobile Vending Machine concept presented earlier wherein the customers designed their own version of the product for later delivery. Integration of the firm moves toward this same ideal—self-design of the products by the actual customers. It means that systems automatically enforce exact and financially feasible response to every customer want. The achievement of this goal is still a long way off. Integration does not take place just within the walls of the corporate head office; integration must enter the mainstream of the organization. Kansei analysis in Japan in 1989 and 1990 derives expert systems to represent consumer preference determinations for each feature of a product. These dozens of expert systems become part of the input to the house of quality of Quality Function Deployment quality systems.

Initial Roles for AI in Corporations

Knowledge portability serves to integrate the firm and is one of the six major roles AI plays from the beginning. Some other roles are not so obvious and are the featured topics of the following text.

Capture of Expertise

This is the most well-known role for AI. For instance, a company can simply make a list of personnel most likely to leave the firm. This study determines which of these people has knowledge, either crucial or irreplaceable, that the firm must capture. To prevent critical knowledge from leaving the firm, the company designs an AI project to capture this expertise.

Performance Stabilization

The outcome of many critical functions in firms depends greatly on who performs them. For example, an automobile company headquarters may ask its divisions to estimate how much to charge for future models. Based on these estimates, headquarters decides how much business to give each division. If the division's estimate is too low, costs exceed budget and the division loses money. If the division's estimates are too high, headquarters will never award it any business. Some people, for unknown reasons, do an excellent job performing this kind of estimating. Others do terribly, even though they share the same credentials on paper with those who perform well. For this function, the absolutely best performance is not needed, but rather some lowest common denominator performance below which the function never falls. An AI advisor system can achieve this bottom level platform of performance even where it cannot model absolute best human performance in the function.

Intelligent Documentation

It's an overwhelming fact that today's manufacturing equipment and systems are highly complex. Single robots are so sophisticated that the work force cannot possibly learn everything about correcting defects and erroneous performance. By the same token, anyone who buys a Digital Equipment Corporation Micro-VAX II computer will receive an entire roomful of ugly orange manuals from the DEC company. And, for the most part, these manuals will gather dust. Unfortunately, the paper documentation that accompanies computer and robot systems is inconvenient to store and handle, poorly written, and badly indexed; there might as well be no documentation at all. This situation continues because user manuals represent only a marginal part of each vendor's profits, and these books rarely influence the customer's decision to buy. Companies often use training courses (costing thousands of dollars a day) as a substitute for poor documentation. People simply give up on the manuals and have no recourse but to sign up for training courses in order to learn something about their equipment. Worst of all, course instructors are sometimes no clearer than the manuals. They emphasize repeatedly that the new equipment is still relatively unproven and no one has yet mastered it completely. At least, these instructors are there in the flesh to field questions. They may even give a helpful answer.

AI ends this dilemma by publishing all system documentation in AI expert system rule form. An employee simply types in a question, and the AI expert advisor guides him in the procedures needed. By necessity, the overall number of lines of code in a software package will be multiplied by tenfold for this AI tutorial documentation system. Not only must the system model the correct ways of doing things, it must also take into account the varied and creative errors that humans commit. These "error models" outnumber "correct models" by about ten to one. So each system will be delivered with one-tenth of its code devoted to functioning documentation and nine-tenths of its code for tutoring type documentation. This intelligent documentation system is underway in some large American companies. Actual use patterns (for building models of the task/command sets users naturally use with equipment and software) are being videotaped, then transcribed. Error-prone procedures are being studied and corrected, and system enhancements are being published in expert rule form.

Diagnostic Recovery

Employees sometimes adhere poorly to the complex systems and procedures that are part of the modern business firm. In addition, complicated software and hardware systems often break down or are underutilized. AI can help train people in correct procedures for social and technical systems including, for example, correct sign-offs for computer and manufacturing systems. Surprisingly, an adequate scope of application for AI diagnosis is not found in most industrial AI programs. Any complex system, no matter where located in the corporation, can benefit from using an AI diagnostic facility. However, firms today create diagnostic systems for only a few kinds of equipment rather than for all complex systems.

Program Enhancement

Increasingly, the computer terminal or the workstation is becoming the workplace itself. Work is becoming more and more professionalized in numerous industries and with only software between an individual and his tasks, much depends on how effectively that person interfaces with the software. People who manage themselves well and perform their software tasks with competency lead their companies to major savings and competitive advantage. AI enhances these extant software systems. It turns a procrustean interface into an intelligent dialogue with domain common sense behind it. Additionally, AI translates data across complicated protocols and operating systems in a firm's entire computer network. With AI, the user is not burdened with knowing operating system and network protocol keywords and commands. AI serves to lubricate the flow of information among complex computer system components.

Cognitive Load-Lifter

Many errors that hurt the firm are due to the small window of information access into and out of the human brain. Short-term memory in humans is a constant source of error. Many jobs and job fragments have local cognitive intensities at the very edge of human short-term memory capacity. For example, if a manufacturing line uses dies, a human operator must examine a production schedule and then orient each die and be ready to re-orient it every few seconds. The work is repetitious, boring and involves working at the very limit of human short-term memory abilities. The end result is substandard job performance. An AI expert system, however, can make these orientation decisions instantly and efficiently, thereby reducing the mental load on the operator so that time can be spent improving the system, rather than suffering from it. In every firm there are hundreds of sources of these short-term memory errors which AI can help correct.

Knowledge Portability

The six points just discussed depend upon knowledge portability. Even though it was explained before, it is included here again because of its importance. Conservative corporate managers, hoping to minimize career risks to themselves when new technology is introduced, often implement elitist, isolated expert systems. By doing so, the portability of knowledge is lost, and company department structure is merely duplicated in the guise of AI expert systems.

Some Advantages Inherent with AI

Many industrial AI programs look for special AI applications. That is, they look for things that AI alone can do without ordinary software. This creates a lot of work and is somewhat futile. AI is a revolution in software practice, not just part of software itself. As such, it is useful wherever software exists. Since software is used extensively in design and manufacture, it is relatively easy to find applications for AI by simply enhancing all existing design and manufacturing software with AI.

It takes a pretty deep appreciation of the history and evolution of software to view AI application this way. Concepts like "specification programming," "non-deterministic procedure invocation," and "data abstraction" that have concerned mainstream software people for twenty-five years, contain in their histories the contributions that AI can make to ordinary software. Unfortunately, many new AI practitioners are educated in the following ways:

1. They get very little exposure to good AI developers who don't teach because of low university salary structures.
2. They get precious little understanding of the entirety of software practice because specialization sets in too soon.
3. They get constant exposure to all the latest fads in AI which are denuded of the history of software concepts that motivates contemporary software features.

This means universities are graduating people who know all of AI's features but have no understanding of the strategic reasons for the usefulness of those features. For example, the first major LISP environments (BBNLISP, MacLISP, ZetaLISP) were a specific AI tool that solved a problem in ordinary programming practice by creating "evolutionary programming." This evolutionary programming ended the old, time-wasting software development cycle of: 1) keeping a logbook of problems with existing systems; 2) hiring a software vendor to turn the logbook into code; 3) waiting months or years to get the code and then spend even more time correcting it; 4) keeping a logbook on that code for a year or two. The cycle then repeats itself. This meant that whatever software a person worked on was usually considerably out of date. In the early 1970's, people involved with Xerox's Palo Alto Research Center (PARC) realized that the inability of users to update the functionality of their systems was a critical issue. The reliance on outside vendors meant delay, outdated software and poor carry-over from specifications to actual systems delivered. These developers at Xerox envisioned a programming environment that allowed users of the code to update its functionality. Hence, they developed major LISP environments with incremental compilers, intelligent error-correcting facilities, and automatic implementation design assist facilities. Contemporary university graduates know all about these features but don't understand the strategic importance relative to software practice. That is, these features enable "Evolutionary Programming" by users of a system. This is but one of many examples. By not grasping the strategic thrust and worth of the techniques they have learned, these university graduates join companies and create their own exclusive AI domains. They don't envision the revolutionary position of AI. By isolating AI in this way, they soon run out of easy, "pure" AI applications and start to lean toward research and development projects which dilute AI's impact on a corporation's bottom line. When AI is freed from this limited vision, then effective application to manufacturing can begin. All existing software is then examined to see in what ways it can be enhanced by AI.

Simulation and Estimation

Before a firm spends millions of dollars on a new technology, it must have some idea of the payback. Since these technologies are complex, all sorts of ancillary factors are critical, such as training time for the work force, quality of equipment delivered, optimal transport of parts through the plant, efficient floor layout, emergency exits, future changes of equipment, and just-in-time delivery of parts to their exact spot of use on the production line. These secondary factors dramatically affect a system's payback. In most cases the pure cost of the hardware alone is less important than the cost of using the hardware well. Therefore, management must analyze all factors and not just the initial cost of the hardware. There must be estimates available so that alternatives can be considered. AI, with its object-oriented programming paradigm and with the decision process modeling its rule-based paradigm allows, can do this estimating and simulation. For example, I was involved in a sneaky AI project to estimate another firm's plant capacity for a major manufacturer's materials manager. This man had outside suppliers he would call up on occasion to place an order for parts. Often the contractor would back out by claiming that his people were already working overtime and there was no possible way to fill the order. The manager doubted these excuses, but he had no data to tell him when the outside contractor wasn't telling the truth. So, he hired me to make an AI plant capacity estimator system that would calculate the vendor's capacity for manufacturing various products. By using this program, he got reliable figures that allowed him to get tough with the vendor. This "lie detector" AI estimator saved him millions by making plural supplier contracts unnecssary.

AI vendor companies sell expensive simulation kits along with their AI tools. However, it takes only about three weeks for a mediocre AI worker at the master's degree level to write such a simulation build kit from scratch. Moreover, the usefulness of such simulation kits depends upon the naturalness of the simulation building primitives, and those tend to be domain specific (factory floor layout primitives, plant capacity primitives, robot cell simulation primitives, and so on). AI itself, especially object oriented AI, makes simulation so easy that special kits are hardly needed at all.

AI Process Control

In the future, an automated factory may have twenty thousand sensors reporting conditions from fifty robots, twenty automatic guided vehicles, ten machining stations, thirty-eight workers, three shifts, nearly five thousand part types, and over two hundred coordinate measuring quality machines. Unmanned manufacturing is on its way. Vendors are selling Optimized Production Technology (OPT) as a good factory scheduling system for such plants, a system consonant with kanban just-in-time production. The first managers to try OPT in their industries, however, found it inflexible and incompatible with kanban. Its status categories were too narrow to handle such normal variables as machine breakdowns, people arriving late or leaving early, product orders needing correction in the middle of manufacture, new priorities that altered production schedules, and inaccurate bills of materials. In other words, existing factory process control and scheduling software excels only when things are working right. When things go wrong—as they inevitably do—the process falls apart.

AI has whole subdivisions that deal with uncertain knowledge, fuzzy values, and qualitative reasoning with equations whose variables don't have discrete numeric values but rather regions of value. The chemical process industry has placed under AI control entire production plants that manufacture millions of dollars worth of chemicals every day. The capacity of AI to model the uncertain, the partial, the wrong, and the nearly right surpasses anything traditional software can do. (Lately the Finns have speeded up OPS83 and modularized its working memory feature to allow real time control by AI.) Moreover, in real time process control, the "evolutionary programming power" of AI is a powerful asset. Nobody now knows exactly what a "right" control algorithm will be in these future unmanned factories since there is no actual use experience at present to determine optimal performance. Through its "evolutionary programming," AI allows new rules and objects to be added to the system in real time as human operators determine what response should occur in real situations. This means the functionality delivered with the initial AI software is one-tenth the functionality achieved a year later. Factories of the future will rely on this ability of AI to allow for the continuous updating of software.

One Data Model of the Part

Many firms develop a physical model of a part and then proceed to take surface data from it and port that information into a different surface representation through analysis programs. From the analysis results, a new surface is created using Computer Aided Design (CAD) systems. The analyzed set of surfaces is translated into another set of mathematics for Numerical Control (NC) path programming. Finally, machine vision inspection is performed based on the data of the original model. This adds up to five different mathematical/physical models of the same part surfaces with many translations between representations. This situation with pluriform models of the part is a disaster. Each model induces errors; each translation induces errors. Inane political struggles go on in the firm as different factions promote one of these diverse models as the "authoritative" one. (This is a meaningless distinction since each "authoritative" model undergoes changes in every translation.) America's leading firms are rapidly eliminating this diversity; Japan's leading firms hold a two year lead in this area. Companies are adopting this one model of the part concept that all areas and processes of the corporation update. No duplication is allowed. AI has an object-oriented programming feature that permits firms to achieve this integration neatly.

With object-oriented programming, one conceptual structure can be built that relates parts to assemblies, assemblies to assembly processes, and so on. There results a one-to-one correspondence of real world attributes to programming "objects." And this one-to-one correspondence makes programming simple. The uniformity of the "objects" makes this modularity safe, because no object gets inside another object's procedure codes. Firms can then build within these objects incompatible mathematical models and gradually whittle down the various mathematical models into one. The conceptual structure never has to be built again. Indeed, AI objects are natural translators because each object has routines that define its behavior. It might have one set of routines to define its behavior in the CAD world and another to define its behavior in the NC world. Since all such behaviors stem from one set of software objects, they can be integrated easily in software form. Then, over time, the plurality within the procedure defining parts of each object can be reduced to one unified model.

Process Planning

AI programs can automatically classify parts from drawings into a group technology system. They can invent new manufacturing processes for never before encountered new materials or parts by using rules to handle different situations. They can optimize processes along several simultaneous criteria like cost, speed, and quality. In addition, AI programs can simulate new, untried processes and produce detailed estimates so the firm can discover even better ways of processing. These programs can add design for assembly features to the manufacturing design specs. In this way, designers create designs that lead to the more efficient manufacturing of parts.

Diagnosis and Recovery Procedure Design

Artificial intelligence can use causal reasoning to understand breakdowns and identify the causes. AI can estimate correct answers and processes from initial task descriptions and then guide parameters to achieve optima in that vicinity. AI can explain its reasoning as it diagnoses the cause of a machine tool error so that mechanics educate themselves in the process of repair. AI replaces all the logbooks that operators keep on hand to assist them when a machine starts to work irregularly. AI can put these logbooks on the screen so that operators can have English-like dialogues that ask no unneccessary questions and require no scanning of technical manuals. There is a kind of AI application called the "Help Desk." Often when complex software or hardware breaks down, companies call an outside source for assistance. The advice they receive is frequently late and imperfect because the person on the other end of the line may have to search through hundreds of pages of data to find an example of a similar problem. AI can replace that notebook, eliminate the scan process, correctly diagnose problems, add data from new problems to a knowledgebase, and coach people in the best procedures to recover from a process breakdown.

The "Help Desk" will be part of a true revolution: billion dollar manufacturers will probably need a minimum of ten thousand such "Help Desks." This one AI application alone could save firms one-fifth of their total costs. Any and all complex pieces of hardware and software could be accompanied by an AI "Help Desk" from the first day of use. Some leading U.S. firms are doing this now. Most firms, however, don't realize the strategic power of this application, because their university-educated AI staff over-emphasizes "diagnosis." As previously mentioned, these university-educated developers limit AI and fail to understand its commercially strategic roles in the firm.

"Diagnosis" is just a small subcategory under "Self Explaining Devices." All new software and hardware systems installed by the firm will, utilizing AI, teach themselves to the work force instead of requiring coursework and maintenance manuals. "Self-Explaining Devices" publish all system documentation in AI Tutor form. This means a machine teaches a worker its own operating procedures and diagnoses its own malfunctions directly on the screen. Some estimate that in a decade, seventy percent of all industrial AI will be this type of self-educating device.

6

Some Practical Applications

Preventing AI from Becoming Isolated

The typical student spends six years studying computer science and AI hoping to be hired by a large firm for an attractive salary. After graduation, he visits the various divisions in a company and talks to the engineers about possible AI applications. These engineers know little about AI beyond what they've read in the popular press and almost always specify complicated hybrid projects as a starting point, rather than pure AI applications. Perhaps one of these projects involves straightening up some FORTRAN I analysis programs and capturing some design rules. Chances are, the new worker will avoid the project, wanting to do AI programming instead of graphics, analysis, or database programming.

This scenario illustrates why AI becomes isolated. The tragic fact is, ninety percent of a firm's AI programs should mesh AI with traditional software systems. Newly hired AI practitioners will do one or two "hybrid" projects but, over time, they will resist learning graphics and perhaps even move to another firm to conduct research. By immersing themselves in research, they avoid having to learn all the related knowledge that can lead AI to help industry. Hence, it is foolish for a company to create AI groups containing exclusively AI people. Rather, the AI groups should contain a cross section of employees that combines the talents of AI people with the expertise of people in areas such as finance and engineering who have been trained in basic AI knowledge extraction and coding techniques.

Gradually, over the next five years of AI application in industry, two things will occur that will downgrade the work life of those who apply it. First, they will find that seventy-five percent of the code they write is not AI code but code that integrates AI systems to traditional software systems. Second, they will find many jobs in AI application that pay under $25,000 a year. AI jobs will not automatically command hefty salaries. Universities are training all computer science graduates in AI, and personal computers provide very powerful AI tools cheaply enough that eventually sharp twelve year olds will be able to provide intense competition. For those AI workers intent upon performing pure research in industry at a high price, the future is bleak. AI is in the process of corporate evolution that all previous technologies have undergone. The high-paying positions will be for those responsible for management of the overall AI program and the further development of all AI network and connectionist hardware. AI will be resocialized to the values of industry as its DARPA beginnings recede into the background. An amusing clash occurs at AI conferences between the old-timers and these industry-need appliers of AI. The old-timers understand the contexts of AI features but not AI's future form. The industry-appliers envision AI's future shape but are wrong about AI's ultimate strategic potential.

Initial AI Application Projects

Those who "professionalize" AI and keep it "pure" to avoid learning graphics, analysis, and all the other disciplines with which AI must interface to be of use to industry, are too "literal" about AI. They seek only pure applications for AI. They ask for budget money and create esoteric "AI projects." Within just a few weeks, they have evolved into just another technology interest group whose main goal is self-perpetuation. There is an alternative approach.

This approach does not seek resources and attention for AI on AI terms. Instead, it identifies already existing high priority campaigns and programs and explains how AI can accelerate or amplify these already approved projects. Rather than requesting central money, seed money, or R&D money to launch new AI projects, the AI group simply asks for money already allocated to these existing projects and campaigns. It turns out that this is easy, for AI has very powerful and unique contributions that can be applied to the most profound and widespread industry projects.

The following paragraphs describe nine major new technology campaigns to which most large industrial firms are committed. Associated with each is a description of the role AI can play. Many of these campaigns are of such high priority that any technique that helps firms obtain results will be readily embraced. Most of the campaigns have been forced on reluctant American and European firms by Japanese competition. In some companies, these campaigns are survival tactics rather than improvement tactics. They are powerful magnets for revenues and management attention. They are also excellent proving grounds for first AI efforts. AI makes specific, unique, and powerful contributions that can substantially reduce costs and boost the effectiveness of these campaigns. So, instead of seeking "pure" AI projects, firms should introduce AI to already existing projects. Not only will there be an increased likelihood for success, but management will show greater attention.

Design for Assembly

Most major firms have implemented programs to train designers in ways to make their designs easy to manufacture. As training programs, these efforts yield only modest results. But AI "design assistant" programs can be built that incorporate not only formal rules from "Design for Assembly" texts but also use rules of manufacturing from actual process planners, NC programmers, and machine tool operators. When these expanded rule-based instructions and references are made available to designers through the AI Design Assistant, the advantages are quickly perceived. With this assistance at the designer's disposal in the early stages of the design process, much more effective compliance (indeed, the compliance is automatic) is achieved using optimal design for assembly principles. This would apply not only to those workers who had trained in special courses but to all designers who use the AI Design Assistant, including new hires.

Simultaneous Engineering

Many firms are constructing new facilities and moving hundreds of design engineers so that they are in close physical proximity to manufacturing engineers. This is an attempt to buttress design for assembly by the actual simultaneous co-design of a process or part by the manufacturing engineers and the product design engineers. It is an amplification of design for assembly on the sociological level. Unfortunately, in most firms, these two camps of engineers use incompatible computer systems. Through shared knowledgebase networks, AI can enable engineers from separate departments (even in different cities) to share and update one AI knowledgebase of rules for the design of certain parts. The shared knowledgebases allow each department to use a different subset of AI design rules. These subsets can overlap, however, so that process planning rules can be used by designers using the system and vice versa. This achieves in computer network form what simultaneous engineering achieves in physical body transfer form. By making computer systems match social systems in this way, AI can overcome the over-individualist assumptions that exist in both traditional DARPA AI practice and ordinary engineering practice.

Variational Engineering

Engineers are discovering that they do two fundamentally different kinds of engineering. One is "routine" engineering wherein the design and manufacturing rules are well within past practice traditions. The other is "research" engineering wherein new ways of doing things, new optima and new product parts or materials are explored. Many firms are handing over all routine engineering to subcontractors and concentrating their energies on research engineering. For routine engineering projects, AI offers design assistants that take the human designer out of the loop for all design rules that are tried, tested, and known. For research engineering, AI offers variational engineering features. In research engineering, the engineer looks at a screen to see the part or process being designed. A lot of estimating and playing hunches is involved for which immediate solid model graphic feedback is needed. AI provides automatic construction of three-dimensional models from two-dimensional inputs, automatic equation solvers, and general design rule sets. These three functions interact to create variational engineering software.

Variational engineering displays a solid model on the screen with two sets of equations that automatically control the model and the geometry behind it. One of these equation sets is purely geometric and determines how other dimensions change if one dimension is altered. The other set of equations relates to physics and determines how dimensions and other properties change if heat transfer, stress, and other conditions are modified. AI can provide image matching techniques for automatic generation of 3-D models for manipulation on screen. Finally, AI can constrain the model by rules and relations not analytically determined like the equation sets, but by involving human heuristics. All three aspects of variational engineering software can be significantly enhanced by AI.

The Massachusetts Institute of Technology (MIT) has built a solid model driven by an equation solver called Mathpak. It has severe limitations, however, due to the mathematics underlying its equation solver. Enhancements that are needed to augment the overall engineering abilities are:

1. Object-oriented AI representation of solid primitives;
2. Interpreted driving of solid model aspects from the AI design rules in interactive sessions;
3. Automatic dialogue driven acquisition of design rules from experts;
4. Enhancement of the equation solver so it uses symbolic equation solving algorithms of MACSYMA in addition to the simple Newton-Raphson method of Mathpak;
5. Automatic finite element mesh creation on the model driven by AI rulebase capturing mesh expertise;
6. Automatic interpretation of the results of finite element analyses by an AI rulebase interpreter;
7. Artwork to math compiler to translate aesthetic and styling work in design shops into mathematical surface geometry forms for analysis and CAD processing.

Today, major American firms are actively pursuing these enhancements.

Dimensional Simulation

With dimensional simulation, the actual "statistical" measurements of parts to be manufactured are simulated and then related to assembly tolerances. In this way, the overall fit of the product can be predicted based on a company's ability to control quality. Dimensional simulation is responsible at present for the production of the highest quality products in the United States and promises one day to integrate itself automatically with process control so the simulation can adjust processes to conform with dimensional "fit" criteria. The development of a workable model of the part and process variations that conform to actual production in the company is the main thrust of this undertaking. Once a working model has been built, it is tested and the results are interpreted. AI can help automate the building of the model by diagnosing potential problems and suggesting corrective measures. AI can also help interpret model results since the criteria for interpretation (now done by humans) can be accurately captured in AI rulebase form.

Kanban

Many companies are adopting kanban, a "leaner" form of inventory. Kanban makes a mockery of computer inventory systems. For instance, rather than relying on immense computer systems to control inventory, Japanese firms outperform American and European firms by using little blue cardboard cards. (These little cards have never been known to crash at inopportune times.) Kanban requires suppliers to adhere to a tight delivery schedule. Moreover, it requires the immediate and accurate repair of any assembly or production problems in the plant so that delivery schedules are not disrupted. In factories where AI has been implemented, those who schedule deliveries and those who manage the machines must provide fast recovery from exceptional conditions to meet tight kanban schedules. Conventional software simply cannot handle the uncertainty, variability, and growth of function; AI easily copes with all of these.

Process Inspection

Most Japanese firms are moving major product lines into the process inspection arena. Instead of randomly inspecting parts for flaws after manufacture, the Japanese maintain such a stringent inspection of the manufacturing process itself that faults and errors cannot result. This moving of inspection from part to process is one of the major goals of Japanese manufacturers for the 1980s. Processes, however, must have enough flexibility to respond to many variables, such as new product features. AI machine controller programs offer this adaptability and growth of functionality whereas conventional software is so cumbersome to update that it is of little long-term help.

Generic Documentation

Most companies are aiming toward a distant goal of one generic documentation system that automatically manages memos, reports, bills of materials, invoices, and engineering drawings. AI systems currently on the market offer "intelligent document" capability in which each document, indeed, each shape or field on each document, manages itself intelligently in relation to hundreds of other documents, fields, and shapes. These "self-managing" document systems afford industry immense opportunities, because no overall "right answer design" of a document system is needed. AI allows users of the system to add (in increments) new rules and objects to the system's functionality as new situations arise or new understanding of previous situations arises.

Supplier-User Co-Design of Process/Product

Japanese competitive pressure causes many firms to ask their suppliers and users to help design next generation parts, products, and processes. In addition to physically bringing these people into the company, there must be computer networking between companies and their suppliers. AI allows such networks to capture and disseminate the expertise of all members of all involved firms so that no gaps develop when immediate response is required.

One Mathematical Model of the Product

Many firms suffer from too many models (mathematical, physical, CAD, etc.) of their parts. Because of these diverse models, slight discrepancies arise in engineering. Some firms have vowed to achieve one mathematical model of each part and product, but find, in practice, that it is an extremely challenging integration issue. AI object oriented databases can unite in one conceptual database structure all the physical attributes of parts and products while allowing multiple calculation methods to co-exist. Such AI objects then permit a gradual incremental merging of calculation methods without changing or rewriting major portions of the database. This "encapsulation of representation problems" provides firms a cost-efficient path gravitating toward one mathematical geometry for all processes in the firm—from artwork to machine vision inspection.

Chances are these nine technological opportunities already exist as funded programs in most companies and are begging for implementation help. AI can offer practical help right now. Moreover, one of AI's ultimate roles, the portability of knowledge, can be incorporated in many of the abovementioned programs. AI, more modular and more easily updatable, can integrate deeper levels of knowledge than conventional software.

What AI Offers Design

In the past there has been a clear cut separation of design and manufacture. However, Japanese simultaneous engineering accomplishments are making this division disappear. Ideally, AI should not be separated into design and manufacturing applications, but the corporate real world intrudes here. In most firms, design and manufacturing are separate entities each with its own budget. Corporate politics require that both constituencies endorse AI before implementation begins. For this reason, this book will retain the false distinction between design and manufacture.

The future will see not a design/manufacture boundary but rather a geometry/expertise boundary. There will be one set of mathematics for representing part and process geometry that will, in turn, mesh with the expertise driving it. That expertise, like the geometry driving it, will be in computer form. And between this geometry and expertise comes analytics—finite element analysis for such things as stress and temperature that make use of determinate mathematics. In essence, this is physics. Therefore, we have three fundamental layers: geometry, physics, and expertise. Those lacking a full understanding of AI expert systems will say, "AI must be the expertise layer." They are thinking of how AI captures expertise and makes knowledge portable. In fact, AI encompasses all three layers. AI objects will house the geometry. AI code generators will automatically generate analytic software from specs of physics applications. AI rules will capture the estimating and aesthetic trade-offs of the best actual designers.

Early in the design phase, the geometry is generated from artwork. Then it is meshed for finite element analysis and subsequently translated into a "semantic geometry" wherein the functional and meaningful subshapes are identified for process plan creation. Then the geometry is translated into its inverse for machine tool path creation, that is, the geometry of removed material which leaves the desired shape. AI translates "brute" geometry into its "semantic" form; AI chooses proper "meshes" for finite element analysis; AI designs proper machine tool pathing of inverse geometry.

To appreciate the global analysis of AI's role in design, you have to know something about the way software and systems integration influence design and manufacture. The multiple geometries that companies use today to build any one part are giving way to hundred million dollar programs to achieve one geometry that all parts of the design/manufacture process use. Firms not understanding this principle will use AI indiscriminately. The ultimate role for AI will become confused with the ultimate role for integration. This will result in redundant AI and missing integration at great cost to the firm. It is absolutely essential that firms grasp this global view for applying AI to the design process.

Enhancements to Variational Engineering

Earlier in the book, I described seven ways to enhance variational engineering software. It was pointed out that AI will take humans out of the loop for routine designs. When nonroutine change, inventiveness, or tough constraints are needed, human intervention will be required. These situations will necessitate a solid model on the screen that the human operator manipulates. Associated with that solid model is a set of equations governing the geometric relations and all the physics relations that constrain it. This includes the spatial envelop within which deflections of the part must take place. An automatic equation solver will manage that equation set. Driving both the solid model and the equation set is an AI rule set embodying current expertise for a particular part or process that spans all departments of the firm. Chances are the solid model graphic primitives will be in AI object form and the equation solver will be a system like Mathematica. The AI rulebase, of course, will also be in object form.

Design Process Backtrack Facility

The design process embodies human hunches, estimations, backtracking, and retrials of previous design paths. To say the least, it is an unsequential sequence. In routine designing, AI follows the same tortuous path of execution. In nonroutine design, AI allows the designer to recover easily from wrong design paths and explore alternative paths. Also, AI gives the designer the ability to return effortlessly to any previous point in the design process.

Construction of Solid Models

Extrusion and rotation of basic shapes are two principal ways of generating solid models convenient to research. Although automatic construction of three-dimension drawings from two-dimension has been achieved, there is little demand for it. New designs and old drawings that are not in vector or raster form cannot presently be input at all except with the use of expensive scanners. Constructing a solid model is less an issue than getting the drawings in electronic form. Boolean subtract operations of basic shapes are useful but not enough. Voice generation of a solid model is hindered by the still primitive state of voice-input technology.

AI can derive a three-dimensional model from two-dimension inputs easily enough. AI can automatically classify drawing or solid model features into meaningful machining features or attributes. It can create a solid model from similar solid models, supporting "distortion" and "borrow" operations from those similar models. In the real world, a company wants an AI system that knows in principle what the "rotation flange on the choker" of a transmission is and puts it on the screen automatically, awaiting modifications.

A number of companies are betting on sketch pad input, that is, preliminary solid models created for proving concepts in the initial phase of design. AI also recognizes the intended solid model from two-dimension human input on a sketch pad and projects that solid on the screen for dimensioning. Drawing complex solids, however, even in sketch form is extremely tedious and few would tolerate it for long, but it may fill a void in present systems.

Automatic Dimensioning of Parts

The rules for good dimensioning are well-known. Unfortunately, the wrong people, the manufacturers, know these rules. The designers perform the dimensioning and drafters complete the process, but only manufacturing people know what form of dimensioning will tell them the best way to make a part. AI, which makes knowledge portable, can capture these dimensioning rules and make them available to designers at the point of design. Moreover, AI can automatically dimension arbitrary designs put up by designers. Such dimensions will be of better quality because they were made using manufacturing rules.

Self-Modifying Database

AI objects for part and process data are modular. This means that a left-hand widget of a transmission has its object which can be removed and a new widget with twice its diameter inserted. The rest of the objects representing that transmission will be automatically recalculated. In effect, this redesigns the whole transmission to accommodate the diameter of the new widget. This self-modifying property pertains to all AI object databases when routine changes are introduced.

Self-Tutoring Environment

This AI feature encompasses more than design alone. Because of employee turnover in their shops, expert designers spend a lot of time tutoring and coaching novices. Research shows the quality of tutoring is vastly improved when the terminology, shop procedures, history of shop practice for particular families of parts, and instructions in software systems and procedures are made the responsibility of someone other than the expert designers. If that someone else turns out to be an AI tutoring system, hundreds of designers can use it and update it across the firm and even across whole industries (as some Japanese industries are currently discussing). AI tutoring is vastly more responsive and precise than the old computer instruction products like PLATO (Programmed Logic for Automatic Teaching Operations). In the full learn mode, an AI tutor can train people in sessions; in the coach mode, it can assist people with particular tasks through example.

Shared Knowledgebase Network

A shared knowledgebase network is potentially the single most productive use for AI in industry. It means that dozens of people in several cities on one AI network can share and update one knowledgebase. In regularly scheduled meetings, these workers can promote the "what if" rules they each added during the year into full authority "green advice" rules, authorized for engineering release. This is an example of a software system built for companywide teams to use rather than software individualized to one person/one terminal as we have today.

A design rulebase that hundreds of individuals in the firm use and update continuously can grow in expertise much more rapidly than design knowledge at present.

Evolutionary Programming

The final point in the preceding paragraph deserves further treatment. Whenever the users themselves are able to update the

functionality of their software while using it on real cases and problems, the functional content of the software grows exponentially. Individually, workers frequently come across problems that overwhelm
their confidence, experience, or time availability. But when the problem is shared among a large number of people, it becomes a fun-
filled group quest for an answer. The problem is divided and con-
quered. Evolutionary programming, as permitted by AI, allows any
user to add to the functionality of the system. Of course, by the same
token, incompetent users can add stupid rules to the system and
exponentially downgrade overall software functioning. For this reason, there must be a security system of AI rulemasters, an appointed
panel that examines all new contributions before promoting them to
authoritative status. Nevertheless, anyone can add new rules to see
how they affect the system and those that are beneficial will be promoted to authoritative status within a few months.

Semantic Geometry: A Step Toward Intelligent Geometry

Companies like Creative Design, Wisdom Systems, Aries, Cognition,
Cissy, ICAD, Cericor, and Artecon are developing ways to enhance
AI's contributions to the design process. They share a number of
ideas but differ on means of delivery. Unfortunately, they are in a
hurry to get a product to market so they promote new technology
that needs better integration with actual business practices. From
these products, however, we can abstract a certain transformation in
geometry itself, a transformation enabled by simple AI capabilities.
AI has had these capabilities for a long time but they have not been
brought to bear on geometry problems, until these pioneering companies appeared.

This new, emerging geometry is Semantic Geometry. Semantic Geometry, in essence, embodies all the mathematics defining all the
shapes displayed on the computer screen of usual solid modeling
Computer Aided Design (CAD) systems indexed by functionally
meaningful constraints and functionally meaningful shapes for manufacturing process determination.

Design may be defined as "a set of particular constraints that
cause the attributes of the figure to achieve certain functioning."
That is, design is the gradual process of selecting the "right" constraints or those that specify the correct functioning of the part. If
you talk to CAD people (engineers, analysts and process planners),
they will tell you that they need "intelligent" shapes on the screen.
For example, a notch must "know" that it is a notch so that if the
engineers move it, they will not have to change edges or surfaces

when optimizing the design for manufacture. For the defining of a design, they need "constraints not between parameters but between conceptual entities." That is, they want general rules instead of specific rules, such as "make surface A always parallel to surface B" rather than "make the surface of area 50 at location 10 parallel to the surface area of 30 at location 2." AI allows both meaningful constraints and meaningful shapes.

Intelligent constraints permit all possible variations to be simulated for a particular part. It means the part can be rescaled or modified in complex ways and each constraint will intelligently re-position and actualize itself. It even means that the part will "warn" when it has come into conflict with the new situation or a new aspect of the new situation caused by another constraint. "Intelligent shapes" means that each part "knows" that it is a functional entity and can "explain" itself to machining operations or "explain" itself to manufacturing constraints that cause redesign. Parts are dealt with as functional units and not as an arbitrary collection of surfaces and edges.

AI creates semantic meaning for constraints by automatically building and maintaining equation sets that represent constraints bolstered by AI production rules that re-input into such equation sets intelligently. For example, a constraint is set to keep the end of a cylinder parallel with the end of a box in which it is embedded and then the cylinder is "Boolean" removed to make a cylindrical hole in the box. The constraint, then, automatically propagates itself to the lower end of the cylinder where it was initially set by the now nonexistent upper end of the cylinder. AI creates semantic meaning for shapes by representing not only the collection of geometric features that specifies shape but also by representing the "functional constraints," "locational constraints" and "interrelated behavior constraints" which relate that shape to other aspects of overall design. In this way, geometry, physics, and expertise are becoming embedded in one another. The geometry itself is intelligent in geometric constraint terms. The physics "knows" geometry and relates itself automatically to geometric constraints. The expertise of the designer interfaces with intelligent shapes that are intelligently constrained by physics.

Beyond Manufacturing

The ways that AI can help a company are best visualized by examining the manufacturing and design process. Increasingly, however, companies in the United States are turning toward services that place a strong emphasis on technology and knowledge. Wherever knowledge is key to business, AI can play a number of major roles.

The Business Intelligence Function

Until recently, major firms have not systematically collected information on their competitors. Michael Porter, the Harvard Business School consultant, has been teaching managements which kinds of competitor data will be most useful. In particular, if a firm knows its rival's goals and ways of thinking, it can then predict how the competition will respond to new situations and events. In addition, it can foretell which initiatives are going to be worthwhile to competitor managements.

There are several ways to approach business intelligence operations:

1. Gather data from the entire work force.
2. Conduct investigative probes.
3. Utilize formal data processing systems.
4. Initiate analysis and distillation of data.

Each approach emphasizes a different aspect of collecting intelligence. The first stresses gathering data from the hundreds of contacts ordinary employees have every day with other firms. The second approach deals with finding particular data in response to specific needs. The third emphasizes the effective collection of data that is already in the firm. And finally, all data must be correctly analyzed so that the firm can take the most advantageous action. AI, which has little or no application to the first and third approaches, can have significant impact on the other two. To the second approach, it can offer intelligent simulations and models that tell management what data is still needed. And AI has profound implications for the fourth approach.

The United States government can serve as an example of the importance of correctly interpreting data once it has been gathered. The Carter Administration had all the data on Iran, but interpreted it all wrong. During the Vietnam war, the government once again had the requisite data but chose to lie to the public to protect national honor and policy investments. The Reagan administration had all the necessary data on Iran, but the check and balance points were excluded from the interpretation and decision process. It is easy to see that our political system fails more often from poor interpretation of its intelligence reports rather than a lack of information. And in this respect, business is no different than the government.

Spreadsheets are an important tool for interpretation. Recently advanced spreadsheets have come on the market that allow backward as well as forward processing. AI can turn a spreadsheet into parallel models of reasoning. As values in spreadsheet cells change, new lines of reasoning kick in and gather or combine new data. Many decisions depend on the ability to view large spaces of various combinations of factors. Trying out multiple lines of reasoning and comparing the results also affect decision making. The four types of AI spreadsheets are:

1. AI Formulasheets—The formulas that control relations between values in one spreadsheet row, column, cell, or formula-selected groups of cells are really AI rule and object sets.
2. AI Cellsheets—The contents of each cell of the spreadsheet are various AI rulesets, and the formulas that control relations between rows, columns, cells, or formula-selected groups of cells are rule manipulating rules.
3. AI Object Cellsheets—The cells themselves and the formulas that control them are all AI objects which can pass messages to any other object in the system with complete generality.
4. AI Viewsheets—Each cell of the spreadsheet is an AI object implemented spreadsheet itself, with each such cell spreadsheet representing a fundamentally different view of the data.

The combination of AI Spreadsheeting and Data views can drastically improve the interpretation capability of managers, executives, professional staffs, and workers. To make these four products useful, the following procedures should be adhered to:

1. Omnidirectional Reversibility—Any value in the system can be "anchored" and all other values recalculated backwards or forwards from the anchored value.
2. Mid-Process View Comparison—Different formulas and logic processes can be set upon the same or different initial data. As the processes work themselves out, different views or snapshots across different lines of development can be monitored in time by the user in a visual form highlighting automatically AI-determined similarities and differences, both trends and values.

3. Genetic Algorithm Competition Between Rulesets—
   Spreadsheets, each cell of which has a different ruleset for controlling values in another spreadsheet, can be set up so all cell
   rulesets compete to produce certain values, and the winning
   rulesets are determined at the end.

With tools like these, business analysts can spot not only key data
from which they can make good interpretations, but they can determine which essential data is still missing.

However, spreadsheets are now the problem. They are so plentiful,
no one reads them. Even graphs of spreadsheet row or column values
do not get read. People want to scan rows of issue statements not
rows of numbers. Further, people want to regularly invent new key
indicators and examine rows of them, for different levels of the organization. Finally, everything in any business is a process that needs
monitoring as changing types of indicators of performance and rows
of issues—current priority ones needing immediate human attention,
automatically solved ones already fixed by the software, waiting issues not yet big enough or frequent enough to be called a priority.
Adding rulebase AI to relational data engines gives all this capability
today.

Retail AI

Many consumer goods companies believe computers may totally
change what stores are, salespersons do, people buy. Computers have
innundated suppliers, trade customers, retailers, and salesforces
with data they cannot digest. AI can be the digester of that data—
transforming it automatically into issues. The retail business is
knowledge intensive and AI can help companies boost sales whether
the business is involved with financial services, computer services, or
retail sales. Here are some examples where application could improve service industries, the retail industry in particular.

1. Fast Transaction Speed—AI can drastically shorten transaction
   time when complex products, services, systems, or sets of op-
   tions are the product being sold.
2. Comprehensive Advice/No Missed Product Opportunities—AI
   can guarantee a thoroughness and exploration of all possibilities that no human operator could hope to achieve in configur-
   ing complex products or services for the customers. Thus, the

customer trusts the AI advisor's advice when retail clerks are doubted.

3. Personalized Treatment—AI can guarantee a certain degree of relevance, up-to-the-minute advice, and demographic appropriateness to service and products delivered beyond what tired, bored or dishonest employees will produce.

4. Special Qualifications Notification—No one wants to miss opportunities because the sales clerk did not think of something or consider all the possibilities; AI systems will explore all possibilities for discounts, loans, and financing.

5. Intelligent Product Spreadsheeting—Customers buying complex products or services will benefit from the kind of intelligent spreadsheets mentioned above, which lays out all combinations, lines of development, product combinations, and their influence on key variables over time or over different initial price or cost investments.

The list extends beyond the five items shown above, but it should suffice to illustrate AI's tremendous potential to improve the quality of retail transactions by increasing accuracy, reliability, courtesy and speed. Moreover, AI will expand how much of the workforce gets to see and interact with key spreadsheets.

The Japanese are currently testing mini-expert system "price tags" that respond intelligently to customer queries about product features.

Office Work

Offices will probably disappear entirely by the end of the century. The functions, systems and people that were concentrated in them can now be technically distributed on a network of workstations. Support tasks that once required a concentrated office of people are now largely accomplished by nonsupport staff on the network computer system. Even the boss will be able to do without a secretary because the input that formerly was typed on paper can now be captured electronically. Therefore, AI will not be used to automate offices—which won't be in existence much longer anyway—but rather to increase the computer capability throughout the firm until each function takes on its own "officing." Office workers will then become a group that improves communication throughout a firm's computer network rather than a group that solely types letters.

In total contradiction to the above, AI will enable offices to take another route. Instead of using AI to eliminate office work entirely, AI can be used in an "augmentation" strategy to enhance the work of offices in existence now. In real life, both of these opposing strategies for AI will take place simultaneously.

Later in this book, an Intelligent Document Platform (in effect, the automation of offices in the firm) will be described. Here I will mention only a couple of basic premises. First, imagine an electronic document on the computer screen. The front side of the document is the usual form with boxes, labels, and places to input information. The back of that electronic document is a set of "imaginary lines" connecting each box on the front, using certain calculations and reasoning lines, to values on other documents, or even to new documents created automatically (if specific values on the original document reach certain levels). In such a system, a user could update the dollar amount for one rental unit and watch as the system created new documents automatically, filled in data by searching for it throughout the system, changed values in particular boxes on other documents, and called certain documents out of existence as they became irrelevant or obsolete. The technical capability to do this across networks of personal computers already exists. One such product in the thousand dollar price range is called Intuitive Solution.

Office Networks

An organization can be defined as networks of promises and commitments. Any social organization exchanges only certain kinds of "points." That is, everything we say to each other has some point. Linguists have catalogued these points into roughly ten categories: promises, requests, and so on.

People envision computer networks as electronic data exchange systems. If we use this vision as an image for social organizations, it looks pretty ridiculous. Social organizations, for the most part, do not exchange data. As mentioned above, they exchange points in the form of promises and various types of commitments. However, we can design the beginnings of an Electronic Social System on computer networks by building software that allows people on the computer network to exchange promises, commitments, and requests. Furthermore, relationships are built up in these exchanges of "points." Any Electronic Social System will allow exchanges of "points" to be managed in terms of degree of intimacy, represented in data structures called "relationships."

The prevailing attitude is that Electronic Social Systems are less human, less emotive and, therefore, less "real" than traditional social systems. But research into mood meters—cartoon faces that each user on the network sets to communicate emotion in reaction to some group network activity—show they reveal more about emotions than would be expected. Shockingly, use of mood meters across computer networks showed organizations ended meetings with the participants indicating abysmal despair. Researchers did not know what to think. Was that appropriate behavior? At any rate, Electronic Social System encounters will include live video and enhancements to the cues of unmediated social encounters.

Social psychology has recently researched the social memory models of social interaction. This is typically when we use other people to perform mental functions for us. For example, we depend on one of our friends to remember sports team standings; we collect the latest on world events from another friend; we use family members to remind us of social obligations. We each manage and live among a distributed group mind. Electronic Social Systems can support this group mind using a much larger pool of people who are not geographically constrained to be near each other.

In managing promises across networks, early products, like the Coordinator, omit many essential realities of promise exchange in social systems. The software of the Coordinator manages promises by reminding us that they were made and the deadlines implicit in them. But, in real life, all of our promises exist in an unfolding, constantly changing space of interest. Add to that a space of priority change. So we may have promised Allen last Thursday to do something for him this week, but now with the passage of time, we may wish to degrade our commitment and turn it into something much more tentative. Electronic Social Systems exchange Interpretive Persona. Part of the social mind that we all build by using the minds of our friends and acquaintances are the roles we play with them. We develop distinct parts of ourselves to interact with each person we regularly encounter. These mini-persons, or persona, we use strategically like chess pieces as tactics in social situations. They allow us to adopt a number of viewpoints instead of limiting ourselves to just one. As part of our social mind, we use these persona, such as the Skeptic (developed with Barbara) or the Intellectual (developed with Terrel) as resources. Electronic Social Systems will have to permit us to build electronic facsimiles of these persona and use them as analytical tools.

What is the role of AI in all this? AI of the future will be implemented in human society and will have to "think" its way through these Electronic Social System situations. Second, AI can create facsimiles of the items above i.e. (promise trackers, request trackers, point trackers and mood trackers). AI persona can be used as automatic interpretation aids that lead us through series of questions that elucidate a persona's values. AI can create social mind secretaries that monitor and manage the social mind we establish among our friends and acquaintances. These are not earthshaking applications, but useful and modest applications of the limited AI capabilities currently available. They do not require full natural language understanding. In fact, they thrive on what are called "semi-structured messages" which in many ways have been found to be more understandable than natural language itself. And this means a better medium of communication opens up between people and machines.

3

The AI Software Revolution

"...when we introduce a computer-based system, we are not just designing its structure and function, but are participating in the larger design of the organization...We are designing work, not just a tool."

Terry Winograd, addressing the first annual Conference on
Computer-Supported Co-operative Work, Austin, Texas,
December 3-5, 1986.

It is not enough to know how AI application revolutionizes software practice in theory. In practice, AI is, and remains, part of a much larger world of software. Some people make the mistake of simply adding AI onto software as an elite specialty area. Others make the mistake of supplanting all software with new AI software. In short, their behavior, in style and in preference, typifies unrealistic alternatives. Rather, AI's relationship to ordinary software must be carefully considered. The various stages of evolution need to be clearly articulated. At each stage, projects must be launched to test the payback to the business. The ways that Japanese factories are using AI, as well as ways they might better utilize it, will be examined.

This portion of the book will discuss the relationship that exists between AI and ordinary software—especially the ways they can enhance one another. Many pure AI "experts" will regret that any compromises at all have to be made with ordinary software. They will see this as the tarnishing of AI's hard won improvements. But we shall see that these compromises make good business sense and lead to the profitable evolution of AI and ordinary software.

7

AI and Exploratory Programming

Disciplined and Error-Free AI

If the present industry styles of AI application continue, disciplined and error-free AI will remain unattainable. (To be fair to AI, there is something called "exploratory programming" in which computers are programmed to perform the arbitrary, interesting aspects of human thinking. But "exploratory programming" is never going to be structured top-down design, and AI programming in industry is hardly limited to "exploratory programming.") Most, indeed one hundred percent of current industry AI application, consists of repeating the achievements made years ago in laboratories. Practically no current AI techniques are being applied in industry. Examples are legion. Pat Langley, who invented a superior learning production rule language for AI called PRISM, has not been deluged with phone calls from industries interested in using his advanced language. Industries are content with the older techniques.

All this non-exploratory programming that constitutes current AI application in industry needs discipline. Other than COBOL coding, the error leader, no part of software practice anywhere in the world leads to more errors than AI. AI groups, writing diagnostic expert system number 21, develop no specification languages or rules for modular AI expert component development. Of course, some researchers are correcting this and their efforts are beginning to appear in journals. In general, industry practice simply omits discipline from AI code development.

AI's origins in DARPA (Defense Advanced Research Projects Agency) are clearly evident. Created in an environment where specifications would be fatally counterproductive, AI (alone among other forms of software practice) has remained free of discipline. AI must be resocialized to industry needs. That means discipline, formal construction methods and error-elimination techniques must be brought to bear on mediocre expert system design, expert design assistant design, and expert cost estimator design.

Americans (especially) and Europeans will object to standards by claiming that they stifle creativity and innovation. Japan, however, has proven otherwise. The Japanese have used forward thinking standardization as "moves" or "ploys" in world markets to achieve an immediate competitive advantage. Industries that have borne the brunt of Japanese technological advances will point out both formal, technical standards and informal, newly created Japanese standards that give Japan a clear field for sales. Standards, as much as they may grate on the American notion of independent thinking, ultimately lead to innovation and propel an industry ahead of its rivals.

For which disciplines should AI be held accountable? How should expert system development be standardized, formalized, and specified? It would seem that the individual differences of expertise in the human experts preclude any uniformity. Yet cognitive science research is uncovering clear shared principles of expertise, of error, of good retention systems, and of knowledge indexing systems across many kinds of experts and expertise.

There is another viewpoint: industry is awaiting the mass production phase of AI. Japanese firms have already geared up for this, because they see mass production as a starting point for AI. They are building software factories in which up to 25% of all code written daily is AI code. This includes automatic code generation systems, intelligent debugging environments, enhanced "do-what-I-mean" facilities, automatic code specification systems, shared code knowledgebase networks, intelligently indexed subroutine libraries with automatic AI matchers of task descriptions to library routines, and intelligent AI secretaries to handle systems administration of distributed workstations. Conversely, American and European firms are looking for AI groups to enhance the entire programming establishment of their industry. Unfortunately, these AI groups are taking the opposite path by attempting to keep AI within their own exclusive and high-salaried realm of professionalism. It is obvious that the self-interest of the AI professionals is in direct conflict with the aims of the company. The former wish to maximize the price the latter pays for minimal actual transfer of technology. Hence, preventing AI from entering the mainstream is the pervading style of current industry application. What is forgotten, or conveniently pushed aside, is the fundamental approachability of AI itself. For example, many forms of AI are no more difficult than BASIC and present no particular challenge to the intellect of a twelve year old. In fact, the line between routine AI and exploratory programming is deliberately blurred by AI professionals in their attempt to protect routine AI applications from becoming a discipline that might harm exploratory programming. Remember, though, very little actual exploratory programming is found in industry campaigns.

However, sloppy procedure and undisciplined AI program development are easily found. Recently I consulted for two firms that had large AI military contracts. They were having general discussions with experts in a specific domain in order to model the experts' mental procedures for working through a particular task. They put an expert in a room and had weeks of general discussions to build a model of what that expert did. This violates a lot of AI history and practice. An expert knows only a fraction of what it is he actually does. This has been solidly proven by cognitive research. These talks with the expert produce nothing more than idealizations. Then code is written to perform this idealization and, no matter how carefully this is done, the code breaks down miserably when it is forced to deal with actual problems later on. There is a discipline to AI code development, but it is not the same type of discipline needed for developing PASCAL, Modula 2, or other type programs.

When Will Ordinary Programming Be as Exploratory as AI?

Life is not a one way street. If the discipline of ordinary software practice has something to offer routine AI application in industry, so too, AI's exploratory programming has something to offer to ordinary software practice. The fact is most major AI techniques are already translated into languages like C and FORTRAN. That proves not that AI could have been conceived easily in those languages, but that people who used those languages for decades could have conceived AI techniques. But they did not.

An explanation for this oversight can be found by careful scrutiny of a great debate between the Napkins and Environments: Which is the Key Tool of the Expert Programmer? To answer this question, one has to know the difference between programmers and coders (from Dykstra). Some people, when presented a problem, rush instinctively to the terminal and start typing code. These are the coders. They are paid $25,000 a year for their efforts, but deserve less. People who think when presented a problem are programmers, and they rely on napkins! (This sounds strange, but I will explain.) In fact, in early AI programs conducted at the Massachusetts Institute of Technology in the late 1960's, two factions, the "Napkins" and the "Environments," squared off for debate.

The "Napkin" adherents believed that the single most important tool for the expert programmer was the napkin. All major problems were solved during lunch, dinner, or breaks by writing out solutions on napkins. Opposing the "Napkins" were the "Environments" who argued that the single most important piece of equipment for the expert programmer was the incremental compiler which debugged the software under construction. The "Napkins" pointed out that debugging environments made it easy for people to make mistakes, thus accelerating laziness as much as accelerating learning. The "Environments" countered that many napkin sessions started and ended with a blank piece of paper which constituted, at best, an undependable and unstructured approach to solving hard programming problems. The "Napkins" declared that programming consists of pure thought and thought is never easy. Hence, there was no sense in trying to simplify something that is inherently difficult. The "Environments" had more to say. They retorted that real experts, when faced with real problems, experimented with changes of representation for the problem as well as changes of viewpoint. And to enable this kind of experimentation, one needed a symbolic language. The "Napkins" countered that the "Environments" let people achieve code using little fixes without understanding the principles of why it worked. Hence, little learning was carried over to the next programming job.

To choose a side in this debate, different kinds of problems must be distinguished. Routine AI problems do not need an environment built for exploratory programming problems. Routine AI problems select a solution method from a body of well known experiences and techniques. Exploratory programming problems represent things in the mind never before represented. It is a case of the known versus the unknown. Traditional programming, by omitting the "Environment" view, got into the rut of handling only well-known problems and stagnated as a result. AI programming, by omitting the "Napkins viewpoint," wallowed and luxuriated in permissiveness and reared bad children, that is, a bad habit set for its own routine parts. Both programming cultures can benefit by borrowing from each other. Traditional programming needs "Environments" and AI programming needs "Napkins." That may seem like an unequal trade, and as unequal as it may be, it is long overdue.

AI as Defined for Businesspeople

Most people believe that AI is merely an enhanced programming language whose features enable programs to do more intelligent things. It's always been a source of deep humiliation to some psychologists that in 1962, AI computers took intelligence tests and received perfect scores in milliseconds. Rather than admit that the machine was smart, psychologists suddenly decided that the tests needed upgrading and modification. Since humans have a hard time defining intelligent people, it is perhaps forgivable if AI has a hard time defining machine intelligence.

Contrasting sharply with the previous definition of AI is the following software practice definition: AI is two disciplines of developing software, one wholly new to software and one an enhancement of a type of software.

Note the exclusive "two" used in that definition: it means not "one" or "three" or any other number. (Three new disciplines of program development are rapidly developing—classifiers, connections, and learning productions. They have not yet become common for applications except in leading European firms and U.S. military AI programs.) One discipline of developing programs is "modeling the mind" and the other is "simulating the world." AI accomplishes the first using production rules or rules. The second is achieved using what AI calls "objects" or "self-managing agents." Both disciplines have a formal mapping process with the object being mapped serving as an authoritative reference or benchmark against which the product of "using AI" can be judged adequate or inadequate. In "modeling the mind" AI, the reference is a videotape of an expert doing something expertly. In "simulating the world" AI, the reference is the number and actual interrelations of objects in the real world. In both cases, there is something objective against which to measure the adequacy of the modeling that AI has been able to achieve. This means rule-based programming without a videotaped session has lost its reference and its adequacy is theoretical and immeasurable. Object-based programming without a bounded subset of the real world upon which it is modeled has the same deficiency and its adequacy cannot be measured.

This model of AI is quite independent of programming language features. FORTRAN and machine language could be used to do both jobs and even, if a person had enough talent and time, a series of zeros and ones would work. This model of AI blurs the boundary between creative traditional programming and routine AI programming. This model also invokes two kinds of optimization. Rule-based AI can be optimized toward perfect representation of the behavior videotaped and it can be optimized toward efficient operations while modeling perfectly. Efficient operation is achieved through altering a "conflict resolution set algorithm" that determines which of the many rules that "match" in one cycle of the program, should fire the next. Object-based AI can be optimized toward perfect representation as well as toward best level abstraction. This is achieved by inventing new types of objects to attain excellent modeling without bogging down the system with infinitesimal modeling of unnecessary details. Both forms of AI are pretty old. Rule-based languages grew out of IPL1 in 1956. Objects stem from ordinary simulation software, in particular Swedish software called Simula 67. The Swedes are good at modularity both in software terms and in social form, for example, autonomous work groups at Volvo plants in Sweden. The actual steps involved, greatly simplified, are presented in Figure 7-1.

Both disciplines of developing programs help eliminate or reduce what the programmer has to know about the overall system flow control of the program being developed. In non-AI languages, a flow chart, or something like it, must be captured conceptually or on paper in order to construct the program. That is, the programmer must envision the general overall flow of control through the program. An AI program has certain entities within its flow chart but no control statements. So, in fact, no flow chart is used. The control that used to be contained in one big bureaucratic pile of procedures in FORTRAN or PASCAL has been split into little local pieces of control. In rules, those pieces of control constitute the left-hand sides of rules (the "if" part). In objects, those pieces of control reside in the "acquaintance list" of other objects with which each object communicates. Any one object can send or receive messages to and from other objects. Their behavior lists tell them what to do if a certain message is received from or sent to it by a certain other object. The following provides a good analogy.

If the Soviet Union lost its central government overnight, chaos would be unleashed because control is concentrated in a FORTRAN-like central government apparatus. Through the years, the government has become hard to modify and hard to find things in. On the other hand, if the United States lost its central government tomorrow, flowers would bloom twice as bright and the economy would leap forward. Creative local control of the economy would not be stifled by inept government bureaucrats. This somewhat tongue-in-cheek example illustrates the efficiency gained by not having to specify centrally and know ahead of time overall flow of control in any complex system. The downside of this modularity and decentralization of control is the likelihood of impossible bottlenecks with too

ARTIFICIAL INTELLIGENCE IS:
MERELY TWO NEW WAYS TO DEVELOP PROGRAMS

The Trade-off is: no knowledge of, or control of, the overall flow of control thru the program is needed, only local control is specified but huge message or rule match bottlenecks are certain unless lean representations are devised or software bus is implemented to control messages/matches

RULES

Programming by:
MODELING THE MIND

Method: Protocol analysis
First lang.: IPL1, 1956 by Herbert Simon

STEPS

1. *videotape process*
2. *transcribe videotape*
3. *analyze into operators and operands*
4. *translate into production rules*

5. *check against videotape*
6. *optimize conflict resolution ruleset*

OBJECTS

Programming by:
SIMULATING THE WORLD

Method: Actor programming
First lang.: Simula, 1967 by Swedes

STEPS

1. *list actors*
2. *match actors to object library*
3. *list acquaintances of each actor*
4. *list, send, and receive message of each actor to each acqfnce.*
5. *list behaviors for each message*
6. *optimize level of abstraction of actors chosen*

Figure 7-1 Two New Ways to Develop Programs.

many rules trying to fire at once or too many objects all trying to pass messages simultaneously. Good AI programming, then, can be defined as knowing how to achieve the localization of control without intractable masses of inter-item (rule or object) communication. Another way to say the same thing: AI makes it very easy to write very bad programs.

At MIT in the late 1960s, AI was defined differently than today but in a way that helps illustrate how AI differs from ordinary software. AI is the way to program when memory is unlimited and either central processing units (C.P.U.'s) are cheap or there is a great willingness to wait days for results. In fact, many of the first AI techniques were originated by graduate students who didn't have to worry about how much memory they used. They played around with very expensive ways (in terms of used memory) of representing things. When the financial stranglehold on programming was broken (programming everywhere in the early 1960s was defined as efficient use of computer processing cycles and memory cells), entirely new domains of functionality were achieved. History did the rest. The price of C.P.U. cycles and memory cells dropped precipitously until everyone could afford to program as if memory were unlimited. AI innovated this by operating at different price ratios than the general computing economy. There is a lesson here for future generations of computing power.

8

Goals for Artificial Intelligence

Artificial Intelligence and Fulfilling Expectation

Artificial Intelligence, like the result of any scientific enterprise, is the product of certain human dreams and ambitions. In particular, AI has unlimited potential to improve software. Many ordinary programming problems have been lessened or solved by using AI. What are these dreams and ambitions that gave rise to AI? More importantly, what good does it do corporations to define AI in terms of these dreams and ambitions?

AI is applied in the United States without imagination or vision. It is done, quite literally, by the book. The more innovative and creative aspects of AI are ignored which leads to the shortsighted AI applications that are so prevalent. Instead of pursuing the solution to a problem to its conclusion, AI programmers are apt to settle for far less. By omitting the deepest applications, AI is reduced to a meager improvement factor in the software development revolution. Much of this timid and cautious use of AI can be directly linked to the conservative management styles of U.S. firms. Whenever people who are basically ignorant of the history and potential of AI are put in charge of its application, they miss its profound purposes and capabilities. Recently, in the past three years, over 1,100 colleges in North America have developed AI courses. How were so many qualified instructors found overnight? Actually, they were not found, but rather created. In a significant number of cases novices were given the job. These new "expert teachers," in turn, are generating thousands of students who lack an in-depth understanding of AI and its future. Eleven specific goals for AI are listed below. They will serve to remind newcomers to the field of AI's profound potential and how it can heighten a firm's financial returns. Figure 8-1 summarizes some of these eleven goals.

One: The Non-Deterministic Programming Potential

In the late 1960s, AI languages like Planner and Conniver exhibited a technique called "non-deterministic procedure invocation." It improved the ways subroutines in ordinary programming were invoked by either name or the numerical value of some parameter. The basic intent was to make a programming language so smart that it could decide which subroutine to invoke and when it should be invoked (instead of a programmer doing this task ahead of time). Examined closely, this amounted to delving into the process of programming itself. A small element of the programmer's thinking process was incorporated into AI programming language. In this case, the tiny bit of thinking was the programmer's analysis of what conditions to put around the invocation of a particular subroutine. The implications are immense. We will have to examine the programmer's thought processes in detail and transfer bits and pieces into machine constructs that can perform them. The entire "automatic programming" effort is just an elaboration of non-deterministic procedure invocation.

A second tier within non-deterministic procedure invocation was called "data driven programming" and was based on observing human behaviors and finding those where the human took actions based on patterns recognized in his or her environment. Programs, too, could do that, it was supposed. If subroutines were the form in which the actions were stored in computers, then the data given the program could make computers decide on their own which subroutines to invoke under given conditions. In edge-of-field laboratories, researchers are modeling the human mind using about fifty different computers each having a unique hardware architecture and using different software. Each computer has a specific kind of memory and ways of interconnecting with some of the other fifty computers. Data-driven programming then lets the computers decide which other computer to invoke so that non-deterministic procedure invocation becomes non-deterministic processor invocation.

How A.I. Differs From Ordinary Programming

Ordinary Programming:	A.I. Programming:	
Prefabricated subroutines	New subroutines are built during each execution	Non-deterministic programming
Specification of how	Specification of what	Specification programming
Data base	Knowledge base	Heuristic programming
Numeric/parametric programming hard to read	Easily read	Transparent programming
Automated calculation	Automated reasoning	Level of abstraction programming
New code must be written	The program by itself can learn	Machine learning programming
One hypothesis	Competing hypotheses	Non-monotonic logic programming
Centralized coordinator	Message passing patterns	Society of experts "actors" programming

Figure 8-1 How AI Differs from Ordinary Programming.

Two: The Specification Programming Potential

Computer students learn in their very first classes that computers will only do what they have previously been programmed to do. If the slightest mistake is left uncorrected, the computer produces nonsensical results which it is unable to avoid or correct. It stands to reason that if data can be put in computers, then certainly rules about commonsense interpretation and manipulation of that data can also be input. Programmers spend far too much time specifying how something should be done. They need a way to specify what they want the computer to do, and then the computer itself calculates how to do it. This is called specification programming.

The key to achieving specification is understanding just what the computer has to "know" in order to calculate how to do certain things. PROLOG, an AI language based on logic, was invented by French researchers intent on achieving specification programming for a certain class of problems. With PROLOG, the user can input a database and rulebase and then input a description of a type of result wanted. The PROLOG program will calculate how to achieve its objectives. Unfortunately, at present PROLOG has a very limited range of computer-calculable actions. This goal has run into a very large stumbling block: building common sense into computers. If specification programming is to work for a wide range of computer problems, the computer must have common sense. It must be able to sense absurd or contradictory results and recalculate the core data until a more reasonable value is available. Leading researchers in AI are currently struggling to give computers the ability to differentiate the "reasonable" from the "unreasonable."

Three: The Heuristic Programming Potential

Most of AI's early work attempted to make computers relevant to commonsense necessities of new areas of AI work. For example, when a child thinks about playing chess with a computer, the child uncovers the concept "search space" which is not a method or technique but the least insightful knowledge possible in the chess playing situation. Search spaces are merely commonsense response to representing all possible moves from any one configuration of a chess board. (Nowadays, executives attend seminars where search spaces are taught as a key AI "technique.") AI researchers spent nearly ten years engaged in little more than searches. At times, it seemed that intelligence was nothing more than searching. Now, some twenty years later, we are returning to searching. All intelligence is in the form of direct association memories in connectionist hardware. Direct association memories replace AI rules in these new systems by matching entities across all previously encountered similar experiences (where a rule was something abstracted from such similar past experiences in rule-based AI systems of the past).

Previously, searching was so expensive (in terms of computer hardware and software) that researchers turned to making the search process itself intelligent (rather than equating search with intelligence as was formerly done). They did not find any good techniques for doing this, however. Finally, they turned to the real world for models of intelligent search. They found experts in various domains to be likely sources for methods to search over many possible relevant factors intelligently. This eventually produced expert systems which to this day are largely compilations of ways to search large possibility-spaces intelligently.

To develop these systems, AI researchers studied doctors, chemists, mathematicians, and programmers and concentrated on capturing the idiosyncratic personal "rules of thumb" called "heuristics." These heuristics, which represented normal ways of doing things, allowed the researchers to avoid searching parts of the possibility space that would not lead to a solution. Instead, heuristics nominated certain space areas wherein they would most likely find an answer. Heuristic programming, then, was creating, in addition to databases, "heuristic-bases" in the form of AI rules. Currently, rule based AI programming is dying out and is being replaced by highly parallel searches over the actual experiences and cases from which experts form rules as abstractions. Most corporations, thinking rule-based/heuristic-based programming is all that AI offers today, are overlooking the future and busily investing in the past. The Japanese are well into their Sixth Generation Computing Project and generating new hardware architectures for Direct Associative Memory programming which will replace rule-based/heuristic programming.

Four: The Transparent Programming Goal

The first programming languages were sets of highly arbitrary rules interrelating abstruse program language keywords. Japanese education theorists years ago pronounced PROLOG a more "learnable" language for school children than BASIC or LOGO. As a national strategy, AI languages are the first languages taught to ordinary Japanese people. Unlike ordinary languages, AI languages have a "transparency" which is explained in the following text.

Ordinary programming underwent a crisis of understanding in the mid-1960s. Europeans, with far fewer computer resources, pioneered better programming than Americans. They found Americans mired in a confusing array of programming languages and constructs. From this hodgepodge the Europeans went on to design disciplined uses. They called it "structured programming" and claimed its principal side benefit was its ability to make systems "self-documenting." Years after they are built, self-documenting systems are programs that can be read quickly, easily and reliably by people who did not design them. Structured programming is a set of disciplined procedures where the keywords and features of the particular programming languages make the code almost as readable as natural English. While these trends were going on in the world of ordinary programming in Europe, AI researchers sought ways to make AI programming "transparent." That is, the code written in any AI program is readable and understandable years later by people who did not design the program.

The Europeans invented the language, PASCAL (now updated in a language called Modula-2), where the program's algorithm is written in structured English called "pseudo-code" as the sixth step in programming. As the seventh step, the programmer chooses an actual computer language into which to translate the pseudo-code line-for-line. The last step is the actual translation. Notice that choosing the programming language is the next to the last step and not the first.

The pseudo-code is easy to read because it is written in English-like syntax. The PASCAL program that results is also easy to read because its syntax as a computer language has specific features that preserve a lot of the natural English. For example, variables have values of January through December instead of numeric codes representing the months. AI programmers develop planning programs with goals and sub-goals along with tactics and strategies which enable them to write highly modular task-oriented code segments that look like natural English.

These planning AI systems gave rise to natural language AI efforts. Natural language understanding requires translating human intent, latent in natural language expressions, into an AI planning code. The problem is detecting human intent in natural language. Furthermore, recent research has shown that natural language is neither the best nor preferred medium for sophisticated adult communication. Semi-structured messages have outperformed natural language in computer conferencing systems and as means of input for doctors and other expert computer users. So, the problem of transparent programming in AI has become a problem of the transparency of natural language itself and finding a medium more transparent to its intent content than natural language.

There are several implications for companies considering AI. First, AI is the best beginning language for newcomers to computing. Second, the usefulness and cogency of AI natural language systems depend on how well an organization's people already use natural language itself. The fact that language use is a critical discriminant of lower level employees from top management suggests that having a companywide AI natural language understanding system will merely allow sloppy language to result in sloppy deeds. Indeed, AI natural language products already on the market are among the least successful AI products. In major corporations, users of these products end up hating them after a few months of use. These products give users the appearance of natural language but lack all the common sense and inferencing capability that makes natural language processing tolerable for humans. AI companies make huge mistakes building demos to show what AI can do by putting natural language front ends on expert systems. This confuses managers into thinking the system is much smarter than it is and leads to the inevitable bitter disappointment.

Five: The Level of Abstraction Programming Ambition

In its infancy, AI modeled human thought. It borrowed concepts from academic disciplines like psychology, engineering control theory, and information theory. From psychology, it acquired the schema concept to explain how objects might be represented in computers with sets of characteristics that occur together. A data structure, "frames," was based on mimicking this schema behavior observed in the psychology of humans. Frames consisted of characteristics that generally occurred together. This included slots representing types of data and default values which were generally assumed unless overruled by the specifics of a situation. For example, the apple object would have a color slot with a default value of red or green unless specific situations called for a yellow value.

As AI ambitiously modeled human thought, it had to represent all aspects of the world and human behavior in computer form. This required prodigious amounts of memory and, given the computer technology of the 1970s, new ways to use memory efficiently. AI researchers found that frames had a property called "inheritance" that mitigated the problem of small memory capacity. Frames could inherit from parent frames default values of slots. For example, apples are instances of fruits and can inherit "form" from the fruit object slots for shape (with defaults for a general roundness property and so forth). That way, the roundness of many types of fruit could be represented in one location in the computer's memory and all the other objects that shared membership in the fruit category could merely point to that shape slot with its roundness value rather than repeat the slot and its value for each fruit object. A parallel processing idea of message passing was added to the efficient memory capabilities of frames. Work with frames that represented major objects in a program (rather than minor details) proved that writing frame-based programs resembled building a simulation of the objects and their behaviors in some domain. If more than one processor was available, then each processor could represent one frame and the frames could interact by performing input-output operations between processors.

During this time, Europeans were learning to build programs based on methods for building simulations. The Swedes even developed a language, Simula 67, with a special software construct making it easy to build programs the way simulations were built. They used a one-to-one mapping ability to transform real world objects into corresponding programming objects. Simula-67 had "classes" that could separate the name space of everything inside any defined programming object and build new objects by combining or modifying existing objects. In university research labs, this led to discovery of several levels of abstraction of primitive objects defined in terms of even more primitive objects. Swedish researchers used these definitions, made in terms of increasingly primitive objects, as a process of program building. Central to this was the efficiency gained by defining primitive capabilities only once and reusing that code again and again in other objects throughout the system.

The work in levels of abstraction made clear the importance of software reusability. Studies showed that the vast majority of all code written in any organization was nothing more than repetition. Libraries of objects that could be shared within organizations and throughout the world became a topic of research. In the late 1970s, researchers working on schema, frames, and parallel processing realized that their work substantially overlapped mainstream software work on levels of abstraction and simulation-styles of program building. Today, Japan's Sigma project is building a national software library of reusable code objects. Simultaneously, the U.S. is researching such an idea in its Software Engineering Institute at Carnegie-Mellon and in the Pentagon's Star project. Unfortunately, most American companies are building AI code as incapable of reuse as traditional code. Americans have too little understanding of the history and intents of AI. Standard object libraries that go across an industry should be part of every corporate AI program. This essential cross-industry component won't come easily to the United States which has a long history of minimal technical co-operation within industries. Instead, Japanese manufacturers, by being the first to implement standard libraries, will impose these libraries on the United States. And these libraries will be optimized for Japanese, not American, production systems.

Six: The Machine Learning Programming Goal

Two learning systems operate in humans: the evolutionary learning through Darwinian mutation of the genome of the species and the situated learning of the individuals of the species. Almost from its beginning, AI research was concerned with getting machines to adopt both ways of learning. At first, however, there was the problem of representing many different forms of knowledge in the computer. Then, it was discovered that not enough was known about the forms of knowledge and their representation in humans. Finally, the processes of adding new knowledge at the appropriate places in those representations of knowledge and modifying the representations themselves as a product of learning became the focus.

Ordinary software does not learn. The code at the beginning of the program is the same as the code at the end. Only the data changes; the code remains the same. In AI learning systems, the code of the program changes with each batch of data or knowledge used in operation applications. This amounts to having a program that is its own data. Interestingly enough, the oldest AI language still in use, LISP, has this attribute as its most primitive assumption and feature. Procedures in LISP are data objects and can be built, operated on, and modified during execution of LISP programs as if they were data objects. Early work by John Holland in Michigan and his research group led to modeling evolutionary process learning on machines making use of parallel processing. These so-called genetic algorithms, randomly mutate rules and then try out these new rulesets on phenomena. When they do well, their constituent features are reinforced; when they fail, their feature sets are weakened. Recently, these genetic algorithms have been used on ordinary AI rulebases to optimize the rulesets for best decision or fastest decision performance.

There are many immediate applications for this type of human learning programming. Many program users experience confusion or difficulty using features of various software systems. The problems they discover—and also their ways to overcome these problems—are lost to others because of the way systems are set up. Simple learning features, when added to all ordinary programs, allow human use of the system to be captured as rules, advice, and diagnosis from which other users of the system would automatically benefit.

Seven: The Logic Programming Goal

For some reason, the French and English concentrated on using logic as a basis for AI automation—as if logic were how the human mind worked. Long ago psychology proved that logic actually plays a small role in human mental processing. Nevertheless, in Europe there has been a consistent effort to automate logic in combination with a huge effort to extend logic to cover enough areas of meaning to make this automation worth doing. One enterprise depended solidly upon the other.

Americans, following a different path, started implementing AI from a problem solving perspective and found that very few problems were solved with logic of any kind. Recently, as the depth of European-developed extensions of logic increased, multiple logic applications have been employed in a kind of "capitalism of thought" where hypotheses compete for computer system resources as each hypothesis draws closer to the desired solution. The Japanese, using fifth generation computing machines (machines that use PROLOG as a machine language in which other forms of knowledge representation are builtup) have applied parallel hardware systems to logic programming.

Logic, then, is as valid a computer language for corporations as LISP lists. Both are such primitive models of mental processes that one cannot be called more advanced than the other. Now that Japan has opted for PROLOG and is optimizing the hardware and software for its applications, the United States, with its pluriform systems, must brace itself for defeat. Ultimately, cost reductions, and/or speed improvement will allow the Japanese to mimic any new knowledge representation in their uniform PROLOG systems. American firms are hung up on getting the "right" language for basic knowledge representation on an individual work group basis. They are not concerned with unity across companies or across industries or even across national economies. Because they won't admit that neither LISP nor PROLOG is much past the beginning stages, they fuss with many incompatible AI languages and tools. The Japanese, having agreed on PROLOG as a machine language, copy all American high level AI tools and languages on their PROLOG substrate. This substrate is now as fast as the fastest American system but less expensive (referring to the first commercial product of the fifth generation project the MELCOR PROLOG engine from Mitsubishi Electric). And soon that substrate will be markedly cheaper. The Japanese do not debate the merits of LISP and PROLOG because both are far too primitive to even warrant an argument. What does matter to the Japanese is national commitment to levels of architecture for economies of scale and, more importantly, economies of national education in AI.

Eight: The Modularity Programming Goal

At one time, people thought some big, centralized ego controlled the human mind and told each part of the brain what to do. However, world wars, arms races, and even the petty transgressions within human relationships convinced many people that if any central control existed, it could be easily swayed by instinct, desire, or situational exigency. Computing in the 1950s inherited a central control paradigm of the program from psychology. A central main outline told all the other routines what to do and when to do it. This central control paradigm disappeared in the early 1970s in both psychology and AI. Research results indicated the human mind consisted of around fifty little computers. Corresponding AI research had fifty expert systems negotiating among themselves to define a fifty-first system for some new occasion. To show how thinking has changed during this time, a hypothetical book of the 1950s might have been titled *Mechanism of the Mind*. In the 1970s, books called *Modularity of the Mind* (by Jerry Fodor) and *Society of Mind* (by Marvin Minsky) appeared in book stores. AI research on building expert systems was replaced by AI research on establishing groups of expert systems, like mini-societies, to negotiate among themselves to achieve interesting results.

Instead of the main routine of traditional programs, AI took patterns of messages passed between autonomous, intelligent "actor" routines. Of course, some diehards suggested a central "Stalin" figure which coordinated all the autonomous actors, but this proved impossible. Given the arbitrary capabilities in each of the expert systems, there was no body of knowledge about how a Stalin routine would coordinate the work. The "Actor Theory" was developed to cover these modular systems. In it, each actor had an acquaintance list. Each acquaintance list determined which actors sent messages to and received messages from the actor routine. For each message sent and each message received, any actor had a list of behavior routines telling it what to do. With nothing more complicated than this, complex systems could be built in modules by defining actors, their acquaintances, messages, and behavior lists. Over time as users gained experience, new actors could be added to the system by modifying just the acquaintance, message, and behavior lists of those actors they communicated with. No overall main routine would have to be altered.

This modularity of update feature is a revolution within programming practice, because all ordinary computer programs are not user updatable. That is because some complex, nontransparent central routine must be searched and updated for even minor program changes. Only the software designers who originally wrote the code can update it. This delays updating and, because the user must try to communicate his needs to the designer, misunderstandings can occur which ultimately lead to errors in the updated program. Conversely, AI programs can be updated by users because control has been decentralized into each actor and no central control exists.

Nine: The Automated Expertise Extraction Programming Goal

Recently, the intelligent part of an expert system, the inference engine, was redirected. Formerly, it directed its inferencing power to the problem to be solved. This has changed. It now not only draws inferences about its problem domain but it also drives an intelligent dialog with the expert whose knowledge is to be captured by the expert system. By doing so, it automates extraction of the expert's terminology and segmentation of the issues of his field. Eventually, it may automate extraction of other aspects of expertise. At present this is done with a handful of experts whose knowledge is to be compiled into the system. In Japan, however, companies are working to apply this intelligent dialog to capture user experience for all users of software systems. That is, instead of capturing expertise for building expert systems, they hope to capture the expertise of all good users of any software system and make that experience-based learning available to other users of the software. This means that what

Kathy learns about using word processor-X can be used by me when I first start learning how to use the same software.

Ten: The Modeling The Mind Programming Goal

Diverse groups of researchers have participated in the modeling of the mind as shown on Figure 8-2. The first AI language, IPL1, assumed knowledge in the human mind was represented in recursive lists—lists whose members could be lists themselves. Shortly thereafter, Europeans assumed knowledge in the human mind was represented as propositions of logic and built logic languages, the most successful being PROLOG. Psychologists thought they had something to contribute to AI, and they added productions as a basic form of representing knowledge in the computer. Each production was a kind of glorified "if-then" rule that assumed nothing about anything else in the program but contained all the knowledge of when to fire and what its relevancy was within its "if" section. Audio and video tapes of experts were translated item-by-item into productions. Another group of psychologists counterattacked with frames. They represented knowledge in sets of features with default values inherited from an ontology or taxonomy of object types. Linguists, who were relative newcomers to AI, wanted to do something different than the psychologists and added semantic nets as a form of knowledge representation. These were enormous interconnections of nodes and arcs where meanings were attached to each other, and attention or system focus was spread along arcs by a kind of "spreading activation" of arcs in the vicinity of interest. (British mathematicians, familiar with lattice theory, applied this to these node-arc conglomerations with astonishingly opaque and computationally useless results. However, the linguists had put their two cents' worth in and were temporarily mollified.) Demons, or active values, were contributed by pure AI researchers who noticed that quality control "critics" existed in the human mind to keep the results of rules or frames from violating commonsense bounds. The "critics" were key to such phenomena of the mind as humor, common sense, and the ability to estimate. Ordinary software developers in the data extraction movement and the simulation people who learned Simula-67 contributed objects. Recently, researchers working with genetic algorithm machine learning have added "classifiers" which compete in generations of evolution. Lastly, parallel hardware developers noticed that the human mind has some memories distributed across many areas of the brain so that if damage occurs to one part, it does not entirely eliminate a

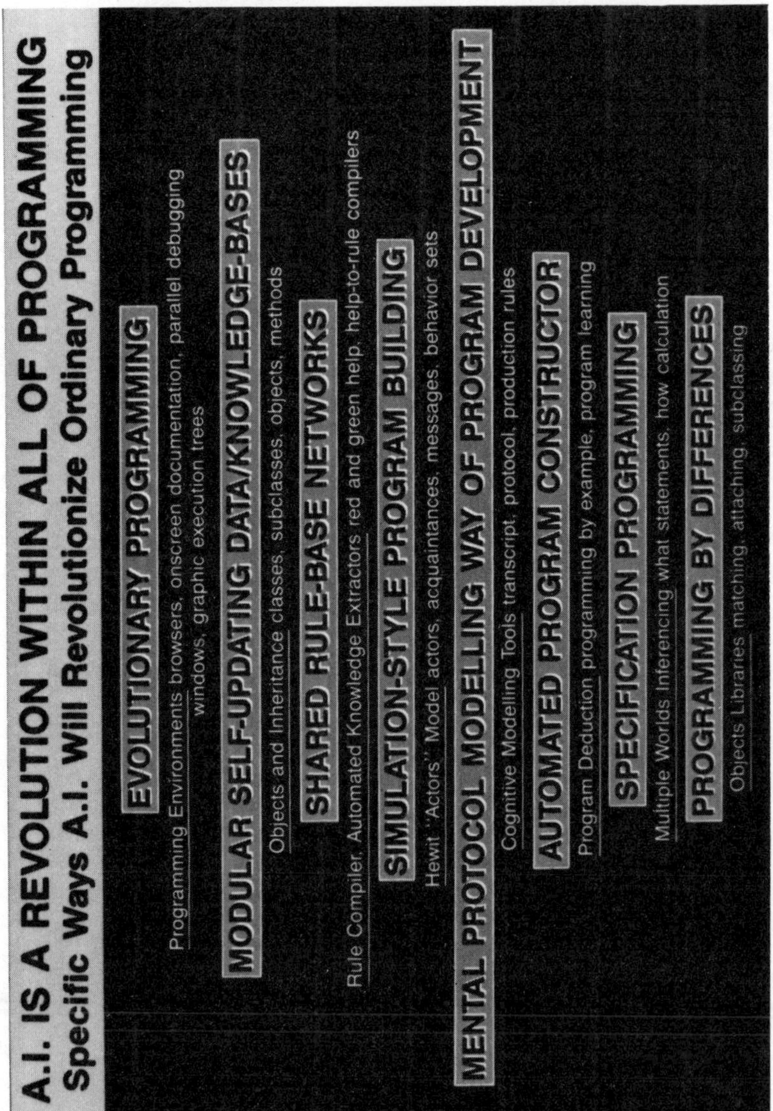

A.I. IS A REVOLUTION WITHIN ALL OF PROGRAMMING
Specific Ways A.I. Will Revolutionize Ordinary Programming

EVOLUTIONARY PROGRAMMING
Programming Environments browsers, onscreen documentation, parallel debugging windows, graphic execution trees

MODULAR SELF-UPDATING DATA/KNOWLEDGE-BASES
Objects and Inheritance classes subclasses, objects, methods

SHARED RULE-BASE NETWORKS
Rule Compiler, Automated Knowledge Extractors red and green help. help-to-rule compilers

SIMULATION-STYLE PROGRAM BUILDING
Hewit "Actors" Model actors, acquaintances. messages. behavior sets

MENTAL PROTOCOL MODELLING WAY OF PROGRAM DEVELOPMENT
Cognitive Modelling Tools transcript. protocol. production rules

AUTOMATED PROGRAM CONSTRUCTOR
Program Deduction programming by example, program learning

SPECIFICATION PROGRAMMING
Multiple Worlds Inferencing what statements. how calculation

PROGRAMMING BY DIFFERENCES
Objects Libraries matching, attaching, subclassing

Figure 8-2 AI Is a Revolution Within All of Programming.

memory. They have built a new kind of AI hardware—connectionist hardware—to simulate this attribute of neuro-anatomy.

Eleven: The User Expertise Programming Goal

AI researchers first assumed that a standard programming language was the vehicle with which to develop AI. They quickly learned that the basic AI language, LISP (and later PROLOG), was merely a language which allowed them to easily build their own language. The first things built in those early languages were "environments." These were tools used to debug AI programs, to trace execution of routines, to organize LISP and PROLOG code for editing, and to guess intelligently the intent from partially correct code instructions. System building tools were added to these environments. Zeta- and Inter- were two of the earliest such environments. These programs made it easier to translate user rules into AI rule form and user objects into AI object form. These environments evolved into expert system building tools. As cognitive psychologists learned more about AI and used it to build models of mental processes to test actual human performance, they modified these expert system building tools (called ESBT's or "ezzbits") and created cognitive modeling tools (CMT's). The best AI systems are currently not found in AI laboratories but rather in these psychology department cognitive modeling tools. Recently these tools have been modified to form cognitive modeling tool generators which allow easy specification of many related models of mental process using one tool. Also, expert system application generators have recently been developed which create generic knowledge structures for specialized domains such as real time process control or machine diagnosis.

All of this has enormous implications for corporations. First, industry completely ignores the great, cheaply available AI power in cognitive modeling tools. Second, for the immediate future, there will continue to be better AI capability in such CMT's than in regular AI environments and ESBT's. Third, the science of knowledge representation does not exist that permits corporations to judge which of these eleven forms of knowledge representation to use. So this selection must be done somewhat arbitrarily, based on long-term emerging standards within AI itself. (Industry will have to nudge the AI community toward these standards as researchers will not standardize on their own.) Fourth, the trend is toward more domain specific tools and more closer-to-user mental categories tools to be developed over time. Companies should steer their AI programs in that direction. Too many companies do not manage AI well and allow pure research-oriented AI staffers to talk them into making new AI ESBT's or environments that are intellectually barren and tactically useless for the corporation. These high tech investments do, however, provide ample fodder for the superficial articles these AI "hackers" write for second-rate journals. We do not need new versions of Zeta-LISP or new KEE systems. We do need good standard object libraries for real time process control, and new tools modeled more closely to the user's mental processing will help realize this goal. Japanese AI Circles Programs have AI Application Generator Conferences in which roughly forty employees will write code over a two day period for a standard library set over a particular domain. A comparable program is not found in the United States.

9

Revolutions in Programming

Although most ordinary programmers do not realize this, Artificial Intelligence has revolutionized all aspects of computer programming. AI has solved some major problems with existing software development systems, and it is no accident that this happened. The early AI developers were frustrated by the arbitrary limits of ordinary software. They struggled to make fundamental improvements while the world of software grappled with incidental, short-range improvements. Companies still show too much caution when implementing AI. This is caused in large part by managers who lack a solid understanding of the new technology and simply add AI to existing tools within the corporation. This poor utilization has become so ingrained in U.S. industry practice that it is now, unfortunately, the norm. Recently, computer-integrated manufacturing (CIM) has frustrated many companies. Integrated systems are an inherent part of CIM, so the isolation and inadequate implementation of AI are incompatible with CIM systems. The norm of underutilization (which had been operational long before the advent of CIM) has now been pushed aside as managements go in the opposite direction and flood themselves in a torrent of automation.

It is easy to detect "added-on" AI in companies. First, the AI groups devote themselves exclusively to pure AI projects even though they know that ultimately 95% of all AI will be meshed with existing software systems. Second, successful beginning AI projects do not spread throughout the company to other similar application sites. Instead, these early projects end up entrenched in niches in the firm where local political support for new technology is high. Younger managers, engaged in career building pursuits, relish AI (a highly visible and "flashy" new technology) as a kind of professional catapult. All of this leads to poorly conceived technology application. When politics alone determine technology dissemination and application, intelligent deliberation is omitted from the decision making process. And many firms are in that very position—they are prisoners of their own internal politics. (Japanese firms act with an authority much more powerful than any internal political faction. This impresses American visitors who have to "persuade" many layers of management to implement a technical project.) Third, added-on AI is detectable in large systems integration projects that omit any AI component. This artificial, often politically caused separation of AI from other technical programs in the firm means the company will never benefit from AI's revolutionary role throughout software systems.

No one suggests that an organization undertake a grandiose, hastily conceived project to add AI to every one of its programs. Rather, a firm must think through AI's ultimate role in each software system and then map out campaigns of incremental AI implementation. These campaigns can be staged as required in response to various productivity and marketing conditions within the company.

Evolutionary Programming

Twenty years ago, Xerox PARC (Palo Alto Research Center) realized the utter futility of the usual software development cycle. It went something like this:

1. Mary Ellen keeps a log of what is needed in her job position.
2. She meets with an outside software vendor and develops specifications for a software product to improve her job.
3. The outside vendor returns six months later with a demonstration program that fundamentally misunderstands and misuses half of the information contained in Mary Ellen's specifications.
4. The outside vendor goes off again and returns with a better demo which is no longer relevant because changes in company conditions have outmoded some of the original specifications.
5. Mary Ellen and the outside vendor agree on some third-rate compromises to save the project in which they have both invested a lot of time and personal pride.

6. The outside vendor makes another appearance with a final program that Mary Ellen spends the next six months debugging before it can be useful in everyday work.
7. The outside vendor fixes the bugs.

The fundamental flaw in this process—and this scenario is played out every day—is obvious. So much time is spent completing and modifying the product that by the time the software is finally delivered conditions in the company have altered so much that the software has been rendered obsolete. Moreover, it is not easy to articulate complex software interfaces and features, so users have difficulty communicating their precise needs to the vendors. Recently, new software products allowing simulation of a software system before it is actually produced have helped some, but the communication problems are still enormous.

The Xerox PARC people realized what was going on and decided that the users of any software system needed the ability to update its functionality themselves. Therefore, vendors had to deliver only a core of functionality with which end users could build customized feature sets and interfaces. But this requires an intelligent platform be available to enable end users to build such features. AI is presently mature enough to furnish that platform. The advantages of user-updatable systems are numerous. The misunderstanding of system specifications between user and vendor is eliminated. The delay between need for a feature and building that feature is reduced to hours. Finally, the experience of the end user with the system is immediately fed back into new system features.

An example may help. Real time process control software uses operations research techniques to schedule passive or active inventory. AI real time process control software allows users of the software to update its functionality in real time. When the software is controlling mainly new equipment with which no one has actual experience, the software delivered with it is a pale abstraction of what is needed to operate it well in real life production. And this has led to some true horror stories in American industry. Real time process control software requires operators to keep a logbook and contact a vendor every six months to receive specification updates. Another eight months is spent awaiting delivery and then the inevitable debugging process begins. A year and a half is wasted before the original update in the logbook becomes a reality. AI real time process control software allows operators to create new AI rules or objects the day the need is first spotted. Because of AI's transparency feature (the language reads like structured natural English) operators can create new rules without being programmers in the obscure algorithmic sense. This is the objective of evolutionary programming.

Recent experience with low level word processors has convinced many companies that end user knowledge of the word processor must be captured. The end users document the system, increase its productivity, and learn about the system's major features that some would regard as too complicated. Subsequent users then profit from the experiences of these pioneers. Until AI is used to capture and make available the experience and advice of a system's first users, there will be no productivity with existing software.

Shared Knowledgebase Networks

Networking and AI are both revolutions within computing and they eventually will interact. In the United States, however, they are seen as separate entities. Because American middle management does not consider various company systems as a whole functioning unit, the systems remain technical factions and projects which only nominally interface with each other. In the 1950s, this kind of "salt and pepper" thinking was seen in the United States when databases first became popular. By "salt and pepper," I mean the tendency of a company to look at its organization chart and to introduce, over time, the latest technology into each box without considering how all these systems might interact with each other. AI is the latest victim of this random "salt and pepper" method of technology implementation.

Networking, the cure for "salt and pepper" AI, takes a practical look at how AI projects are set up within companies. But first, it is necessary to understand how the "salt and pepper" philosophy undermines and limits new technologies. In the case of AI, "salt and pepper" works this way: An AI group approaches departments in the firm that may need (or at least voice no objections to) AI. Some meetings are held, and one department volunteers to have a feasibility study done. An expert system application is worked up, specs are made, and a trial proposal is circulated. After reading the reports, the management committee approves the project. This whole scenario is completely wrong. Instead, when the project specifications are known, several other departments whose data must be input or output to the proposed system should become involved. Together, all affected departments develop specifications for a common knowledgebase that they all will share and update. This amounts to a "Shared Knowledgebase Network" across departments.

Right away, realists see the difficulty and delay this approach will engender. Getting several departments to agree on one expert system project dooms AI to unbelievably slow implementation, they will argue. This is not necessarily the case. One department can tacitly go ahead with its expert system development so long as the multi-department features are included in the project specifications, and other supporting departments do not feel obligated to "buy into" the project via additional funding or through eventual use. When project payback results become available for the one completed expert system project, a full shared knowledgebase network can then be proposed. But there is one requirement: from its beginning, the initial project must meet multi-departmental specifications so that the system can interface and exchange data freely with other systems across the company. Virtually nowhere in the United States can shared knowledgebase networks be found. In Japan, it is part of the usual way middle management thinks through interactions between multiple new technologies at the workplace. Middle Japanese managers can do this because they invite their line workers to help with the planning. With more heads to do the thinking, more thinking gets done.

Shared knowledgebase networks give company software systems an amazing capability. For example, the mental rules that Richard in production uses for process planning, the mental rules that Susan in design uses for product design for assembly, and the rules that Rex in analysis uses for finite element studies can now all be found in one knowledgebase. Members of all user departments can tap these rules and learn. Suddenly, the wisdom and information from the production line is available to someone in artwork who first models a product or process for the firm. Knowledge has been mined, put into objective AI rule form, and made portable. In effect, the firm has become more integrated, more productive, and more competitive.

Simulation Style Program Building

AI allows programs to be built without an overall flow chart being constructed (either mentally or on paper). This modular program construction permits most programs to be built the way simulations were built in the past: a one-to-one mapping from the world being modeled to the software objects that match those modeled objects. This makes programs more readable, easier to update, and more flexible. The programming process becomes safer as modularity encapsulates mistakes instead of propagating them to other points within the system. The computer portion of programming is reduced and replaced with greater time for concern with the problem domain being modeled. This has been a major problem in traditional programming which concentrated on program construction skills that didn't consider the user needs and the problem domain. AI object-oriented programming enables the developer to create a one-to-one map from a good model of the problem domain without intermediate technically obscure algorithmic process construction.

Mental Protocol Modeling Way of Constructing Programs

Although mentioned earlier in this book, a discussion of modeling human thought processes is repeated here because it is truly revolutionary in software development. It opens up a whole new domain of possible software applications. Whenever a key person's mental processes are essential to company performance, it is in the firm's best interest to build a model of the expert's mind. Of course, many people are reluctant to admit that machines can function intelligently like human minds because we like to feel that our ability to think makes us unique. And while we are currently able to model a number of these mental processes, there are still certain limits. Firms pioneering the modeling of the human mind will ultimately prove to doubters that machines can indeed copy human thinking processes.

Automatic Program Construction

Today Artificial Intelligence is capable of automating program specification, program maintenance, and simple program changes or updating. Within the next two years, AI generators that automate a wide range of programs will be commercially available, and thousands of programmers will either be laid off or forced to get into the AI generator programming business. AI allows task descriptions to be input and combined with AI program knowledge of "how-to-program" so that completed code is output. The small domains where this has worked in research are now being extended by major industrial and defense industry firms. Automatic construction of AI programs is being incrementally approached, too. Automation of expertise extraction is complex, but the mundane aspects—gathering terminology and forming taxonomies of relevant categories and issues—have been automated on some systems.

Programming by Differences

Object libraries for interesting practical business domains were commercially released for sale in 1987. These libraries allow programmers to construct applications programs by using a method called "programming by differences." When basic objects in the library are included in the program, new specialized objects are later created by combining the characteristics of existing library objects. Any behavior of a specific object that is the same as a behavior already defined in the library objects can be inherited without new code being written. Only those features of the specific objects that differ from behavior in library objects need to have code written for them and sometimes not even then. For instance, some behaviors from library object A and other behaviors from library object B can be combined if new object C inherits behaviors from both A and B. The resulting combination of behaviors is a new object with a new behavior, and no code has been written other than a line telling the system that C inherits from A and B. Programming by differences allows new features to be added to a program and because each new feature written becomes an object from which future objects can inherit properties, less and less code will be written. In fact, there is an exponential decline of code needing to be written for each new additional feature. Typically, new features will require only one percent of the number of lines of code ordinarily needed; this impact increases for large programs. This is true reusability of code via object libraries; it represents a genuine revolution in software productivity.

How Corporations Can Benefit from the AI Revolution

The Management Information Systems department is under general siege these days. It has the dubious honor of doing more than its share to delay computing innovation in firms today. It generates an atmosphere that is anti-networking and anti-personal computing. This is the result of firms leaving the decisions about technology to their technical departments. Today's problems stem from old ways where company management "added on" computing to older precomputing styles of the firm's organization. When the computing section grew too large, it was promoted to full department status. Incredibly, little understanding of computing took place. Recently though, strategic advantages available through computing have been realized. For example, American Airlines extended its in-house reservations system to travel agents and captured significant new business worldwide. Today everyone's eyes are open to the strategic force of computing and the fact that computers are no longer an appendage of the workplace but rather the work place itself.

The wise AI program requires that certain steps be followed as the program evolves. In the beginning, every person in the firm becomes involved in the planning stages through participation in an AI Circles Program. (Having such circles companywide really requires a whole sequence of new technologies to be delivered through the same circles program.) To deliver a technology like AI through a circles program, certain special modifications have to be made to the technology. It must be implemented in small increments so that work forces can be trained gradually.

Competitive advantage tactics are found in the heart of a sound AI development program. This means going beyond the safe "follow the leader" strategies and breaking new ground. Those in the firm with the technical imagination must divorce themselves from the popular business presentations of other firm's successes. This requires real AI experts in the firm who fully understand and participate in company strategy building. Of course, this combination technical person/business strategist is a very rare specimen who is unlikely to walk in off the street. It is more likely that companies will have to create their own such persons. Finally, a wise AI program results in the Meta-Cognitive Organization—an organization that objectifies, automates, and studies and modifies its own mental processes at work. To avoid tyranny, this must be done with everyone's participation. The work force must enhance and manage its own new mental protocols. Therefore, workers must have tools that allow them to objectify the mental content of their jobs and envision the dimensions of enhancement. The Educative WorkPlace Theory, which applies formal curriculum theory from education to the workplace, can elucidate the cognitive parameters, both rational and affective, of each job. AI, which objectifies expertise, can be a major part of such an Educative Workplace program.

The Genealogy of Artificial Intelligence

Those who understand and can predict the future directions of a new technology automatically have the competitive advantage. They will also know what kind of long-term investment to make in new systems. The Americans and Europeans have distinct approaches to AI which the Japanese studied carefully before devising their own version. The Japanese were able to gain advantage by deliberately waiting for AI developments elsewhere. They viewed the directions of evolution and spotted long-term trends and tendencies.

Israel, Britain, and Japan publish some of the world's best details of new research. All three nations scour the world to investigate the best technologies and compile the results for use at high caliber universities at home. AI, as summarized by the Japanese, can be cogently understood. The history of AI appears as a history of symbolic programming. Symbolic programming simply represents things with symbols other than numbers in the computer. These symbols are basically character strings (word-like entities) and shapes (patterns in which word-like entities are combined). LISP, a second generation AI language, is best taught to beginners as two types of keywords: one set that changes values (the way ordinary FORTRAN does) and another set that changes shapes into which values are configured. AI development as symbolic programming has been in the form of new languages that run on machines performing symbolic operations and producing meaningful symbolic results. Therefore, the history of AI started with copying the most formal and literal components of the way human minds use symbols. AI, then, has been chained to what was known about symbolics. Later, less formal thought was studied and AI developers learned from this and developed new representations of meaning. AI has evolved away from the one symbol/one meaning relationship. First a pluralization direction across time occurred. Here, AI evolved from single sets of symbols and shapes to networks of interconnections between symbols and shapes. These, in turn, became communities of symbols and shapes and then statistical distributions of states representing symbols and shapes. Whereas early AI represented concepts with one corresponding symbol, recent AI represents concepts with millions of feature vectors all set to different values at the moment of representation. Therefore, more things represent any one "meaning." A commensurate step of increasing internal structure accompanies each pluralizing step of this progression within any plural representation scheme. For example, when AI moved from rules to societies of experts, a sort of "social" structure within each society of expert component evolved that was more detailed than internal structure achieved within sets of rules. This evolution of AI parallels progress made in the understanding of how the human mind actually represents things.

Most company AI programs have not reflected the major discontinuities along this evolutionary path. Most companies are using AI rule and object languages and tools like KEE, Common LISP, ART and Knowledgecraft (KEE, ART, and Knowledgecraft are expert system building tools), that are, in most respects, technically and practically out of date. Because firms have charted their course of business around these systems, they will persist. But they are substantially a part of AI's past. These systems are being replaced by new connectionist and massively parallel computer hardware capable of simulating rule and object behavior. They represent "meaning" in a form that more closely mimics the brain's actual circuitry. (Of course, even our most sophisticated machines are primitive when compared to the human mind.) AI rule-based systems, in particular, are abstract symbol statements. Recent work on parallel hardware has achieved rule-base performance using statistical distributions of features across thousands of feature vectors, not AI rules. This is called direct associative memory and it achieves rule-based programming as a kind of "tip of the iceberg" phenomenon. The rest of the iceberg, being much bigger, can represent all of the system's actual experiences from which it deduced an abstract summarizing rule. When the simplifications inherent in that rule cause the system to malfunction, it falls back on the actual remembered experiences from which it derived the rule.

Companies in the United States mistakenly assume that new technologies are, by definition, difficult. Professional communities create a mystique around anything that is new so as to discourage others from entering the highly paid field. So, American firms delegate the best available AI representation schemes to the laboratory and concentrate their efforts instead on past AI achievements. This fear of the unknown causes people to fail. For instance, companies virtually ignore the fact that research AI connectionist systems achieve 1,000 times the performance of rulebase systems over more difficult problem domains. Japanese companies observe from afar the overall trend in this AI "meaning representation" evolution. They better understand the future directions of maximizing AI performance and allow for connectionist evolution as part of their preliminary plans when beginning AI programs.

In truth, firms would be well-advised to split all AI work into two distinct technical delivery platforms. The first would be based on present work, optimizing what is solidly known and meshing it with all other company systems integration criteria. Rule- and object-based AI would be delivered on Sun 5 "Campus" workstations (or comparable hardware) across network file systems (NFS) among departments in the firm using, for example, shared knowledgebase networks instead of individual expert systems. Few companies, however, have this minimal level of AI performance even in the planning stages. The second technical delivery platform for AI would be con-

The Modularity Revolution--Its Social and Technical Forms				
Area of Life	Center One	Center Two	Dysfunction	Corrective
Manufacturing	Large Runs	Fixed Schedule	Slow response	Just-in-Time
Management	Command	Control	Resistance	Autonomous Workteams
Software Objects	Procedures	Data	Search time	Code modules
Modular Minds	One processor	One memory	Search time	50 minds and memories
Simultaneous Engineering	Design Dept.	Manufr. Dept.	Revisions	Cross-function
Parallel computation	Sole processor	Sole memory	Serialization	Distributed cpus
Deregulation	Agency rules	Laws	Adversaries	Competition

Figure 9-1 AI Is a Revolution Within Programming.

nectionist edge-of-field hardware and software networked into Sun 5's throughout the firm. This requires such a fundamental change in vision that it will take months of actual hands-on experience with the system before any breakthroughs can be achieved. And, as can be expected, many companies will procrastinate and finally adopt the new technology when it is no longer state of the art. By developing systems on both platforms, companies can have the best of the present and future simultaneously. They can meet today's bottom line needs and also train their entire work force in tomorrow's radically improved AI systems.

In some politically dominated U.S. technical programs, the boss' nephew (or some other totally unqualified individual) is put in charge of creating an AI group. With any luck at all, this person may be familiar with one of the several forms of AI representation and that will be the only form used in the firm. The others will either be dismissed as "bad" or even non-existent. Therefore, major portions of AI's past and present will be blithely ignored because the person heading the project has had minimal AI training. Japanese firms bar the amateurs from AI group management. They know that AI executive seminars can give, at best, a superficial overview. They prefer to build their AI departments with university graduates who have made an indepth study of AI.

Surprisingly, the evolution of AI parallels a pluralization in many other domains in life as is shown in Figure 9-1 on p. 131. Although the domains are different, the changes they have undergone are similar. Central controllers, which operated over a homogeneous mass, have now become autonomous unit controllers operating over segmented localities. Today we see changes in the modularity of computer programs, changes in the self-direction allowed work groups in factories, changes in parts of organizations that are allowed to co-design systems, and changes in the design of computer hardware. Are these changes all one phenomenon? Does this signal some general change in intellectual history?

This book will not attempt to fully answer these questions. Instead, we will attempt to see how these changes will affect AI. AI constructs (such as objects) have allowed for innovations in modularity of programming, but this advance has not been fully reflected in the United States. The U.S. has accepted the technical aspect of this overall phenomenon, but not the social aspect. The opposite holds true in Europe where the social modularity revolution took place first and led to the invention of modular programming (like Simula-67, the Swedish programming language). In other words, in Europe, social modularity preceded computer modularity; in the U.S, social modularity has been resisted while its technical effect has been accepted. This book will help American firms conceive, develop and deliver AI that embodies both halves of the modularity revolution. The benefits of social modularity will be fully illustrated as well as the tactics for overcoming resistance to it.

Kanban Coding

Over the past decade, most manufacturers in the United States have heard of "kanban"; the Japanese word designating a little cardboard tag put on each part and product in the manufacturing process. This card simultaneously identifies a particular item, serves as an invoice to reorder that item, and traces the location of that item in the manufacturing process. American manufacturers had no such system to keep track of process and static inventory. Typically, they moved parts to several different locations in the plant before the parts finally reached the point of assembly. And while American manufacturers played a time consuming game of musical chairs with parts, the Japanese gained huge market shares at U.S. expense. But the importance of this lesson was not lost. The little cardboard tags that the Japanese use to eliminate work in process and static inventories and to keep parts from moving all over the factory have since proliferated in American industry. Business people have trouble understanding the importance of emerging object-oriented programming in the realm of AI. Some explanations are deceptively simple; others are unnecessarily complicated. Object-oriented programming is "kanban" in the world of software.

Consider the following analogy. There used to be large bureaucracies called programs and each program operated on a larger bureaucracy called a database. The program contained thousands of procedures while the database contained thousands of data records. This separation of procedure from data was originally designed for the sake of conceptual efficiency. When programming was a new field, it was easier to think about procedures and data as separate entities. Unfortunately, when users wanted to update a program, they had to perform a large search operation, going through a huge list of procedures to find just the right place for the update. Similarly, they had to search a huge database. Also, since parts of the procedures were highly interrelated, it was likely that any attempts to update the program would induce some ancillary errors. Unanticipated interactions caused modification of one procedure to unwittingly alter other procedures playing off the instructional values fed to other procedures. The errors and search time made updating programs so tedious that in most firms the task was kept to a bare minimum. Large segments of American industry operated on obsolescent software. This inflexible software froze the social, the competitive, and the strategic responses of the firm.

In the good old days of abundance, American companies had stacks of orders for goods, storehouses bulging with new parts, and mountains of freshly produced goods. This plentiful supply amounted to nothing more than waste. Obviously, this uncontrolled glut meant that it was not worth the firm's time to respond to small orders that required only a few produced goods using only a few parts. So the company went to work only when several sizable orders came in. And by doing so, the company effectively decoupled itself from its market. The enormity of the plant's operations buffered the manufacturing function from actual customer wants. In time, each overstocked area developed its own experts, its own professional societies, its own conferences, its own political constituencies, and its own career paths. The company drowned in its own excess.

Japanese firms offered a solution to the market response problem. Increased Japanese competition goaded U.S. manufacturers to copy the key ingredient of Japanese responsiveness (at least the superficial technique currently in place although generated by a deeper system of responsiveness technique invention). The kanban system in Japan took small increments of customer orders, combined them with small increments of products that could be produced, and combined that with small increments of parts to be ordered from suppliers. That is, each tiny fluctuation in customer orders was found in one piece of paper—the kanban—with one increment of product to be produced and one increment of part to be resupplied. Instead of big piles of orders, large parts inventories and work in process, the company stayed lean and quickly processed the orders in small increments thanks to the little kanban card.

The analogy should be obvious. AI objects were designed to eliminate the procedure and database bureaucracy in software in the same way that kanbans were invented to eliminate the order inventory, the work-in-process inventory, and the parts inventory in firms. In one package, protected by special software constructs, AI objects combined for each type of data all the procedures that told how that type of data behaved. Instead of programs consisting of huge procedure lists and huge databases, programs consisted of only one thing—objects. Each object locally encapsulated a type of data and all the rules defining how that type of data interacted with other objects. Each AI object had the same function in software as kanban

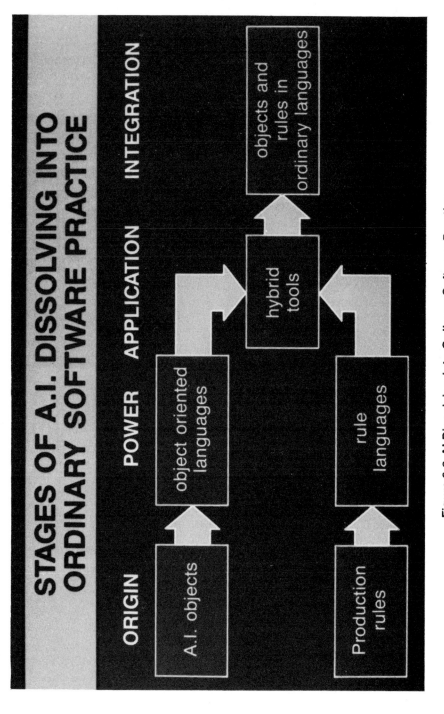

STAGES OF A.I. DISSOLVING INTO
ORDINARY SOFTWARE PRACTICE

ORIGIN   POWER   APPLICATION   INTEGRATION

A.I. objects

object oriented
languages

hybrid
tools

objects and
rules in
ordinary languages

Production
rules

rule
languages

Figure 9-2 AI Dissolving into Ordinary Software Practice.

in manufacturing. Figure 9-2 on p. 135 illustrates AI object representation of data.

Kanbans in Japanese factories are attached to units of inventory and are, in a unique sense, "inspected visually." Special packaging and pallets are used so that anyone can walk down an aisle of a Japanese manufacturing plant and instantly see (from the shape of the packages remaining on pallets) how many minutes of production inventory remain at each workstation. Under usual operating conditions, only an hour or so of inventory is waiting at each workstation. Any flaws in the overall production process shut down all of production and claim the attention of the entire work force. Problems are diagnosed immediately and fixed. Small inventories become, then, a research incentive for the entire organization.

Today, AI objects do not have this instant visibility character. They need it. In fact, AI object libraries need to include within each AI object package procedures for training newcomers to the use and character of each object and procedures for indexing such object packages into functionally similar and functionally interrelated groups. No AI object system on the market at present adds these two essential visibility features. Once added, they will be an even better analog of kanban in manufacturing.

This analogy has importance for industry. Many companies are pursuing Computer-Integrated Manufacturing (CIM) in helter-skelter fashion with few overall principles to guide them. Some pursue it because they think full automation will help them. Others do it because they want to respond to a market with greater speed and more flexibility. In either case, they find themselves facing other aspects of system change, such as the quality of work life and worker quality programs. CIM work, as done today, tends toward large overall systems lacking modularity in direct opposition to the social modularity of work life quality programs. CIM, properly understood, is a modularized form of production process and technology, not a repetition of Ford's Model T assembly line. To stay competitive in the international market, manufacturers must strive toward an overall modular meshing of the firm. In some of the world's most successful companies, even such cognitive functions as executive management and long-range research and development are becoming modular in nature and are being distributed among the work force, using quality techniques such as Policy Deployment, Kansei analysis, and Quality Function Deployment.

10

Making AI a Reality

Seven Strategies for AI

The following sections introduce seven strategies which can lead to a successful implementation of Artificial Intelligence—Japanese Style.

One: The Cognitive Strategy

It is imperative that a firm be aware of its expertise in order to do business effectively. It is just as important that the firm capture this expertise in a way that benefits its business. Expertise in all forms is very valuable, often more valuable than the firm's product or service. The Japanese call this expertise one of the company's "invisible assets" (from Prof. Hiroyuki Itami of Hitotsubashi University.) Management, realizing the importance of expertise, incorporates plans which detail how the firm will gather and disseminate its expertise. To do this, management creates a list of all workers who are about to leave the firm due to retirement, job transfer, or better job offer. Some of these people may have expertise that is crucial to new systems and business. The company could spend years training new people to achieve the same level of performance. Management also notes expertise that doesn't necessarily require great performance but rather avoidance of performance that falls below a certain lowest level. AI projects are planned for each of these types of expertise. The resulting candidate projects are then overlaid onto a list of the real business and competitive pressures facing the firm. The top priority AI projects are those that overlap with key needs of the firm.

This is the most familiar and obvious strategy for spotting potential AI applications and almost all large firms in the world are pursuing it. However, there is no competitive advantage in it unless the
firm is utterly rigorous and thorough in its mapping of corporate
expertise.

Accumulated expertise is becoming less plentiful and relevant as
rapid changes in customer preferences, technology, and so on prevent
any one system from being in place long enough for expertise to accumulate. So a new strategy in which AI captures the experience of
first users working on new systems—a kind of real-time compilation
into new AI rules of users' diary and logbook entries—is replacing
"modelling old Joe's 25 years of experience with an out of date system."

Two: The Software Revolution Strategy

The firm examines all present and planned software systems and
lists those that need AI enhancement. Companies need to consider
the following when making decisions:

1. AI documentation systems that explain and teach complex systems.
2. AI automatic code maintenance and update systems.
3. AI tutors that teach new users how to interface with and use
   new software systems.
4. AI standard object libraries that boost the productivity of programmer staffs.
5. AI software capabilities which capture expertise beyond what
   current software capabilities can handle.
6. Aspects of the software development process that can be automated using AI.

These items are listed by priority and then turned into AI project
proposals. Next they are overlaid on a map of the firm's real competitive and business needs, and then, the final selections are made.

I know of no non-Japanese firm in the world that is seriously pursuing this strategy to determine which AI projects it will initiate.
Many firms have tinkered with AI involvement in their MIS or software functions, but this hardly represents a cohesive strategic
thrust. Recently created Japanese software factories devote almost
25% of all lines of code written to AI development. This effort is not
an application of current AI techniques but rather an ongoing mind-
probing function. The AI developers in these software factories continually monitor the work process of the other programmers as well

as customer demands on the factory as a whole. They devise AI assistance and tools to respond to needs in each area. AI becomes a kind of meta-programming function in these factories. This function continually extends the areas of "modeling of the mind" in software tools and systems that are enhanced or augmented by software systems. This is a revival of the old AI concept of exploratory programming wherein AI was defined as programming machines to imitate the mental processes of the human mind.

Three: The Integration Strategy

This invaluable tool makes knowledge portable. Management surveys the firm to find out what kinds of knowledge underperform because they are available only a few places while needed in many. (This strategy is not to be confused with the current "salt and pepper" tendencies which sprinkle AI projects randomly throughout the firm until every box in the company organization chart boasts an AI project. This achieves widespread dissemination of AI, but at the cost of integration.) Companies identify cross department forms of AI and enforce them as Shared Knowledgebase Network projects rather than independent, non-integrated expert system projects.

Corporations in the United States do not seriously pursue this form of AI. In Japan, the major firms have a vision of standard AI platforms utilized across departments upon which hundreds of AI projects can be built. Surprisingly, the U.S. has many firms valiantly struggling to integrate systems of old technologies, but their actions omit recent and new technologies like AI. These firms allow new technologies to become incompatible gardens of "wild weeds" by a process of omission. Ten years from now, these firms will need a new integration campaign to undo the earlier "wild weeds" AI projects that have overrun the garden. Japanese firms, by comparison, are immune from the "wild weeding" of new technologies. They build AI into long-term platforms and standardize their firms and industries around these platforms. The Japanese realize that this standardization slows down the rate of project implementation, but they understand the long-term competitive benefits of AI platforms. The same does not hold true for the United States.

Four: The Automation Strategy

AI can completely take over hundreds of jobs and activities so that humans won't have to perform them ever again. To implement this strategy effectively, workers are trained to spot jobs and actions that AI (or some other new technology) can totally automate. And even when AI does not constitute the whole solution, it does have a role to play in such efforts. Here the differences between Japan and the United States are most glaring. The U.S. cannot formally recognize this strategy. The American work force, not guaranteed lifetime employment, strongly resists the idea of automating people out of work. The Japanese, who are assured lifetime employment, consider automating their own jobs out of existence as part of the job description. (Of course, the Japanese do face unemployment when entire industries die. Smaller firms do not offer lifetime employment, but do go out of their way to avoid layoffs.)

American workers worry about how AI will affect their job security. After their knowledge is captured by an expert system, they may feel less essential to the company. Indeed, many employees in the U.S. deliberately monopolize areas of knowledge and experience to render themselves indispensable. They see AI as a direct threat, but the fact is, AI cannot automate the essential work they do. AI just is not good enough to fully capture key expertise. It can, however, eliminate the routine and boring aspects of decision making that most experts aren't interested in doing anyway. When people actually experience the advantages of AI, they see it as a form of relief from the more mundane tasks of their jobs, freeing them to do what they do best. To be sure, simply removing routine parts of a job does not mean that brilliant performance will expand to fill the gap. People do not perform at peak brilliance for long periods of time. They arrange to relax their minds with less taxing "filler" activities. Even here, however, AI can eliminate routine activities for these people and cause them to invent new routines that are more productive than the old filler activities.

In many U.S. firms, academically trained AI developers constitute the entire AI group membership. These "experts" spend their time wandering around the firm trying to persuade managers to accept AI. Few managers eagerly embrace new technologies and these "experts" defeat themselves with their salesman tactics. Managers in the past have been burned repeatedly by the new technologies that were foisted upon them. With these feelings of bitterness, they are not particularly amenable to constructive discussion. Instead, the AI developers should go directly to the work force to locate problem areas. Usually the outline of a problem will suggest places where AI could be used to an advantage. Then the firm can discuss the relative costs of the solution. In this case, AI does not fully automate away human involvement with a process, but lightens the load or bolsters the reliability with which the worker performs the job.

Five: The Reliability Strategy

First of all, a firm identifies critical jobs within the firm and the critical activities within those jobs. By doing so, management learns where the reliability of human performance makes a big difference. Estimating functions is one example of a task that requires great reliability. A large firm might send calls for proposals to its in-house parts departments. A parts department might typically be asked something like: "Tell us what price you would charge five years from now for making a new kind of widget similar to past widgets but with thirty percent more titanium. Also, you must ensure that the new widget can be delivered every two hours by a just-in-time inventory system." No one in the world knows the future price of titanium. No one knows how completely changing inventory systems will affect delivery prices in five years. If the parts department bids too high, outside suppliers will likely get the business. If it bids too low, it loses profitability.

As difficult as this estimating function is, many people have a genuine knack for it. But it's not always easy to spot the high performers. Two people who look identically qualified on paper may take two radically different approaches to the job. One may have some uncanny ability to foresee the future and thrive. And the other, who has the same information at his finger tips, may blunder hopelessly. Of course, complete automation of the estimating function is an impossibility. There are too many kinds of knowledge from too many sources with too many attached variables. A lowest common denominator is needed to define minimal acceptable performance. AI can perform this reliability function. A firm needs to examine every place where reliability is critical and let AI provide this lowest common denominator of performance.

By and large, American firms are not attempting these AI applications. The most profound AI applications are not even open to discussion, because the cost would be high and the payback uncertain enough that no one would venture into such a project. Hence, AI is reduced to expensive, but absolutely certain, "copy cat" applications.

Six: The Electronic Manuals Strategy

There exists in Japan a functional vision of AI that is generally lacking in the United States. For some reason, Japanese firms imagine AI in generic terms while American firms envision AI (and other new technologies) in project form. For example, many Japanese have discussed AI as a form of documentation for existing systems. AI, then, becomes a replacement for paper. It is an electronic manual that is intelligently and flexibly indexed. The U.S. has done a lot of research on Hypertext, a kind of wildly indexed text system. The United States, however, is not currently considering this use of AI to replace the text materials that accompany each piece of hardware and software.

The different perspective in Japan may be due to the joining of the white-collar and the blue-collar workers in the same union structure. Because office and plant floor employees have comparable status and opportunities for promotion, they are not separated by artificial boundaries. They combine their expertise and work together on teams to explore new roles for AI. In the end, an AI application program is developed that is equally appropriate to office work and plant systems. AI developed documentation is identical on the plant floor and in the office file shop.

The Japanese have another generic role for AI: the "question/answerer" role. Japanese firms envision AI as a system to automate the answering of questions. Across the firm, the Japanese examine all of the places where simple and straightforward questions are asked and identify where AI systems might enhance the general quality of answers received. (Earlier in this book, Help Desk AI systems were discussed.) Japanese firms see AI as a kind of omnipresent question answering facility attached to all systems in the firm. This is a broader but less profound role for AI than usually found in the United States. The Japanese do not imagine full natural language processing as being possible or even desirable for this question answering facility. Instead, they imagine nothing more is needed than subsets of natural language for specific functions. They simplify and broaden AI applications. On the other hand, American firms have a mania to turn any new technology into a showcase of endless projects. When I returned to the United States, it amazed me that U.S. firms were so insistent that I design "projects" for AI. In Japanese firms, discussions considered AI in more holistic and strategic ways. Projects were properly seen as an outgrowth of these preliminary discussions. Long before new products were launched, companies considered strategic vision, system integration layering, standards development, and the generation of competitive distinctness. In America, discussions of new technology don't even take place until it is already packaged in the form of specific project recommendations. When technologies are thus localized away from systemic viewpoints, managements view superficially without thought to long-term financial benefits to the firm.

Japanese managers delegate all their work, leaving them free for cross-functional strategy and consensus building and competitive benchmarking. Hence, they envision ultimate roles for new technologies before endorsing specific projects.

Seven: The Knowledge Compilation Strategy

This is Japan's ace in the hole. In the United States, highly paid professionals monopolize the expertise in new technology. The Japanese automatically separate the technology from the experts at an early stage. Hence, programs in Japan are well underway to:

1. Make PROLOG, one of the AI languages, the first computer language taught in schools.
2. Teach all engineering students AI as a required part of their college training so they can make use of their own expert knowledge rather than relying on a highly paid knowledge engineer.
3. Teach all engineers in a company the AI systems as well as any standard language platforms which are standardized nationally or unique to the company.

At present, the U.S. puts forth no concentrated effort in any of these three directions. For example, any attempt to make one computer language the standard would ignite a bitter debate among the adherents of all the various languages.

By eliminating the expensive knowledge engineer from the AI process, Japan gains an immense cost advantage in building expert systems. Engineers in Japan can build their own expert systems without the highly paid (and redundant) knowledge engineer.

AI vendors and knowledge engineers in the United States are very much wrapped up in an ideology of elitism. They attended elite schools, they represent an elite technology, and they are well paid for their skills. I like to give these people a little test when I meet them. I suggest that they give an AI programming language to a friend who has built some FORTRAN programs before, but has no experience with AI. This immediately ruffles their elitist feathers and elicits these kinds of responses:

1. AI is a special way of thinking and I don't think my friend will understand it.
2. Giving an AI tool to a beginner is just going to confuse and discouage him.
3. Giving that tool is fine if my friend also signs up for a series of AI seminars that I will be teaching.
4. AI is not the right tool and is just too complex for beginners.

In the United States, this test produces a nearly unanimous negative reaction. There is always some lame excuse for not disseminating AI expertise beyond those already initiated. The same test elicits a different response in Japan. The Japanese Knowledge Compilation Strategy is based on transmitting AI as a basic tool for all of engineering. It is not something to be jealously hoarded.

American engineers are smart enough to teach themselves AI without the intervention of the knowledge engineers. In the firms where I worked, I gave the engineers the Teknowledge tool "M1" and after three weeks they called to say that it was too weak to represent what they were attempting to do. I then gave them OPS83, a much more profound AI tool in pure AI capability terms, and they readily understood it. It cohered better as a set of concepts. Indeed, the deeper AI tools are often more intuitively obvious than specially simplified commercial tools. Worldwide, the whole field of knowledge engineering is less than a decade old. Simply put, there has not been enough expertise built up that an enterprising tenth-grader couldn't understand most of it.

AI Versus Ordinary Software

The software revolution has been explained in preceding chapters. Regardless of that revolution, AI software still has to relate to the billions of dollars of software already in place in industry. No one is going to rewrite all of that software just because AI techniques offer some improvements. This is not enough to justify redoing work that took over thirty years to accumulate. Therefore, it is imperative that AI relate to ordinary software.

AI, however, is not static. Like any emerging technology, it is dynamic and explosive. The way that it will eventually relate to ordinary software is not some fixed property at the present. Every day new discoveries are being made which have enormous implications.

There is a distinct evolution of AI. At first, AI existed as separate concepts in research labs that dealt with the representation of knowledge in computers. There were "objects" people and "rules" people who pursued separate issues in AI. (Recently new groups have evolved: clasifier, connections, and learning production people.) To expand on their work, they initiated a second phase of building languages that ran on computers and supported either objects or rules. This allowed powerful experimentation with the properties of rules and objects as separate entities. In time, a third phase arrived, the hybrid languages which combined objects and rules. Almost all AI tools, systems, and languages in use today are of this hybrid variety. Even the tools that give the outward appearance of being one type are in actuality a combination of the two. Smalltalk is a language wherein everything is an object. But Smalltalk, as it is delivered to the customer, contains objects that are rules and allows rulebased programming within a world of objects. PROLOG is a language set based on logic processing, but most PROLOG, as delivered to the customer in the past twelve months, has included special packages that contain the definition of objects in PROLOG rules. (Note that objects and rules are just the two most widely used representations out of five used at present. The other three are classifiers, connections, and learning production rules.)

These third phase hybrid languages mix programming based on modeling of the mind with programming based on simulating the world. This double possibility then creates a subcategory within the third phase. When two fundamentally different disciplines of program development coexist in one system, their interrelations are pluriform. A generation of languages with endless features was created: KEE, ART, and Knowledgecraft are three examples. These feature-proliferation languages generate excitement by combining objects and rules. (They also generate inefficiency and error.) They are immense systems with one-thousand-plus page manuals that list hundreds of keywords. Actual programmers use only a fraction of these features. While these languages are impressive in scope, they are dangerously flawed. For one thing, with so many hundreds of features, it is next to impossible to produce good disciplines of program development. It is extremely expensive to train people to use these endless languages effectively and foolish to put software systems in place that are built up on hundreds of new features with which no one has any real experience.

In sum, this subcategory of phase three languages suffers from:

1. Problems learning the features.
2. Problems with error.
3. Problems with discipline of development.
4. Problems with cogency of thought and expression.
5. Problems with standardizing practices and building up experience.
6. Problems with efficiency and low cost production.

A fourth phase is well underway. AI developers have realized that an endless proliferation of language features does not solve problems but compounds them. Features quite simply do not substitute for thought itself. Also, major problems have appeared with the interfacing of AI programs to ordinary software from which the AI systems must get data. More cogent languages have been invented that embody AI features captured in ordinary languages. Hard decisions have been made about the nature of the core of AI languages. OPS83 is the purest form of AI rulebased programming embedded in ordinary PASCAL. VICI (also called Interpreted Objective C) is the purest form of AI objects embedded in ordinary C. OPS2000 is the most robust frame and rule system embedded in an object-oriented C++ interpreter. These fourth phase languages offer the best of both worlds. They provide much more than a cornucopia of features. This is the beginning of a trend to add on AI features to all languages. Back when data structures were new, only a few languages allowed a person to put different types of data—numeric, character string, or Boolean—into the definition of one data structure. In time, more and more languages included structures. Now virtually all languages from TrueBASIC to PL 1 to C to Common LISP include structures. Similarly, rules and objects (as well as classifiers, connections, and learning production rules) will become features for which all programming languages contain primitives. The world of separate AI languages is coming to a rapid end.

Resistance to this trend is centered primarily in the AI community. Venture AI businesses have staked their future on an elite, expensive form of AI. Should AI become embedded in ordinary languages running on ordinary hardware, many of these businesses will find themselves without a clientele. So they fight doggedly to create the impression that this fourth phase is an adulteration of AI that completely misunderstands its inherent uniqueness. But these visions of elitism can have costly consequences.

Given these four phases, there are four kinds of AI that can be related to ordinary software:

1. Conceptual AI (which is in the research laboratories today).
2. Power AI (special purpose AI languages testing new representation forms—these are also in laboratories).
3. Hybrid AI (AI languages containing several knowledge representation or interfacing types).
4. Integration AI (AI features embedded in ordinary languages).

Obviously the fourth type interrelates the best. It provides, as features of the language itself, immediate passing of data from AI to ordinary code within one language. It invites the user to apply the same disciplines of software development used everywhere for PAS-

CAL and Modula 2 programming to AI programming. It invites the same disciplines of C programming to application of object programming. Data passing and discipline sharing are two immense benefits of fourth phase languages. Cogency and power of AI expressions are also important benefits of these smaller but more meaningful tools.

Relating AI to Ordinary Software in Seven Stages

Having discussed the direction in which AI tools are evolving, we can examine the implications for relating AI to ordinary code.

Stage One: Potpourri of Old Programs

Most organizations do not offer "pure" AI applications to AI groups. Instead, they propose chaos. Companies use obsolete, poorly written programs that have been doctored through the years with assorted gimmicks, kludges, and repairs to give them some semblance of being up-to-date. Overly isolated software systems have their performance limited by past assumptions about the availability of real data integration possibilities. In some cases, human judgment has been excluded from the software design because AI wasn't available as a tool. Most AI systems in industry end up having to blend with these messy components.

Stage Two: Parametric Programming

Tired old programming can be fixed by updating procedures. Even without the assistance of AI, superannuated programs can be resuscitated into models that are varied by the changing of certain parameters. This allows one profound model of the situation to simulate many actual variations of the situation. It requires careful design and testing to verify that the model and its variant parameters actually do represent the situation well. AI interrelates better to something well-conceived than something hastily thrown together.

Stage Three: The Above Parametric Model Recomposed as an Object-Oriented System

Translation of the parametric model into AI object form drastically reduces the amount of programming time and programming code. By doing so, it reduces ancillary coding errors. It also builds an inherently more cogent, conceptually clean, and communicative software simulation of the analytical model of the situation.

Stage Four: AI Capture of Heuristic Rules

We will not stop research at the point where ordinary analysis type software gave up on modeling the human mind. AI rules allow us to model aspects of human expert behavior not formerly represented in software form. So we extend the reach of the analytical software by capturing heuristic rules that allow the program to modify or rebuild its own analytical parametric model based on the input data and output data results.

Stage Five: AI as Manager of Old Programs

AI can intelligently manage a set of old analytical programs. It can set up each program with its correct inputs; it can interpret the results of running each old program, and based on that interpretation, select which other old programs to set up inputs for and run. Firms that have hundreds of old programs, each written by a different person and each poorly documented and understood, will find AI to be a lifesaver.

Stage Six: AI as an Object-Oriented Database

AI's role can still grow beyond managing old programs. The different data formats used by various old programs can be reduced to a cogent taxonomy of AI object definitions, and each local database can be recompiled into one overall AI object-oriented database shared by all the old programs.

Stage Seven: Automatic Construction of New Programs

After all the old programs have been made to share one common object-oriented database, the separate routines for processing data can be conceptualized across programs. These concepts can be combined with heuristics of the domain represented by each old program. The result is an AI program that knows how to generate each old program and variants of each old program beyond assumptions made in the past. Old programs create a big problem when they lock a business into old theories and practices. By capturing the procedural side of each old program in a common AI code generator guided by heuristics in each domain, a much broader and easier to update system can be created.

When skeptical engineering or office managers ask how AI will relate to their libraries of old programs, the answer is sevenfold. AI will start as just an intelligent manager, handling the front and back ends of the old programs. Gradually, AI will infiltrate the basic building blocks of each old program until an automatic generator program results. It may take ten years to accomplish this for any one part of the firm, but speed is not the issue. The issue is long-term strategic evolution of software in increments that are cost-effective with complexity that is locally manageable without expensive experts and mistake-laden results from distant developers.

Earlier, we discussed object-oriented programming. When each object contains within it all the routines defining its behavior, object-oriented programming absorbs within the data structure the procedures of ordinary programming. This is a key feature that determines a path of easy evolution from ordinary analytic software systems to AI software systems. By setting up the AI to manage old programs, the inputs and outputs of programs can be modeled as AI objects. By setting up an AI database that all programs write to and read from, an AI form of the objects within each old program can be built incrementally alongside procedures in the old program code. This leaves two easy steps: 1) the encapsulation of the procedures themselves into AI rule form and 2) the enhancement of them by heuristic (beyond analysis) rules from the area of expertise each old program represents. You can reasonably expect to see the entire edifice of old program code transformed into fourth generation AI languages in the coming years.

Overcoming Barriers

Those who wish to start AI programs in companies often have to run the gauntlet of "problem" managers. Many managers have a hard time understanding exactly what capabilities AI has and how it differs from ordinary software. Other managers detest anything that is new and requires a concentrated effort to learn. Here is a brief sampling of the types of unreceptive people an AI group might have to deal with:

1. The Curmudgeon—refuses to believe in the existence of AI at all and if by some chance it does exist, it shouldn't.
2. The Reactionary—claims that BASIC can do whatever AI does, only better and more understandably.
3. The Bottom Liner—states that the small increment in functional improvement that AI can bring does not justify the cost.
4. The Omniscient—boasts of being on the leading edge of AI for over fifteen years.
5. The Badly Burned—has seen too many complex, over-hyped technologies ruin profitability in the company.

Each type requires a different approach by the AI developers. As a rule, never waste time with the Curmudgeon. His mind is set in concrete; his game plan is determined; and AI is the loser before the game even begins. At times, for his own amusement, he may invite AI groups to make presentations. And once he has an audience assembled, he will use the occasion to express his own hostile opinions. Curmudgeons, once spotted, are best ignored.

The Reactionary is often one of the old pioneers in an organization's programming department and he's been hurt (in principle) by new innovations. He's observed the inconsiderate way the world jumps on new technology bandwagons to the detriment of the old ways that had worked so well in the past. To defend his position, he will convene AI conferences and engage in fierce arguments. He will hold BASIC to be superior to recently arrived AI programming. If he had his way, all programming would be reduced to ones and zeroes. In ones and zeroes, AI code is just the same as BASIC. It is all a matter of convenient representation. But it's a matter of convenience that can increase a programmer's productivity one hundred times. Ask anyone who programmed on the IBM 1401 which had an eight digit size limit on numbers. It was necessary to make arrays to multiply 23,445 times 123,443. It could be done, but it certainly wasn't conducive to high productivity.

The Bottom Liner is inconsistent. He firmly states that once all the dust has settled, AI will not bring enough benefit to the firm to justify the expense and trouble of implementing it. And yet, he enjoys playing the devil's advocate. He will challenge people to debates, relishing the opportunity for a good scrap. Why does he waste his time challenging the worth of AI if he already feels it is not cost effective? Obviously, this type should also get the brush-off. There are bound to be other people in the firm more receptive to AI. The poor attitude of the Bottom Liner encourages AI groups to give top priority to others.

The Omniscient has been doing AI for years—or so he says. Somehow, his salary is not commensurate with the salaries of those who are really in the field. He is the type of manager whose inflated self-image requires him to be on the leading edge. He claims all new ideas are his. In fact, he will summon AI experts to meetings so that they can marvel at his exploits.

The Badly Burned is the only one of these "difficult" people that might end up being receptive to AI, but it takes the correct approach. His complaints are legitimate. He has seen all sorts of new innovations arrive with a lot of accompanying fanfare that ultimately didn't deliver. If he can be convinced that the firm is interested in implementing a lean Japanese-style AI program, he may become quite interested in working towards smart automation.

Once the "problem" people have been dealt with (either through avoidance or persuasion), the firm can seriously consider the types of problems and functions that AI can handle.

Figure 10-1 shows eleven distinct types of problems AI can handle. To the left of each level is a kind of function often associated with the problem described in each level. These functions are somewhat abstract. "Planning," for example, includes most design problems— sheet metal design, electric circuit design, and so on. "Writing" includes general composition problems like construction of simulations or construction of figures on a blackboard. "Deciding" is the first level and the easiest for AI to handle while "Inventing" is the last and most difficult. Missing from the figure are items like "natural language understanding" and "common sense understanding" which are beyond AI's current capabilities.

An organization wishing to apply AI should examine all crucial activities that fall under each of the eleven levels in the figure. The same applies to the AI staff. Their skills should be assessed under each of the eleven levels. When the firm decides to "beef up" an expert system, that system should also be examined under each of the eleven levels to decide what new functionality should be added. A peculiar vision of the firm emerges from this kind of function level analysis. One sees, for example, many types of situations being monitored across the firm. Is there some generic monitoring assist or monitoring automation technology that the firm should design? Or should the firm allow the local task in each situation to define a local project? The Americans choose the latter option; the Japanese choose the former.

THE ELEVEN TYPES OF PROBLEMS A.I. CAN SOLVE

Deciding
FEW SOLUTIONS, RELIABLE KNOWLEDGE
A.I. uses exhaustive search, single line of reasoning

Interpreting
UNRELIABLE DATA AND KNOWLEDGE
A.I. uses multiple evidence lines, fuzzy logic

Diagnosing
DATA AND KNOWLEDGE THAT VARY WITH TIME
A.I. uses state-triggered expectations, multiple contexts

Monitoring
NEARLY DECOMPOSABLE PROBLEMS
A.I. uses a hierarchy of abstract goals, local hypothesis

Predicting
FRAGMENTS OF THE SOLUTION CANNOT BE PROVED PART OF THE
SOLUTION TILL THE FINAL SOLUTION IS ALREADY REACHED
A.I. uses "match" a fixed ordering of solution steps

Planning
PROBLEMS WITH NO FIXED SEQUENCE OF SUBPROBLEMS
A.I. uses top-down refinements of plans, from general goals to specific goals, using predetermined generality levels

Repairing
INTERDEPENDENT SUBPROBLEMS
A.I. uses least commitment, the making of decisions only when absolutely necessary

Learning
AT PLACES IN THE PROBLEM, GUESSING IS REQUIRED
A.I. uses assumed states, belief revision, to determine which assumptions to revise when an assumed state is untenable

Writing
WHERE SINGLE LINES OF REASONING CAUSE GOOD SOLUTIONS TO
BE MISTAKENLY UNDER-EVALUATED
A.I. uses qualitative reasoning along simultaneous multiple views of the space of possible solutions

Tutoring
WHERE SINGLE SOURCES OF KNOWLEDGE ARE INADEQUATE
A.I. uses a "society" of experts which "confer and conference" using an opportunistic scheduler, a capitalist competition of possible right answers

Inventing
MASSIVE KNOWLEDGE BASE SYSTEMS, EFFICIENCY LIMITED
A.I. uses format-less data representations "compiled" into any of many different formats as subgoals dictate

Figure 10-1 Types of Problems AI Can Solve.

American industry has harmed itself by its unthinking acceptance of the subdivisions of AI. Americans simply don't see the forest for the trees. They focus their energies and monies on showcase AI projects that appear outwardly impressive but do very little to help the firm as a whole. Their projects are organized around hackneyed AI categories: robotics, machine vision, natural language, expert systems, and parallel systems.

These projects don't take into account the broader perspective. They offer little insight to the firm as a whole. The Japanese concentrate on projects that span the entire organization and serve to integrate it. All complex systems in any corporation need the following seven types of AI system, and each system will include several of the eleven levels.

1. Documenting systems—all systems must be intelligently indexed.
2. Teaching systems—these automatic facilities allow anyone to be trained to use the system at any time whether at work or at home.
3. Controlling systems—these facilities intelligently control the systems' activities.
4. Fixing systems—these facilities investigate trouble and produce probable causes and means of correction.
5. Augmenting human activities—these facilities interact with human operators to make the person's interactions with the system easier and more interesting.
6. Secretarial services to systems—these facilities allow humans to assign tasks to the system so that the system itself can figure out how to perform them.
7. Societies of systems—this will be dealt with in a later section.

The different approaches that the Japanese and Americans take have great consequences. In the United States, for example, firms assign AI developers to specialize in robotics, and they end up applying far more AI than is necessary. This has the unwanted effects of increasing the cost, the complexity, and the failure rates of the robots. On the other hand, firms that assign AI developers to broad areas (like documentation) develop uniform across-the-company integrated AI systems and enhance existing systems. This is done without overemphasizing any particular technical system. Once this companywide documentation system is in place, it can be built up using the previously mentioned seven steps which utilize AI to transform outdated computer programs.

The Japanese are aware of these two different views of AI application. They envision documentation, fixing, and teaching systems that cross department and function and, using strategic design, spread initial projects throughout the entire firm. They do not make one technical area "top heavy" in AI at the expense of the whole firm. They emphasize incremental implementation across a wide spectrum of locales inside a strategically important layer of functionality (such as the documentation of all systems). While the Japanese carefully disseminate AI in their companies, the Americans, victims of their own "bigger is better" philosophy, make huge investments in single local projects where the ultimate payback is much less. It is important to remember that both the Japanese and Americans rely on their social systems when they choose their approach. In Japan, the entire work force designs their automation systems and for this reason, the systems put in place will be of use to all. In the United States, however, small project teams congregate around functions and particular boxes on the organization chart and keep all new systems strictly local.

Standards and Dynamic Technologies

Many companies suffer from a myriad of incompatible systems in the office and factory. For decades, computer vendors feverishly pushed any and all equipment with little regard for the consequences. As a result, many of their customers have been left in a strategically weak position. Some companies have Computer Aided Design (CAD) equipment from more than a dozen different vendors. And each vendor's equipment has its own attached political lobbying group with heavy investments in that particular system. What is to prevent AI from developing along these same lines? Surely AI salespeople are no different than CAD vendors. They are trying to earn a good living and are apt to overlook a system's overall standardization. If AI goes the way of CAD, it is safe to predict that fifteen years from now companies will have AI systems written in ten different languages running on a dozen different kinds of hardware. AI vendors argue that standardization is impossible at this point. The technology is moving so fast that today's new feature is already yesterday's news. They maintain that it is their duty to the customer to offer the latest advances. But more and more businesses are learning the hard way that the newest gimmicks are a poor long-term substitute for standards-integrated systems. Of course, there are some companies in very competitive industries that must buy the very latest and the very best. They simply need the extra one percent cost savings that the new systems offer no matter how incompatible it may be with present equipment.

In a dynamic technology like AI, interconnectivity—not features—becomes the criterion for standardization. The ideal standard would encourage reverse engineering. That is, when new AI features appear on the market, a company's AI staff could copy them (without violating copyrights) and implement them as automatic upgrades that talk to all of the existing AI systems in the firm. That way, all AI components could interconnect, new features could be published annually across the system, and standardization could be accomplished without denying the company the competitive advantages of the latest features.

The Japanese are pursuing just such a form of standards for AI. They envision a day when there will be hundreds of expert systems within a single firm where each such system talks to the rest. (They imagine a day when hundreds of knowledgebases will exist all across the firm with arbitrary new inference capabilities added yearly after being reverse engineered.)

While I was in Japan, one factory estimated that it would ultimately need 1,400 knowledgebases to be built and that was probably an underestimate. They specified that those knowledgebases could each be combined with others for any one expert system. Similarly, they imagined fifty or so different inference engines in the firm with new ones added annually. They wanted those inference engines to be able to talk to each other and to each knowledgebase.

The future of AI consists of populations of expert system components. There are knowledge extractors that automate the extraction of various kinds of information through intelligent AI driven dialogs with expert humans. There are knowledge representations and also knowledge representation translators that translate between representations. There are inference engines of various sorts. Finally, skipping over a few components, there are already constituted expert systems themselves. Therefore a population of both expert systems components and already configured expert systems exists. Ordering and organizing this is a peculiar expert system called the "community organizer" that gives birth to new or destroys obsolete expert systems. It is an expert system that itself designs and makes other expert systems. What features within AI are needed to achieve such an overall system of populations? A scaledown and self-ressemblance principle is the key. Embedded in each expert system and each expert system component is another smaller mini-expert system. That means each knowledgebase contains a mini-inference engine and knowledge extractor within it. This embedded mini-expert system allows each component to calculate how it interrelates with other components of the same or different type. The overall system design, takes on a three level nature. The community organizer is an expert system that creates and destroys expert systems; each component expert system has embedded in it a mini-expert system; and each expert system component has embedded in it a mini-expert system. The same pattern is repeated on three size scales.

The point of all this is to allow reverse engineering. No doubt, exciting new AI features will come on the market every year, and the firms that buy them will have a difficult integration job. It costs a lot of money to buy the most advanced features and then struggle for years to integrate them. Instead, this proposed system copies the best features and utilizes them as one member of a large population of similarly standardized components. The Japanese will adopt this kind of standardization. The United States will continue to confuse the "new" with the "difficult" and miss this opportunity. Americans consider all new things to be difficult until proven easy. In Japan, new things are merely new and they have to be proven difficult or easy. Newness is not synonymous with difficulty. The Japanese have a long tradition of self-teaching and tutoring each other and do not shy away from new things. It was because of this tradition that in just one hundred years the Japanese absorbed much of Western technology. Learning has been an integral part of job descriptions in Japan for decades. This self-tutoring concept is notably absent from U.S. job descriptions.

Common sense tells the Japanese that new AI features are not hard to copy. They are not hard at all; they are just new. The same common sense tells Americans that new AI features must be hard because they were invented by an elite group of scientists. Hence, the vast majority of the people in the United States who are learning AI never attempt to replicate the truly innovative feats. American college curricula in computer science compound this confusion. Many programs make a study of past computer science a prerequisite for the truly useful classes that deal with present day technology. In some schools, the student has to master PL 1 before learning LISP. Cognitively, this makes no sense at all because newer forms of computer science are, by and large, simpler than the older forms. Computer science is, at most, one hundred and fifty years old and nowhere as symbolically intense as mathematics. It is still a new and relatively easy science. Of course, graduate students, with their shaky level of understanding and their inability to express themselves well, have trouble making their knowledge accesible to others.

But just because they have trouble expressing themselves does not necessarily mean they are doing anything hard. It is just new.

The Japanese recognize that during the early stages of a technology, when many people still seek to understand it, confusion may occur. They are patient enough to sift the wheat from the chaff and transmit the wheat. They are patient enough to distinguish the new things from the hard things.

In the United States, this confusion of the new with the hard causes colleges to delay presenting edge-of-field content (or eliminate it altogether) from many curricula. This frustrates the aspirations and lessens the understanding of students who read about it in the press and hear about it on television but find it omitted from their classwork. It also hurts their chances of landing a really good job. Twenty years ago, even MIT made IBM machine language a prerequisite for learning LISP. A poorer preparation for understanding LISP cannot be imagined! This counterproductive tradition forces American students to study useless, out-of-date material that has no bearing on current applications. It leads to a striking competitive disadvantage with students trained overseas. The Japanese understand that LISP is simpler than BASIC and more useful than LOGO and therefore the second best language for beginning programmers after PROLOG. Because AI is a new (not hard) technology, Japanese industry knows that it can reverse-engineer new AI features as they appear.

4

A Tri-Level Approach to AI Implementation

"As work becomes more interdependent, a particular kind of skill becomes increasingly crucial to effective work performance. I call it 'organizational reflexivity,' and by that I mean the capacity on the part of members of a work organization to systematically reflect upon their own organizational practice and to engage in the ongoing modification of work procedures and tasks."

Bob Howard, "Systems Design and Social Responsibility: The Political Implications of 'Computer-Supported Co-operative Work'"; delivered at first annual conference on Computer-Supported Co-operative Work, Austin, Texas, 3-5 December, 1986.

Companies that have just one type of AI program are headed toward failure. One AI program may make it simple for managers to keep in mind what is going on, but companies that reduce their work loads to accommodate the mental capacities of their managers fail in the market. Furthermore, when there is just one AI program in place, it usually means that it is in the hands of one political faction. This unnecessarily subjects a technology to the political whims and fortunes of one set of people. Japanese firms involve larger groups of people in new technologies than American firms. They end up with several centers of activity for any one technology with more human heads inputting their talents.

It would be unrealistic to ask U.S. firms to copy all aspects of Japanese methods. The United States is not Japan. But America must realize that its current procedures for the delivery of technologies are suicidal. They just don't work in the market. American firms will find that they will have to consider many approaches. There is no one right way. As will be seen, a combination of ways will outperform any single method. This part of the book outlines a three part program for AI delivery that accounts for and overcomes the differences between American and Japanese workplaces.

11

The Aggressive AI Program

The Seven Components of a New Technology Delivery System

The over-cautiously managed AI program has already been dealt with—so what does an aggressively managed program look like? Oddly enough, it does not look like an AI program at all, but instead, it looks like a general program for delivery of all new technologies. That is, a bold AI program looks like a particular instance of a general new technology delivery program.

As can be seen in the Figure 11-1, the foremost objective of an AI program is the automating of automation. Top management presents the business case and workgroups throughout the firm strategize with their particular functions to achieve business goals and planned competitive advantages. This is not some vague, hypothetical concept but a system of policymaking in which the entire work force participates. It is a series of policymaking events wherein the work force of the firm constantly improves the ways it implements successive new technologies. It is a system of events, meetings, workshops, and conferences within the firm where the organization as a whole learns from implementing one technology better ways to implement the next one. It is a system of measures and accounting changes that hold the firm to a discipline of implementing one technology better than the last, because without comparative data, no improvement in new technology implementation can be expected.

The second layer consists of the two delivery vehicles. They are normal parts of all jobs in the firm. All employees have at least three components to their job: normal assigned work, social delivery vehi-

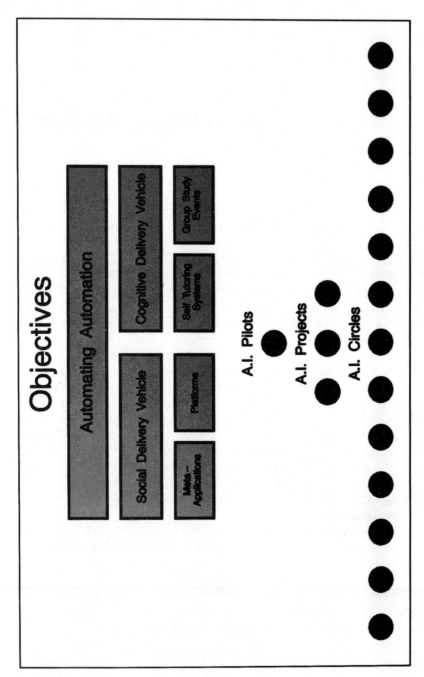

Figure 11-1 AI Program Objectives.

cle participation, and cognitive delivery vehicle participation. This adds an anticipatory content to the present content of each job. Each job, then, splits into two parts—one part that is dedicated to doing present work well and the other dedicated to automating away present work. This means reward systems, job specifications, and performance appraisals must reflect this split. A work force without employment security, however, is unlikely to tolerate this level of automation. A work force unable to tolerate this level of automation is unlikely to be employed five years hence.

The Social Delivery Vehicle (in the tier below "Automating Automation") is a series of activities and coordinating events that consistently deliver new technologies to the workplace. The components of this concept will be presented later, but here it suffices to say that it amounts to perpetual activity.

The Cognitive Delivery Vehicle is the system which trains employees to handle the new technologies being implemented. In the case of AI, the Cognitive Delivery Vehicle is complex because AI serves as the Cognitive Delivery Vehicle for other technologies. AI's diagnostic, intelligent indexing, and tutor facilities ultimately make it the new form of all system documentation.

Next come two of the many components of the Social Delivery Vehicle. First is the Meta-Applications function which replicates first project achievements in all similar sites in the firm. The company concentrates on commercializing the first key accomplishments in a technical area before the market itself commercializes them and charges high prices. Its other functions will be taken up later. Platforms—units of automation—are the second component. Platforms combine several hardware systems and several software packages (including AI languages) into one overall integrated system with one unified interface and one unified data format.

The Cognitive Delivery Vehicle for new technologies is divided into self-training systems and group study events. These prevent the failings seen in usual company training programs in new technologies. The customary study formats contain loopholes that allow people to pretend to be educated when this, in fact, is not the case. In time, large numbers of these supposedly trained people are allowed to simulate knowledge rather than actually demonstrate and use knowledge. Somehow companies get the idea that every employee's contributions, regardless of merit, are worthy of respect. This practice can make serious training nearly impossible. With this kind of policy in place, people hesitate to point out the weaknesses they see in their colleagues' performance. It is an unwritten rule that everyone pats everyone else on the back. If strict standards are not enforced, hundreds of people can go through a training program and not derive any practical benefit. Real training implies real failing in some cases. People must be tested on what they have learned. There is no such thing as social promotion in the well-run firm. The General Motors Hamtramck Plant had immense problems with automation largely because of this insidious social effect. Self-training systems and group study events can prevent this from happening. They are part of a much larger Japanese system for consistent truth exposure and are key to achieving quality.

With the simultaneous arrival of so many new technologies, it is hard to ensure high quality training for all employees. Often, the training is done in a rushed fashion to get a jump on the competition. Even the vendors of new equipment may not have one single person well-versed in the new system as an integrated whole, but rather a half dozen "specialists" who are familiar with individual parts of the system. Since the vendors themselves may not have qualified instructors for their own systems, it is not surprising that companies have a hard time training people. And, unfortunately, they try. When the task is clearly impossible, the companies secure the services of an "expert" instructor to teach employees. More than likely, this results in an amateur teacher spreading amateur knowledge with employees accepting it as the final authority.

Self-study is deeply rooted in Japanese culture. In Buddhist temple schools, students taught themselves new material and new technologies (guns, for one example). After World War II, Japan adopted a more Western approach to education. They built hundreds of new colleges and conscripted people with any kind of knowledge to teach in them. To their dismay, the Japanese found that the students did not learn much from their professors and instead formed self-study groups that met in homes and coffee shops. In Japanese firms today, each workgroup is also a self-study group. This inclusion of study as part of the normal functioning of any workgroup is a key difference between Japanese and American corporate organizations. Study is not part of the job description (sometimes it is even actively discouraged) in American companies and this works to the detriment of American competitiveness. People who have no experience with self-study just can't jump into it. It requires self-confidence, serious application, and the ability to grasp and summarize the main points of a text. The Japanese use Structured Reading as a basic cognitive skill to discriminate top management people from middle management people. This program will be more fully detailed later.

Group Study Events are a real challenge to American mores. Common sense tells Americans that programming is an activity best done individually. Years ago, when I worked for a major American computer firm, I noticed that the senior expert programmers whose knowledge was most valuable to the firm had very little contact with the majority of the programmers. Their expertise existed in a vacuum. Almost no knowledge flowed between the expert performers and novices or middle rank people. In one firm, I worked across from a woman who was a genius at programming, but I was forbidden to interrupt her. After several years, I made modest improvements as a programmer, but if I had had access to that woman's expertise, my progress could have been much greater.

Group Study Events are a social system that includes everyone in the firm from the experts to the novices. At these meetings, the experts explain key aspects of their real work—not just simplified problems. The others in attendance are ranked by skill level and assist the expert in accordance with their capabilities. The lowest ranked make protocols of the expert's decision processes. Specific investigations of literature or tests of possible best algorithms are performed by middle ranked attendees. Top ranked people solve major problems aloud on the board before the expert. Work with this format in Japan has proven that three hours a week is enough to triple the learning rate of 80% of the people attending.

These four items—meta-applications, platforms, self-training systems and group study events—comprise the third layer. They interact with the delivery vehicle layer and the automating automation layer. If the third layer is treated merely as a component of the second layer and the second layer is treated merely as a component of the first layer, a vague, overly general abstract system will develop and fail. To keep the system concrete and well-defined, these three layers have to be managed with equal emphasis. It is common sense in Japan that the concrete and the abstract both have to be welded into one system and managed together so that neither dominates to the exclusion of the other. In the United States, we frequently assign "concepts" to one part of the organization and "practice" to another group of people. This results in concepts that do not get implemented and implementations that contradict key concepts. A Japanese AI system is managed as a three level mixture of a concept evolution system, a concept delivery system, and a system that embeds concepts in reality.

The Three Sizes of Development Platforms for AI

AI hardware and software, if not properly managed, can become a source of disintegration in the firm. To prevent this from happening, it is imperative that firms think through carefully the kinds of equipment they will need from the very inception of their AI program.

Whatever decisions are made, they are likely to include at least three sizes of AI platforms. At the expensive end of the spectrum is the connectionist or massively parallel hardware platform. This level is one of vast performance increases and experimentation. It is where the future is deliberately embedded in the present. The mid-level platform is the engineering workstation. And at the small and inexpensive end of the spectrum is the personal computer.

Anyone examining these platforms immediately wonders where the mainframes and LISP machines are. They are omitted here because the trend is going in another direction. Companies promoting LISP machines and the large, unwieldy environments they run on are increasingly losing money. Mainframes are no longer part of the growing hardware market, although they are in place nearly everywhere. AI software tools are still being developed for mainframes, but they are feeling pressure from an increasingly important super-computer and mini-supercomputer segments. It is predicted that mainframes will become background data repositories front-ended by more user-friendly systems and back-ended by more powerful super-computers. When add-on Intel 80386 boards are put into slots on personal computers, it will bring minicomputer performance of dedicated LISP machines to the world of personal computers. New AI environments are being developed for engineering workstations that embody fundamentally new features not found in dedicated LISP machine environments. Connectionist hardware and massively parallel hardware run fundamentally different kinds of AI software and offer enormous improvements in efficiency.

Corresponding to these three levels of hardware are three different types of knowledge engineers. At the top are the genuine AI experts who are needed at the connectionist and massively parallel end. In the middle, domain experts trained in AI techniques are needed. At the low end, the typical worker learns AI on a personal computer.

An AI program utilizing these three size scales develops one delivery mechanism that delivers connectionist platform AI, another that delivers workstation AI, and a third that delivers personal computer AI. At the connectionist end, well-trained people are necessary. At the workstation end, training is given to those domain experts who are interested in AI or who are involved in a critical function that AI needs to handle. At the personal computer end, anyone in the firm is invited to learn AI in self-training work groups or an AI Circles program.

To some extent, the kinds of AI application attempted will correspond to one of the three platforms. First, the connectionist platform is key to immense AI program development, like AI tutoring systems or AI vision systems. Second, AI applications like planning and designing belong to the workstation level. Third, AI applications like diagnosis, help desks and document indexing belong at the personal computer level. This implies that well-trained AI people are required to handle AI tutoring systems on the connectionist platform. Ordinary engineers or designers can be given AI training sufficient to allow them to extract their own knowledge and make AI design or planning systems. Anyone in the firm can build a diagnosis system on a personal computer. It is critical that domain experts interact with workstation AI users and that the general work force employ their personal computers for AI. This leaves only connectionist AI for highly trained AI experts.

An inductive approach to developing an AI program looks around the company to spot sources of interest in AI and then create projects. Often hundreds of people in the firm have a lot of interest in new technologies. The press and television bombard them with all the latest breakthroughs. They know a reasonable amount about AI based solely on their exposure to the media. Yet, the company does not tap this source of interest. Instead, new technologies belong exclusively to the "specialists" or certain political factions. Those on the outside feel demoralized because they feel an anticipatory element of their job has been removed.

Paradoxically, it is the AI experts within the firm who most strongly resist the dissemination of AI throughout the company. The specific excuses they made for keeping AI from the masses were presented earlier. And on the surface, it seems obvious that AI groups should be composed solely of AI experts. But this just does not work well. Such AI groups stubbornly refuse to learn the other kinds of software necessary to fully utilize AI. To derive the fullest benefits from an AI program, a company needs to form AI groups that include people of varied backgrounds and experiences. For example, a group could be composed of a few connectionist AI experts, experts representing every business skill domain, and part time representatives from every work group. The AI groups currently found in most companies would balk at including those they deem to be less qualified into their aristocratic club. They are secure in their righteous conviction that AI is beyond the ken of the ordinary worker. And if this elitist attitude prevails for every new technology introduced, the firm pays dearly for placing its future directions in the hands of a few.

Tri-Level Training Systems for New Technologies

A dynamic study program accessible to everyone in the work force is the core of a good training program. In addition, there must be a wide range of material available that can be easily updated. Most importantly, the training program must include all employees within the firm. Customary training programs do not do this. Americans simply do not grasp the importance of this principle.

New technology training programs in America deliberately omit the effects on surrounding systems of implementing a particular new technology. In case after case, the accounting and financial procedures and expectations remain identical across generations of new technologies. This is highly unrealistic. The paybacks, the implementation cost, the expense of learning, and the learning curve itself all change with each new technology. To push each technology through a static accounting system causes the firm to lose touch with the real paybacks and costs. The innovation process is uncertain. The paybacks and cost cannot be based on inflexible criteria, or the stage will be set for expensive surprises. In conservatively managed businesses, surprises are unwelcome. If, however, the finance office and all its work groups are directly involved in companywide campaigns for each new implemented technology, then they can adjust the accounting system to reflect the unique characteristics of that particular project in terms of costs and paybacks. In Japan, the finance office participates in just this way, and its systems account for the idiosyncrasies of each new technology.

In addition to dispersing technology implementation across the work force, Japanese company training programs foster other learning properties. There are three levels of training: the canon, the survey, and the everyman principle. In any new technology, the canon is the fundamental, unchanging determinants of the field. New technical means of reaching these determinants may be attained, but the functions themselves do not go away. The technical content of the canon may vary from year to year, but the functions are constant. The survey (or update) component sends workers traveling around the world to bring back innovations, directions, products, and research results that could lead to products. The firm concentrates its attention on international research in a particular field. The everyman component modifies a new technology so that everyone in the firm can understand it and participate in its implementation. The workers seek to identify the ways it will be of use to their area. This component leads to the transformation of technology from something incomprehensible to something accessible through self-teaching.

In the final analysis of the three components, the canon is by far the most important. It defines the company's basic competency in the technology. It is the whole scope of the technology, all the key aspects that enable a person to achieve using it. It is where minimal levels of quality and understanding are set for the entire firm. It defines the firm's lowest common denominator of use for the new technology. The requisites of quality performance are instilled, measured, and practiced according to the dictates of the canon.

It should be obvious by now what happens to firms that perform AI training without the formal canon component. They establish no minima. Moreover, they cannot tactically maneuver their minima as competitive situations dictate. They have trouble managing the long-range competitive component of their technology. In effect, they condemn themselves to borrowing from others. By default, they let publications like *The Wall Street Journal* and *U.S. News and World Report* define the minima for the technology. Training is the key component in setting style, process, and quality standards; companies that do not control their training cripple their technologies.

The mass participation training component performs an essential cognitive function on new technologies. It simplifies them and establishes them in needs of the company. Moreover, it allows everyone in the firm to become familiar with new technologies. Workers who understand technologies are more likely to support them. Many firms leave new technologies in the hands of elitist staff members who enshroud the technologies in mystery and obscure jargon. Only reluctantly will they condescend to enlighten the uninitiated. They are convinced their job security and salary depend on hoarding their expertise. The company may use these people to train others, but there is a subtle current of sabotage at work. The first-class knowledge of these experts becomes something less at the lecture podium. They refuse to divulge all their secrets. Novices to AI will not detect the corners being cut, but the true experts will.

Firms with a well-established everyman component, introduce new technologies to all their employees. The hallway conversations, the lunchroom debates, and the chatter at social events all familiarize people with the cutting edge of technology. You can sense a different ambience in these firms. Secretaries know which technologies are important to the firm and why. Janitors know what equipment they sweep around. Employees in the firm date their employment by the various technical campaigns in which they participated.

The survey component allows firms to constantly model the edge-of-field. It permits the aggressive incorporation of techniques years before they are expensively commercialized by venture businesses. Workers are sent to learn new techniques while they are still relatively unknown and inexpensive. The applications of new techniques can be worked out internally with real experiments long before the competition does the same. Moreover, the survey component brings the whole world into the firm in a cultural sense. Ordinary AI Circle members can cite leading research names from around the world. This awareness of the ordinary worker elevates the imagination of the firm. The workers in the firm see beyond the technical society in which the firm is embedded. In turn, this convinces each employee that his firm is indeed special.

Those teaching the canon component often rely on the same texts year after year. Because new information is added to the field daily, these outdated texts destroy the relevance of the canon. Rather, the faculty should use the best available new text each year. This consistent updating of texts gives the faculty a deeper understanding of the subject matter. Therefore, the firm's collective knowledge of a technology is edge-of-field and not out of date.

In training sessions, the faculty includes domain experts who know both AI and an expertise like design or finance. These domain experts can lead, along with the faculty, the everyman conferences and problem solving events that enhance self-training in AI. The materials used in these conferences are developed through a joint effort of faculty, domain experts, and first line supervisors. The faculty teaches the survey component with the assistance of key employees who traveled abroad to investigate new technologies. Upon returning, these people compile their findings into the update/survey curriculum. They summarize conference proceedings and turn them into exercises for training classes. For several years I ran such an AI survey training group, and we were probably the only people in the whole world who scanned and summarized the entire American Association of Artificial Intelligence (AAAI) or International Joint Conference on Artificial Intellgence (IJCAI) proceedings each year. We built key insights into exercises— some of which the company later adopted as strategies.

There is a rough correspondence between the levels of AI training and platform sizes. The connectionist platform, the workstation platform, and the personal computer platform correspond to the survey, the canon and the everyman training levels respectively.

Three Sources of AI Projects

In addition to the three training levels and the three platform levels there are three levels of project sources. Top-down projects are started by the highly skilled AI connectionist groups. Bottom-up projects are started by social tactics that extend into the entire work force of the firm. Lateral projects start out as homework in the canon training curriculum.

These three levels of project differ substantially in type. The top-down projects pioneer new AI techniques or applications so that the rest of the organization can copy and replicate them in other relevant locations throughout the firm. The bottom-up projects are initiated by any ordinary work group, perhaps working in an AI Circles program, and these projects, instead of pioneering new techniques, find new, economically beneficial applications for already existing techniques. Also, as bottom-up projects spread throughout the firm, the enhancement of existing bottom-up projects with new AI techniques continues. Lateral projects represent the current official state of the field as embodied in the AI training canon. These projects declare the firm's current minimal state of the art. New students, allowed to do this kind of work, are extremely motivated, and their accomplishments suggest to everyone else in the work force that the new technologies are not too hard for beginners. The opposite message comes from "professional" AI groups who actively dissuade people from copying their achievements.

American firms seldom tolerate three independent sources of new AI projects, although it is the norm in Japanese firms. Three sources serve to keep each one working hard because they are in head-to-head competition. And having three sources differentiates the level of performance expected by all players in AI. All roles are highlighted—the connectionist core role, the single work group role, and the new student role. With this role definition, each group knows exactly what is expected of it. The AI experts are prevented from "frittering" away their time doing simple diagnostic systems because newcomers can perform this job adequately. Surprisingly, I found this very situation in several firms that I visited. The Ph.D.'s avoided the latest massively parallel hardware platforms and channeled their considerable educations into nickel and dime projects that untrained circle workers should have been doing. Management simply did not know any better.

These three levels are more profound still. They develop AI along different directions of insight. The top-down people capture the most complex aspects of AI techniques and research and bring them into the firm in ways that pay off. The bottom-up people, who are familiar with work and business routines, develop AI applications that simplify their jobs and improve efficiency. The lateral people revise and advertise the new minima expected of AI applications and techniques. These three different functions are actually an education system that teaches the whole firm about AI's role and potential. They can be summarized this way:

1. Top-Down captures the best of all AI research. This equals DEPTH DIMENSION.
2. Bottom-Up captures company experience and needs of work. This equals NEED DIMENSION.
3. Lateral advertises current minimal level for the firm. This equals QUALITY DIMENSION.

These functions interact as well. The depth dimension challenges the current quality dimension by pioneering things better than what is included in current best minimal practice (as taught in the canon courses). The quality dimension challenges the current need dimension by proving out a new level of skill and application sophistication. The need dimension challenges the current depth dimension by attempting to satisfy needs that sometimes outstrip what current AI technique in the firm can satisfy, thereby forming a kind of agenda of problems to be solved for each dimension group. There is a competitive component to intergroup relations: each strives to be the best. Over time, they attempt to hone competitive advantage out of their own peculiar structural roles. Those in depth dimension scout the world for advanced techniques. Those in need dimension seek big payback applications that exist within the firm. Those in quality dimension distribute a higher level of expertise and technique throughout the firm. Because each dimension aspires to do its very best, new technologies are broadened, deepened, and made more relevant.

In a poorly managed organization, this tri-level system can run into trouble. Although the sources compete with each other to offer the best projects to the firm, they ultimately share the same goal: they all want to help the firm better its strategic position. It is essential that the boundaries be maintained between their distinct roles, because the three have separate missions. Managers who are looking for fast and dramatic results may actually undermine the other two sources as they seek to further their career goals by embodying the other two roles in the groups they lead.

As this tri-level system succeeds, a number of people scattered throughout the firm learn AI and become involved in successful projects. Gradually, these people start to challenge the tri-level system. That is, about every two years the system generates a certain minimal level of AI throughout the firm that acts as its own source of new AI projects. The three levels should act by reflex and invite these outsiders into the canon training classes, the Circles program, or the AI core group. But often, whether for reasons of time, interest or convenience, the outsiders choose not to participate. Quite simply, many want to implement AI on their own. This attitude can best be handled by new generations of AI Circles programs that are distinct enough that they can compete with previous circles throughout the firm. Instead of funneling all newcomers into a single system, it works better to create several smaller, differentiated entities. In the end, this maximizes the learning of AI in the organization as a whole. Within three of these cycles (about six years), virtually every person in the firm will have been touched by AI. When this occurs, every person in the firm seeks out uses for AI. This phenomenon is at the core of Japanese AI programs.

12

Program Development and Corporate Polity

A Three Part Development Rhythm

The need for expert time is the single greatest factor that slows down the spread of AI in companies and reduces the total number of applications. By definition, the experts in a firm are its busiest people. There simply are no experts with free time on their hands. Even more important, the typical expert outperforms ordinary workers by a factor of eight to one. So the use of an expert's time is worth a multiple of the actual dollar cost of that time. Many companies undertake AI programs with only the vaguest idea of the amount of expert involvement that will be required. Engineers in several firms that I visited spoke frankly about the concerns they had about AI programs and expert time. Many said they avoided meeting with the AI groups because they didn't even want to think about tying up their key personnel on an AI project that could drag on for months or years. They felt there were other more pressing priorities. Since the AI group had glanced over the expert time factor when making their initial presentations, engineering managers became extremely apprehensive about AI project involvement. This vagueness exacerbated fears, and the projects that the AI group sponsored seemed questionable at best. Engineering managers have been around for decades, and they know all the tricks. They've heard technical groups promise to use an expert's time only a few hours a week. When the projects became more complicated than originally anticipated, they begged for more of the expert's time to save the company's investment. Now when AI groups assure these engineering managers that only "a few hours" of expert time will be needed each week, they fear the worst.

There is a remedy: at the outset, a schedule must be drawn up which clearly indicates how much expert time will be devoted to an AI project. And AI groups will have to adhere to this timetable. Naive AI group managers have just the opposite approach. They are so afraid of failure that they squander all sorts of unnecessary resources on their projects to make sure that they will have something to show for their efforts. Unfortunately, by wasting expert time, they make other company managers leery of committing their experts to time-consuming AI projects. Therefore, a company must know exactly how much expert time is needed to strike a balance: the expert's time is expensive and should not be misused and, equally important, valuable projects should not be shortchanged. The Japanese excel in this area. They envision new technologies as a foundation for all the work the firm will do until an even better technology arrives on the scene. They see AI as something independent of time. This allows them to try out various applications which range from modest to all-encompassing. American firms see new technologies as a solution to today's bottom-line problems and not as investments in the firm's long-term competitive capabilities. The Americans explore a much smaller universe of AI application and demand an unrealistic certainty of a new technology before committing to a project. They do not envision a firm living with a new technology for the long-term nor the skills workers will build up by dealing with it on a daily basis. Because of this shortsighted view, American firms emphasize brief product-oriented training courses that teach just enough AI to get a particular project done.

There is a trade-off between the amount of expert time needed each week to get a project done and the time to complete it. If the project can be completed in a relatively short time, the expert must be used full time. A more lengthy project might use just an hour of the expert's time every week. There is another part to this trade-off in the area of multiple sources of knowledge. Cognitive psychology research has shown that second-best performers are truly second-rate. They are astonishingly less effective than many first-rate performers in various domains. The only practical use of this trade-off is one between a terminology component of an expert system and the rules themselves of an expert system. For example, if the knowledge engineer is someone who knows AI, but not the domain, then having a second level performer help the knowledge engineer become familiar with the terminology and the basics of the field is a good idea. An even better idea is to bypass the middleman altogether and not involve the AI knowledge engineer at all. A firm is way ahead of the game with a domain expert (already familiar with the basics) who has received AI training.

I built an AI program for one firm that clearly announced from the very first day that no more than four hours a week of expert time would be required for any AI project. This put everyone's mind at ease. As a corollary, it was also announced that it would take two to two and a half years to bring a project to completion. Had we decided to use the expert two days a week or more, we could have halved the completion time. How can an AI group survive with so little access to expert time? There are a number of factors to weigh. First of all, the quality of time spent with the expert is more important than the quantity. Many poorly managed AI groups have no idea what to do with an expert once committed. They utilize the expert for general discussion sessions, asking questions about general knowledge. In all likelihood, the AI groups have not done formal protocol analysis. They have not videotaped experts nor used a probe question to prompt the expert to reveal knowledge. Instead of expert systems, they end up building computer embodiments of the expert's favorite theories about job task performance. Research has shown these theories we have about our own behavior correlate poorly with the actual procedures we go through. The bottom line is this: If the time with the expert is properly disciplined and all protocols formally analyzed, then much less access will be needed. Second, the knowledge extraction process, when done with skill and discipline, is exhausting. To attempt to do this day after day will surely degrade the quality of protocols being observed. Rather, this knowledge extraction process should be regularly interspersed with normal work. It will be far easier on the expert. Third, when the AI staff member and the expert meet for only four hours a week, they both have ample time to analyze and reflect upon past work sessions. These periods of review focus the perceptions of both the AI person and the expert on the expert decision process.

As can be expected, politics play a part in the development rhythm for AI. I designed a two-week development rhythm that included one day of knowledge extraction every two weeks done on-site with the expert. Not only that, but code for modeling the last session was developed biweekly and shown (on screen) to the expert at each session. Below is a list of the effects of this two week development rhythm:

1. Regular knowledge extraction rhythm.
2. Seeing the customer every two weeks.
3. On-site demo of new functionality every two weeks.
4. Disciplined AI coders consistently producing code.
5. Automatically scheduled meetings every two weeks.
6. Final user participation in interface design every two weeks from the beginning of the project.
7. One new project generated from an old project every six months due to regular biweekly on-site demo.

Most important of all is the interaction that takes place with the customer during this entire project. Both the customer and the AI developers are in contact with each other the whole time. First of all, customers are people, and they don't always make their needs clear. They order one kind of program when in reality something else would suit their needs much better. These misunderstandings upset me when I was younger, but there came a point when I just shrugged my shoulders and adapted. In this case, "adapting" means doing business exactly opposite to the style of outside AI vendors. These vendors "spec out" a project with a manager and then disappear for three months. When they finally emerge, they have a demo that is so fundamentally wrong that weeks would be required to correct it. After a brief discussion, the vendor hides out for another three months and materializes once more with an only slightly improved version of the original.

The two week development rhythm, however, has a totally different approach. To avoid misunderstandings and long delays, a constituency is developed in the customer's own organization. Every two weeks, this constituency sees the latest versions of the software and is involved with every minute decision about the interface and properties of the system. When the top manager comes by to approve continued support of the system or has a question about some aspect of the system's functioning or design, a query is directed to the constituency within the company. This group owns the sequence of decisions that defined the product and can explain to their boss why things were designed in a certain way. An AI developer could not be in a better position. The customer's own staff defends the design decisions of the product. This two week development program also keeps AI coders working steadily and productively. Some coders have a strong tendency to become all wrapped up in their own cleverness and neglect the hard work issues. They turn into "prima donnas" badly in need of discipline. If a manager requires that new code be delivered to the customer face-to-face every two weeks, the developer knows exactly what is expected—there is a deadline to be met every two weeks. The developer is free to work in any style. During this period, the developer can be creative or lazy, just as long as good code is visible on the screen at the prescribed time. If the code is deficient, there is just cause for increased supervision during the next two week period. This policy has the dual function of maintaining discipline within a staff and giving it freedom as well. I carried this out so far that I refused all reports on paper on any project. The only reports I would look at were on-screen demos of working AI code. This kept paperwork from being a substitute for customer service.

There is yet another advantage to this development rhythm process: everyone stays interested in the project. Once a contract has been signed for a project, people's enthusiasm may wane. New technologies, particularly AI, are often implemented on faith, and people's belief in the validity of the project must be constantly bolstered. Because the customer is visited every two weeks and can witness the progress being made, faith does not falter. This constant communication between the customer and AI workers wards off major problems. Sometimes, AI developers work for three months on a prototype system only to have their efforts torpedoed by the customer. A majority of the time this happens, not because the prototype was bad (although it may be out of touch with the customer's needs because the customer did not co-design the system) but because no one was with the customer for three months to keep the belief system in tact. The skeptics had intervened in the meantime before there was a real opportunity to see what the project was all about. However, when people see new functionality on the screen every two weeks, it creates momentum and enthusiasm. The AI developers gradually relax and start thinking of ways they can improve their contributions. The customer feels a pride in the project and invites others to chart its progress. And like clockwork, every two weeks at the same time on the same day of the week, the demo is presented. Hence, over time, each AI project conducted in this way becomes a sales pitch for further AI projects—and these sales pitches are delivered by the customer's own staff. Eventually, the overall AI program can be disciplined so that every existing AI project produces another AI project every six months. This doubling factor leads to exponential growth.

We can summarize by saying that development rhythm consists of 1) a main anchor (the two week development rhythm) and 2) two ancillary parts (a six month prototype horizon and a biweekly four hour meeting with the customer). There is another dimension to this delivery of code. Most AI projects require not one, but four different types of code. And all four types are delivered to the customer at these biweekly meetings. The four parts of every AI project are: the analytic engine, the heuristic engine, platform enhancement, and brute integration. The environment in which the AI code operates uses them to determine the final effectiveness of any AI project. The analytic engine is a "neatened up" version of the ordinary software component that the AI code must manipulate. The heuristic engine is the mind-modeling component of the system. The platform enhancement code formally integrates some AI languages with other key software and hardware systems in the firm. It is designed to support hundreds of AI projects over the years without systems disintegration. The brute integration code ties in to local customer systems that may not be strategically wise or recommended, but are nevertheless essential to getting any one project fully functional in the customer's real world of operation.

Any AI project that does not include these four different kinds of code will be abandoned soon after final delivery. To my shame, my second expert system in Japan suffered this fate. I went on a tour of my employer's plant to see how things were going with the first projects I had completed. I found my second system sitting in the corner, unused and covered with dust. It was a pure AI system that used only AI code. I did not build in automatic tie-ins to other essential sources of data needed for the AI code to operate. When the system was designed, the customer had agreed to hand input the data. That proved to be too troublesome, and the AI system was abandoned rather than have someone hand carry data to it. For the final usefulness of the system, it is imperative that it have this integration feature.

So both the six month and the four hour components of the development rhythm system develop and check, respectively, four kinds of code delivered every two weeks. In the six month time frame, code development moves toward achieving three kinds of prototypes. First, the most difficult part of the AI code must be prototyped within six months of start. This prevents overinvestment in impossible projects. Second, the optimal performance part of the AI code must be prototyped. This keeps big paybacks to the firm a goal in everyone's mind. Third, the integration tie-in code must be prototyped in six months from start. This counters the natural tendency of AI groups to put off system integration until the end of the project, which results in excellent systems going unused by the customer.

So far I have not mentioned the reason for a two-week development rhythm as opposed to a one-week rhythm. To begin with, no single AI project will satisfy AI staffers. Businesses are full of boring, trivial and simplistic needs for AI. They really need these AI applications, but they just don't present a very interesting challenge to AI developers. To keep motivation up, an AI group must be offered a mixture of projects. Some will be boring but have bottom line profitability, and others will be intellectually stimulating edge-of-field projects. By alternating work on these projects (one project one week, the other project the following week), all AI developers can be kept professionally content. Since an AI staffer does not have to face any one project all the time (especially one that is unfavorable), the developer is less prone to the "burn out" syndrome.

This leaves the worker free to structure development time based on individual work habits and bursts of creativity. If the developer wishes to read the newspaper all day Monday, this is fine. If the developer temporarily falls off the face of the earth, this, too, is fine. Nothing more is required than placing a demo in front of the customer every two weeks, written using the four kinds of code. If trouble with this on-screen code appears, then discipline in the development week can be explored. Usually, it is best if each day is devoted to one very clear AI function in system development. For example, Monday can be for protocol transcription from the videotape of the expert. Tuesday can be for protocol analysis. Wednesday can be for protocol analysis translation into objects and production rules. Thursday can be dedicated to analytic engine code, software platform enhancement, and systems integration code. Friday can be a trial demo before the system is shown to the customer sometime the following week. Four hours are needed (probably between Monday and Wednesday) to extract expertise from the expert and to present the demo of the previous week's system to the customer.

The two week development rhythm also benefits new AI programmers who are still unsure of themselves. Every two weeks the experts examine their work and give them feedback. This kind of guidance helps shore up confidence, and when AI Circles are present in the company, this becomes crucial. Newcomers need support and encouragement as they go along. At the same time, they are glad to know that someone will be on hand to monitor their output so that they don't invest months in mistaken code. Too many industry AI programs leave novices to flounder for months without help. Gradually they acquire an unproductive set of work habits. They complain of nothing to do and a lack of direction. Newcomers who work on a rhythmic timetable with expert supervision don't experience these feelings of frustration caused by a lack of focus.

A development rhythm is different than a regular schedule. It implies that all AI staffers hold themselves to the same discipline. This makes the work of the expert programmers and the novice programmers similar on particular days of the week. The customer can sense the overall positive mood of the group as they display their latest accomplishments. The group immediately locates problem areas because everyone is involved in similar work each day. The immediacy of this feedback is overpowering. Furthermore, AI groups often count some "neurotic" technical types in their ranks who totally lack people skills. By having to meet the customer every two weeks, they gradually learn about communication which is essential to the delivery of technology. Over time, the customer and the AI expert can develop a rapport as the AI developer expands his people skills and transfers his technical knowledge to the customer.

The New Authority—Meta-Polity

There is a paradox in Japanese firms. Corporate group participation programs have a strong element of coercion in them. Certainly the involvement of thousands in technology campaigns attests to a kind of participation. However, the predominant mood of any one session, group, or campaign is something other than selfless volunteerism.

In the United States, firms have strived to unite their employees in group participation programs in the manner of their Japanese rivals. Some segments of these companies—most notably the human resources departments and the organizational development sections—become overzealous supporters of participation programs. These programs are hard to implement because there must be a clear task/participation link. Once this link becomes blurred, the participation program is viewed as merely another management fad and excesses appear everywhere. Furthermore, it must be recognized that not all tasks are assisted by participation. This is the key to explaining the paradox that exists in Japan and the imbalance found in the United States. It must also be recognized that not all tasks are suited to autocracy, bureaucracy or any other single form of polity. Individuals and organizations mature as they learn which tasks are best performed under which forms of polity.

Recently, in Sweden and Japan, a few management theorists coined the term "meta-polity" to describe a peculiar management structure that evolved from failed participation programs. These theorists had observed firms that went overboard on participation but later learned to rely on a new position and method. They discovered that participation is imperative in some aspects of a business, but more than that was necessary.

In this new position, each work group discovers the existence of various areas of decision. Some are appropriate for group participation, and some are appropriate for autocratic supervisor command. The group then establishes norms that define which type of polity works best with each issue the group faces. This constitutes a new body of knowledge peculiar to that specific work group, but can still be generalized to a considerable extent across all other work groups. Each group clarifies which issues require which polity. This is "meta-polity," an awareness of the different kinds of authority and how each type of authority relates to the varieties of issues developed in each work group. Meta-polity solves a number of troublesome theory and practice problems which concern participation, circles, and other work situations.

What is the appropriate amount of involvement for industrial managers and workers? There are two schools of thought: those who favor increasing participation and those who favor increasing central control. Everyone has endured outside consultants and their "gung-ho" presentations on worker participation programs. By the time the veneer of enthusiasm has worn thin in the firm, the outside consultant is selling his brand of snake oil in the next county. Similarly we have all suffered from the excesses of the petty tyrants of the workplace who view worker participation as anarchy. These people, traumatized perhaps by a miserable adolescence, turn the workplace into an elaborate military surveillance network of supervisor spies. The workers spend a lot of company time devising cunning ways to outwit their supervisors. Both of these examples, of course, are exaggerations but there is a genuine need to strike a balance between those who advocate mob rule and those who support a dictatorship.

From a Meta-polity perspective, both of these positions seem like oversimplifications. Participation is not a cure-all. It works well with some issues, like designing new equipment, and horribly with other issues, like deciding what day to meet next week. The problems created by a permanent dictatorship are too obvious to mention. The Meta-polity theory has something more to contribute. It makes available a number of polity types for any one work group. Certain types of issues are associated with each type of polity. Multiple, parallel polities evolve within the firm. More than that, it goes so far as to suggest multiple, parallel, simultaneous organization structures for the firm. How can a firm live with plural chains of command and plural organization charts for the same people?

Earlier, the Management by Events Theory showed how a firm could actually be two firms in one. For example, one firm exists from nine to five on Monday through Thursday and from eleven to five on Friday. The second firm exists on Friday from nine to eleven. The first firm does the major present-day work of the company; the second one does new business pioneering and development. For two hours a week, all employees work for the new trial firm. This allows companies to embed the future into the present. The entire work force has the opportunity to experiment. People become familiar with corporate strategic moves that are still a couple of years away from being actualized. Management by Events is merely the simplest embodiment of the Meta-polity principle of managing organizations. It uses the entire work force for a few hours per week to bring about a new polity for future oriented work.

It may seem like a radical proposition, but in fact, almost all major firms are already operating this way—not necessarily by design but by happenstance. The recent generation of computers is a networking generation. One computer can communicate with most other computers in its section of the firm or, in some companies, across the entire firm. Studies of electronic mail systems and electronic conferencing systems show that people who have never met face to face communicate easily with each other. Indeed, people who have never met in person form project teams and get funded work done for the company. This adds a whole new dimension of polity in the firm. Company managements, out of their traditional timidity, at first forbade workers from communicating with others on the network. They feared it would create an immense underground form of communication that bypassed the rules. But after living for a couple years with this underground polity, managers overcame their misgivings and officially sanctioned what had been going on for years.

The issue, then, is not "Shall we try Meta-polity?" but "What shall do with the Meta-polity we will inevitably have?" Meta-polity clearly explains the paradox of Japanese firms. A great deal of participation occurs without anyone in the firm subscribing to the idea that everything ought to be participatory. Indeed, the issues handled by participatory polity and the issues handled by bureaucratic polity or autocratic polity constantly change as experience is gained with the practice of this theory. The Japanese benefit because no one sees one form of polity as a panacea. Outside consultants cannot distort participation programs with overinflated claims. By the same token, it prevents autocratic management from making all decisions. Companies must answer two questions: what form of polity applies to a certain type of issue and what decision is obtained by applying this form of polity to this issue?

Inventing and nurturing a Meta-polity system require deliberate experiments by each work group with different polity forms attached to different kinds of issues. It takes years of effort to push each of these experiments through the stages of copying, perfecting, mastering, and celebrating. These four stages are the cognitive progression of all learning in Japan. Sword fighters traditionally progressed from copying their masters to perfecting their own technique. They subsequently mastered technique and finally fought "celebrationally." But simply going through the motions of a new technique does not truly test it. Any technique must first be thoroughly mastered before a good understanding can be obtained. Often, modern organizations change systems and manager assignments so frequently that nothing is mastered anywhere in the firm. A kind of cognitive profit is missing from the workplace.

The new computer networks of workstations allow software to embody polity assumptions and concepts. Software is extremely flexible. Any type of assumption in respect to polity can be designed into it. This means a lot of experimentation will take place. Also, totally novel forms of polity will be discovered and be engineered into the software.

Ultimately, there will be an interplay between the social and technical systems. Experimental polities in the social system will interact with experimental polities in the technical system. These interactions will then determine productivity, learning characteristics of work, work organization, quality, and the other essential business properties of organizations. This opens up a whole new universe of design possibility.

Many firms, victims of their own unaggressive management style, will implement their old social system on the new electronic media by default. Every bad habit and fault will remain. Indeed, many industrial computer systems have software systems that embody methods used in the 1940s—only put on faster computers. The result is a speedier performance of obsolete designs and programs. One firm had a CAD system that required the operator to input thirty-two digit numbers (taken in eight-digit units from two separate drawings and two separate books) for every wiring part on the screen. This was not Computer-Aided Design, but a new category, Computer-Hindered Design. One observer pointed out that the number of atoms in the Milky Way could be expressed in fewer than thirty-two digits. Did the company really have this many electronic parts? Of course not, but that numbering system, invented in the early 1940s, had worked its way onto a 1986 CAD system. No one thought about what had happened and redesigned the program. Companies can and do implement outdated polities in new electronic media form unless trained, rewarded, and disciplined workers do otherwise.

In conclusion, Meta-polity shows how a trilevel AI system can be realized. The connectionist core component resembles the autocratic component although it also performs some democratic roles as an enabler of workplace learning. The lateral component is similar to the bureaucratic component even though it performs participatory roles by consulting with AI Circles. And finally, the bottom-up every-man component is the participatory component but it performs other functions as well. While each group has its own area of emphasis, each group also has more than one polity role within the firm. When groups start to lose their distinctiveness, they must be reshaped into plural polity forms again.

5

Computer-Integrated Manufacturing and AI

"This reasoning might also go some of the distance toward explaining the tentative finding that Japanese factory organization resembles the structuring of advanced technology plants. In highly automated process industry, technology no longer determines factory social organization, because workers are separated from direct production tasks. Thus, as Woodward (1965) argued, the design of the organization becomes detached to some degree from the technology process and more attuned to the needs of the human work force. The parallel between the structures of advanced production plants and Japanese organization is thus explained by the substitution in both cases of a 'social' for a 'technological' imperative."

Lincoln, J.R.; Hanada, M.; McBride, K.; "Organizational Structures in Japanese and U.S. Manufacturing"; *Administrative Science Quarterly*, vol. 31, no. 3/338-508, September 1986, p. 362.

Computer-Integrated Manufacturing (CIM) is, to a great extent, an overreaction to the isolated way technologies were implemented in the past. From an excess of isolation to an excess of whole systems, we lurch from error to error. Nevertheless, technology has now progressed to the point where the direct labor cost is an insignificant cost of manufacturing. The important costs result from the following:

1. Responding to market change.
2. Responding to competitor copying.
3. Fighting for market share.
4. Customizing production.

These costs depend on the responsiveness of the production system per unit produced. This applies to both service industries and manufacturing industries. Flexible Manufacturing Systems (FMS) and airline fare wars are part of the same phenomenon—mature markets with new entrants. These new competitors are here to stay. As the Third World learns new technologies, they will eagerly compete with the more industrialized nations.

Companies concerned with this responsiveness to unit produced ratio will implement AI and the other new technologies. This changes the character and form of AI by creating new aspects and new roles. The Japanese are implementing Competitive Automated Socio-Technical Systems (CASTS) now instead of CIM. They build a Socially-Integrated Manufacturing (SIM) system that implements CASTS. These new approaches to manufacturing transform AI. The following chapters portray how this new form of AI differs from the usual American style produced by CIM programs.

13

New Social Systems

Effects of Learning Properties

Implementation of Computer-Integrated Manufacturing in the United States parallels the implementation of Socially-Integrated Manufacturing in Japan. When American managers visit the New United Motors Manufacturing Inc. plant—the joint venture between Toyota and GM in Freemont, California—they see much leaner automation than in other automated U.S. plants. It is in these plants, with scaled down automation, where workers consistently defeat the more highly automated factories. How is this possible? The answer is SIM. SIM integrates people in the same way CIM integrates computers. The Japanese consistently obtain a reliable and creative performance from the hundreds of workers and managers in a work force. This is the core of a successful SIM program. When human beings are responsibly employed, they constitute a network of human mental processors much more powerful than computers will be in the near future. More importantly, on a cost performance basis, maximally employed human operators outshine the computers.

Twenty years ago, the Institute of Cultural Affairs and the Ecumenical Institute of Chicago experimented with the concepts that led to SIM. This was somewhat after the Japanese discovered it, but extended far beyond Japanese practices. They did the following:

1. Defined a cognitive methodology to be used corporationwide:
   • a formal methodology for conducting all meetings
   • a formal methodolgy for reading and reporting

- a formal methodology for work group planning
- a formal methodology for organization planning

2. Used their entire work force as a distributed array of human processor computers:
   - distributed research and development conducted by every work group in the company every week
   - distributed planning conducted every quarter by every work group in the company
   - conducted a participatory annual meeting as a mass workshop event involving all employees

3. Split the work week into more than one job per person:
   - added a study component to each work group each week
   - added a management by events component to each regional center each week
   - gave each employee two fundamentally different jobs per week
   - balanced these job tandems to achieve cognitive, administrative, emotional, and social health

Other American organizations paid no attention to these experiments but the Scandinavians and Australians did. From the example of the Swedes and the Australians, the Japanese became familiar with these new concepts of social integration.

These experiments had several positive results. First, when the work of the organization was done through a formal cognitive methodology, the work done per unit time increased. At the same time, it created a methodology-mastery route to career success that supplanted politically based or power-based career building. Second, with basic functions like research and development distributed over thousands of workers, great amounts of research were quickly accomplished. Third, the entire membership of the organization designed its own structures and work in a group assembly held each year. This, over time, trained each employee in the overall methods, aims, experiences, and purposes of all parts of the firm. Fourth, employees with multiple jobs had some work that was oriented to the present day bottom line and other work that looked to the future of the organization. This prevented the employees from splitting into two groups: one trapped in present day work and the other groping in the future. It must be stressed that these experiments that pioneered SIM tactics were performed in America. It was only by way of Sweden and Australia that the Japanese found out about these forms of social integration. American organizations proved impervious to social tactic learning. This, in the long-term, will render the American manufacturing sector less innovative and less competitive.

On the surface, it may appear that SIM is a viable cost-effective alternative to CIM. But this is not the relationship at all. Rather CIM is preceded by SIM. The best businesses develop SIM, and once the SIM system is in place, it designs and implements a CIM system. Thus, companies achieve maximal use of their most cost-effective processors, people, and translate that lean, cognitively-balanced, and healthy social system into technical system form. Recently companies have revised their thinking on that last point. They found that replacing people was a poor way to take best advantage of CIM. Instead, a system is evolving in which CIM does not replace people but instead augments a well-designed SIM system.

What then constitutes SIM? A number of the components that lead to a functioning SIM system have already been mentioned.

1. The Eleven Management Theories of Meta-Cognitive firms.
2. The Five Areas of Management Theory creating the Meta-Cognitive Firm.
3. The Meta-Applications function in corporations.
4. The Tri-level delivery system for new technologies.
5. The High Tech Circles system for everyman implementation of new technologies.

SIM can be achieved only when organizations realize certain truisms of the business world. Above all, companies must manage change. New technologies arrive daily, and customer needs change accordingly. To keep up with new conditions, all employees must be encouraged to learn more about their jobs and their company. The market constantly fluctuates and quick response to shifting customer preferences is essential. The company that is adaptable to the dynamic world outside its doors will have an edge on its competitors.

As previously mentioned, the Tri-level AI program delivery system was designed to maximize both individual and organizational learning. The Japanese custom of lifetime employment has powerful repercussions—it encourages people to become more inquisitive and more interested in learning. In addition, people who enjoy job security are less likely to get involved in labor disputes, because automation, one of the major issues, is no longer seen as a threat. The organization becomes a cohesive whole in which all the individual components learn from each other.

The Japanese management structure informally measures "cognitive profits" as shown in Figure 13-1. That is, the bottom line is not the only consideration. Particular efforts and projects may be deemed profitable on the basis of experience gained or techniques learned. Since employees may spend their entire career with the firm, experience and learning are a form of long-term investment in the company's future. Moreover, the three cognitive profits of lifetime employ (doing more with the same inputs, turning people loose to build new businesses, and dropping costs) can even turn fluctuations in the business cycle to the company's advantage. In the past fifteen years, the Japanese have realized the business opportunities presented by these cognitive profits. Just after World War II, some Japanese companies had a glut of employees during a depressed business cycle. Instead of laying them off, they were given jobs sweeping the grounds or tending the gardens. Gradually, as better trained workers were hired, this pool of labor was given bolder assignments like devising new lines of business.

The Daiken Company, makers of refrigerators, provides a dramatic example. During a slow business period, it assigned its idled workers to find a new CAD system to design its refrigerators. These employees discovered that CAD systems were too expensive to buy, so they designed their own. As it turned out, their cost of production was much lower than that of the leading CAD companies in Japan. Daiken then made CAD systems as a sideline, and within three years, the sales of their CAD terminals accounted for one-third the sales volume of the refrigerators.

Another cognitive profit—dropping costs, not market share—is achieved when underutilized employees are made to fight for a product's share of the market. The recent rise of the yen has forced Japanese firms to maintain their market share while real costs rise. To do this, they must counteract these cost increases with programs redesigned to lower costs within the firm. The entire work forces of most major Japanese firms are engaged in finding ways to reduce costs. In some companies, the workers have an internal vision of achieving absolute costless production by vertically integrating suppliers and making each supply step so efficient that cost of the final product approaches zero. This particular cognitive profit has resulted in both SIM and CIM being scaled down.

During boom times, Japanese companies cannot hire new employees. This is because new employees are hired for life and permanently raise the overall cost of all products. Therefore, as a substitute for hiring new employees, existing workers are asked to conceive of new ways to achieve greater production while using the same number of human inputs. This requires inventing new devices and methods, changing work schedules, and adding more automation. With the entire work force involved, good results are obtained. Japanese firms use subcontractors and part-time labor to buffer these three cognitive profits. And, recently, big firms have avoided slough-

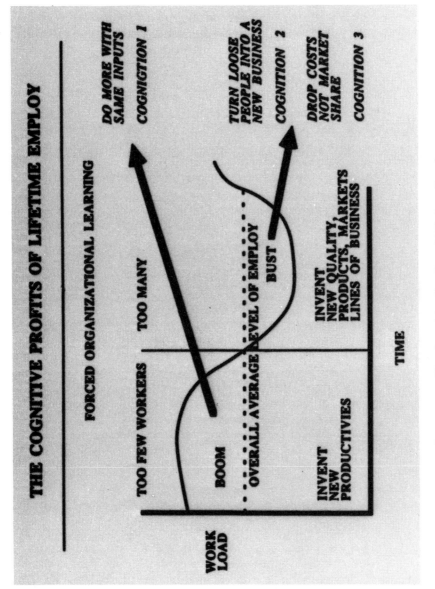

Figure 13-1 The Cognitive Profits of Lifetime Employ.

ing off subcontractors and part-timers when the boom is over. Instead, a more gradual reduction is attempted. In time, this part-time labor force will become absorbed within companies.

The inventiveness of the whole work force is the key to maintaining lifetime employ in Japan. New methods are invented so more work can be done with fewer people. New lines of business are invented when orders go down. The work force finds ways to decrease costs when market share is threatened. American companies trying to move toward a lifetime employ system must realize that merely trading job flexibility for job security will not make this system work. It is only the addition of the three cognitive profits that pays for any lifetime employ system.

Learning properties of organizations, then, are important to achieve SIM systems capable of implementing lean CIM systems. The social factor that leads to CIM in Japan is lacking in American firms which believe in hardware first. The SIM system gives a new perspective on a capital-equipment view of CIM. CIM conference proceedings in the U.S. are rife with networks, protocols, and workstations—pure hardware and software projects. American methods lead to excess automation implemented with great difficulty and less flexibly designed than competitive Japanese no-man production systems.

AI helps companies achieve these powerful learning properties. AI, as a Cognitive Delivery Vehicle for other technologies, promotes each new technology in the workplace. For example, in some companies, AI acts as a repository for key human expertise in systems that distribute expertise around the firm. On a pure automation basis, AI helps machines learn from other machines and build models of different kinds of events and ways to recover from them. With SIM, artificial intelligence becomes the intelligent secretary and advisor at each point of the human interface with the technical system. AI can be used as a new dimension to enhance the learning properties of organizations. There are two directions to distinguish: AI enhances the learning properties of organizations, and the learning properties of organizations determine the effective delivery of new technologies like AI.

Incremental Implementation of Technologies

A new technology must undergo two modifications if it is to be delivered by a SIM system. It must be adapted to fit the SIM system delivery vehicle, and it must also be modified to fit the company's

CIM style. Very few companies attempt these two modifications although some Japanese companies have unconsciously effected these adaptations through their long-standing habits for handling new technologies.

Figure 13-2 illustrates that new technologies must be broken down into small, manageable units for SIM to be effective. Large units of understanding and implementation have to be made into smaller units so that thousands of workers can train themselves to perform the actual implementation. In Japan, the first step is drawing up a prioritized list of business functions that the new technology is expected to fulfill. Then, under each business function, the list specifies the social functions that the technology is to perform. Each social function has cognitive functions that the technology must handle. AI, being a cognitive technology, carries the process further. For each cognitive function, several knowledge types must be specified, and these knowledge types have several meta-rules. If each of these categories has an average of five items, any full expert system then has 3,125 components (five to the fifth power).

Most expert systems implemented in industry today consist of far fewer components. This creates problems. Over time, humans who interface with installed expert systems demand increasing functionality. An AI advisor, if it performs well, will be asked to monitor a process. If it is successful with this task, it may be asked to troubleshoot a process. That is, the system will be promoted to perform new and increasingly complex tasks. Any one AI project implemented must be designed from the beginning with this eventual and inevitable evolution of the system in mind. A responsible AI program has long-term "intelligent" platforms designed into it. (Several of these platforms will be discussed later.)

Because AI can be implemented gradually, it is attractive to industry. Over time it can be given more responsibility. The system can be used as an advisor with a human still in the loop to disagree if necessary. When disagreements become infrequent, the AI system can be promoted to full control, and the human then acts as the advisor. Initial AI systems are often implemented as mere advisors and are not part of a larger, integrated system. By merely performing as an advisor, the AI system doesn't need any electronic ties with the whole system. Hence, many firms are mistakenly implementing hosts of "stand alone" AI advisors without realizing that all these systems in time will be promoted from advising to higher functions— monitoring, troubleshooting, predicting, controlling, tutoring, and inventing. Each promotion requires deeper integration with the rest of the system. This initial "stand alone" implementation of AI hides the

1. A.I. can be safely implemented because it can be incrementally implemented.
2. When A.I. is just advising, it is standalone; hence, software integration does not appear to be an A.I. issue.

   But when A.I. evolves, as it always does, from advising to monitoring, to troubleshooting, to controlling, it must more and more integrate with existing software.
3. There are approximately 625 components to any full "expert system" towards which any initial pilot evolves during actual use.
4. When developers are using A.I. systems, the systems do not need additional social functions of the system, needed by undedicated naive users of the system.

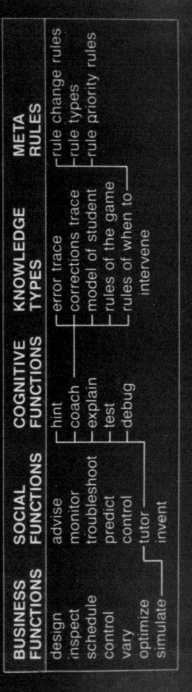

BUSINESS FUNCTIONS	SOCIAL FUNCTIONS	COGNITIVE FUNCTIONS	KNOWLEDGE TYPES	META RULES
design	advise	hint	error trace	rule change rules
inspect	monitor	coach	corrections trace	rule types
schedule	troubleshoot	explain	model of student	rule priority rules
control	predict	test	rules of the game	
vary	control	debug	rules of when to intervene	
optimize	tutor			
simulate	invent			

Figure 13-2 The Incrementality of the AI Revolution and its Consequences.

integration costs of implementing AI over the long-term. It also encourages poor AI platform decisions that will make later integration more expensive and harder to achieve.

When well-trained AI developers make and use an AI system, they do not need further social functionality from it. However, when the AI system is on the job, it will not be the AI elite who use it, but the entire work force. These novices will require a great deal more social functionality of the system and may refuse to use AI systems implemented as mere advisors. For example, if the data has to be input by hand, many people will avoid using the AI advisor. AI developers often start first AI projects in areas of the firm where interest has been expressed. Often the people expressing interest will not be the ones who end up using the system. Later on, unmotivated people will refuse to use systems for the most trivial reasons. A company has to beware of implementing AI systems that are technically right but never used. This is where SIM comes in. In Japanese firms, all workers participate in new technology campaigns. Social tactics and events keep the level of interest high in the project. Hence, new AI systems are implemented among users who will remain interested in the technology for years. In the United States, the opposite holds true. Few employees know about or understand the new technologies. At the slightest sign of difficulty, they reject the new technology and revert to old, familiar ways. Companies without a strong SIM system will pay for their shortsighted strategies.

More practically, there must be a procedure within the firm to modify AI and make it incrementally implementable by whole work forces. The latest AI results and techniques must be translated into curricula that work groups can use for self-teaching a few hours each week. These classroom texts should be written in clear, concise easily understandable language. In Japan, there is an abundance of people who are able to render complicated concepts into everyday terms. In the United States, those with the knowledge prefer to keep it that way and write texts in obscure jargon.

There is a technique I implemented in Group Structured Readings in a Japanese firm that allowed ordinary work groups to break down the texts into self-teachable components. With only minimal outside help, these work groups taught themselves from edge-of-field texts without problems. For example, people without college educations correctly implemented parallel PROLOG simulations of AI objects. (There will be more information on Structural Reading techniques later in this book.)

The Eight Levels of Future CIM Systems

Dozens of technologies are involved in the average CIM implementation. These technologies can be grouped by the different operations each machine type performs, or they can be grouped by method of implementation. The former view includes robots, guided vehicle controllers, and other similarly implemented manufacturing systems. All share eight levels of implementation which are called "busses." The bus concept is used in computer hardware. Simply put, a bus allows parts of a computer to exchange data rapidly among each other. Moreover, as firms struggle to design final computer architectures in offices and factories, these eight busses define the levels of complexity of systems implementation. Each level requires its own special forms of integration and its own standards. The eight busses are split into four technical levels and four social levels. Overall, this is consistent with a socio-technical view of systems.

As shown in Figure 13-3 on p. 200, there are four technical busses: hardware, software, applications, and applications programs. Briefly, the hardware bus connects computers to each other in basic communications networking. The software bus is something more subtle. All application programs in the workplace have a common interface look and a common data exchange format that all software programs read from and write to. The applications bus includes three functions needed for any application program: expert platforms on which applications are coded, self-tutoring capability that allows each application to teach itself to new or occasional users, and an update and standards facility that permits application functionality updates to be added without interfering with system integration. Finally, there is the application layer itself, the actual computer application program.

Many firms are working toward a hardware bus architecture, although few have seen the software bus revolution. In the old days of computing, software companies would create a program and then later add a data facility and interface facility. This meant that the end users of computer systems were confronted with dozens of different interfaces and dozens of different data formats from all the various applications. Engineers complained that they spent more time learning computer interfaces than they did engineering. With the software bus implemented, software vendors no longer construct a myriad of interfaces and data formats. Instead, they deal in standardized interfaces and data exchange formats for which each vendor will create "links." This system of links will let the vendor's software talk to the standard interface and data format, so that one interface "look" and one data exchange "look" will be shared by all applications programs in the company. This immense revolution is underway in Japan as standards committees and software factory designers specify the standards for Japanese software development. When this revolution is complete and standardization is a reality, the cost savings will be enormous. By contrast, companies in the United States will drown in a profusion of interface and data formats.

The applications bus with its three subdivisions is a more profound concept than the software bus. It envisions a world where training in a system is automatically included as part of the system itself. The self-tutoring utility receives prepared lessons that instruct new and occasional users using the application itself. It sees an AI component to all software applications whatsoever. That is, the expert platform utility receives the accumulated expertise of users as they interact with any application program. It imagines a standard way to update system features without disrupting system integration. The update standards facility receives new code updates of the application and meshes them automatically with the rest of the system. These three software utilities which all applications programs interface with and assume, capture the local content of the application. These new forms of automatic integration go beyond data exchange and interface "look"—and are essential to obtain automation of the Cognitive Delivery Vehicle mentioned earlier.

Note that these utilities are applied to all software applications in the firm. Each application meshes and interfaces with these background utilities. They are not one shot, temporary additions to any one program but general facilities that receive particular kinds of data from the application program itself and use that data to achieve powerful enhancement of the application in the overall system.

Figure 13-3 also shows four social levels for a Socio-Technical AI System: meta-applications, meta-participation, meta-cognition, and mission. The first of these, meta-applications, pioneers early commercialization of latest R&D results in any technical field and replicates initial project achievements to all similar application sites in the organization. It acts as a bridge between research and application and keeps both focused on their specific jobs. Then comes the meta-participation function of Management by Events and Monastic Management techniques. This function embeds the future in the present work of each job and transforms ordinary work into precisely articulated ways to defeat competitors. This is followed by a meta-cognition level that monitors and manages the upgrading of cognitive protocols used by all people in the firm. It elevates the basic level of imagination in the firm so that it is superior to the levels found in

A Socio–Technical A.I. System

Social

- Mission
- Meta–cognition
  - Cognitive monitoring
  - Protocol management
- Meta–participation
  - Management by events
  - Monestic management
- Meta–applications
  - Pioneer commercialize
  - Replication management

Technical

- Applications programs
- Applications BUS
  - Expert platforms
  - Self tutoring facility
  - Update standard facility
- Software BUS
  - Common interface
  - Common data format
- Hardware BUS

Figure 13-3 A Socio-Technical AI System.

the industry and society in which the firm is embedded. This superiority feeds into a daily discipline of work and ideas that outproduce the entire society and industry. The so-called 7 New Tools and 7 Old Tools of Japanese quality programs are examples of this. Finally, the mission level is an information system that orchestrates whole work force embodiment of, understanding of, and achievement of the organization's changing statement of its mission. The mission level uses the meta-applications, meta-participation, and meta-cognition levels to produce plans for the firm's response to precisely articulated competitor accomplishments and threats. Simply put, the mission of the firm is to defeat particular competitors and their tactics. Those projected defeats are automatically broken down by the mission layer into data and strategies. This data then illustrates the level of excellence each workgroup must achieve to defeat particular competitor product and market strengths. Quality Function Deployment and its "house of quality" data system are one way of leading companies to achieve this mission layer.

For each of these eight levels—both technical and social—there exist standards. The first of the technical levels, the hardware bus, is already being standardized by industry forces and merely needs conformity. This requires nothing more than choosing a strategic computer hardware architecture and forbidding exceptions to it.

The software bus standards are set by defining a basic interface look to which all functional subdomains on the system must conform. Of course, an infinite variety of applications run on a given hardware system, so functions in one application program may differ from the functions in another program. But they both must have the same interface "look." This means where functions differ between applications, deep analogies between different functional domains will be developed to keep a similar "look" to the way a person works in both systems. Common data formats can be standardized readily since there are very few new data representation innovations in any given year. This permits PDES solid graphics and other international standards for data to be used easily.

The applications bus standards are specific capabilities of minimal expertise capture, automatic tutor building, and automatic updating. This aspect of system integration is still in its infancy. Even minimal progress along any of these three dimensions will dramatically improve performance for the next few years. But soon standards like the following will be practical:

1. Automatic capture of user experience with the system, constituted as creation automatically by the application program and applications bus utility of an expert system representing each user's expertise for using the system.

2. Automatic transformation of the application programs into sessions that tutor users in necessary basic tasks to get work done on the system.
3. Automatic propagation of implications and optimal uses of new features added later to the system throughout the application program and its tutor facility.

Applications program standards require that software vendors build "links" into their software that allow it to be used on the company's own interface and data formats constructs. Also, applications program standards are designed to furnish adequate data for full functioning of the applications bus level functions: expert platform functioning, self-tutoring system functioning, and update standards facility functioning.

Meta-application standards search for absolute perfection in terms of making complete use of one application in every similar instance. They also search the world for new techniques to commercialize before competitors do. These kinds of standards are set by formal measures of the entire innovation content of particular fields each year. They measure the number of innovations that relate to workplace problems and measure as well the number of relevant innovations that were actually commercialized within the firm during the past year. Replication management standards are set by the number of new applications found later for a given technique. (This was after all the possible applications had been presumedly included in a major project victory replication campaign.) If no unforeseen applications arise later, then the replication team performed well. If applications are discovered later, it means the surveying was performed inaccurately.

The meta-participation level standards are consensuses in the firm about what issues should be turned over to participatory polity methods and Management by Events. These are formally set in some organizations and informally in others. Often these standards are negotiated and agreed upon in annual study events. These standards are based on actual experience with trying different polities with different issues. Monastic Management demands managing a firm toward the goal of absolute customer satisfaction so that attention and intensity is focused solely on serving the customers of the firm itself. Standards for Monastic Management require training management and the work force to achieve an absence of distracting problems. The customer need issues that arise are not seen as interruptions of normal work but are responded to as the very essence and content of normal work itself. It is not easy to get thousands of people to accept unpleasant surprises, changes, speed-ups and disappointments as part of the mundane normal work routine. Most organizations mistakenly seek an unconscious repetitive routine. An eventful routine, however, raises the adaptability and responsiveness of the entire firm.

The Japanese system of delegating authority provides a good example. Unlike American companies, the Japanese distribute the most authority to the lowest level workers. A Japanese blue-collar worker who spots a new robot on the loading dock never hesitates to organize a group to take it inside and install it during work hours or free time. The worker takes responsibility for this without filling out forms or waiting for authorization by a supervisor. Conversely, in American companies, robots could rust out on the docks for two months because none of the lower level workers had enough authority to take commonsense actions and do the obvious. American workers are fearful of stepping beyond the narrow limits of their job definitions. What Americans consider to be a problem, the Japanese see as a nonissue that requires no authorization.

At the meta-cognition level, the standards describe minimal companywide cognitive performance of each meeting, discussion, workshop, and computer conference session. By requiring all cognitive activities to achieve certain minimal levels of efficiency, the whole work force is encouraged to monitor and enhance the company's cognitive performance. This is not nearly as difficult as it sounds. A quick reflection on the efficiency shown at the average business meeting will indicate how much more progress can be made without even asking people to work harder. Indeed, when companies employ minimal cognition levels of performance and formal cognitive methods in business meetings, discussions and reports achieve a higher level of animation. Workers show a heightened interest in all company activities. Higher cognitive intensity allows people to suspend all the effort they usually spend protecting themselves from boring, poorly-managed company use of their time. The standards of cognitive method and performance are set by a dynamic weekly companywide study meeting in all work groups. All work groups in the firm study the same thing. The material they study is improvements in the minimal cognitive methods to be employed in workshops, discussions, and business meetings.

At the mission level, the firm establishes successive standards to articulate the competition's level of performance at each function and job in the firm. These Articulation Standards become platforms the firm tries to improve upon by gaining better estimates of competitor performance.

These eight levels of standards development amount to a reversal of relations between vendor communities and firms. Firms must join together in Societies of Industry (like the Japanese groups Sumitomo and Mitsubishi) and negotiate with their vendors. On the other hand, vendors thrive in a world of incompatible systems. Each incompatible feature protects one vendor's products from influence by overall firm systems and needs. By eliminating incompatibility as an option, vendors are forced to co-design their future generations of equipment with their customers. This is the way it's done in Japan.

14

Competition and Societies of Industry

The Polis Principle

Computer-Integrated Manufacturing suffers from an image problem. People tend to see it purely for its technical content and disregard the social and political events that must occur to make CIM work. Americans place all their energies in creating new technical systems at the expense of social systems; they end up losing on both fronts. Firms cling to their traditional culture which pits groups and individuals against each other. This policy dooms their new technical systems as factions fight to control them. This chapter explores the consequences of this worker versus worker competition and depicts a practical alternative. The solution is based on Greek tradition (the heart of Western culture) and is implemented nearly everywhere in Japan.

Initial AI groups in the United States literally have to run the gauntlet when trying to implement projects. Among those who want part of the action are:

1. New technology promotion sections in the head office.
2. Various AI groups scattered in several divisions.
3. AI vendors rummaging around corporate divisions for new work.

4. AI vendor "hostage" groups in the firm. These people are skill-fully manipulated by AI vendors to think they are on an inside track for AI development.
5. Favored vendors, endorsed as "the" vendors for the firm, whose main interest is making sales.
6. Key divisional engineering managers, proud of their AI pion-eering work but unwilling to admit that they don't know every-thing.
7. Research and development groups that boast about trivial ex-pert systems that a twelve year old could have developed.

Each of these groups, hoping to jump aboard the AI bandwagon, allies itself with political factions in management. These seven groups, all of them promoting their own selfish interests, can throw a company's technical program into turmoil. And worse yet, most firms tolerate it. Management is unimaginative and unwilling to put forth the effort to compete with domestic and overseas rivals.

Sometimes the corporation imposes a truce on these warring camps. The groups may coalesce into two or three major alliances and then be granted official sanction to monopolize AI. All future technologies become the exclusive turf of these favored few. They ef-fectively prevent the ordinary workers from gaining access to the firm's future paths. The consequences are immediate: morale and motivation plummet. Some of these groups are populated by ama-teurs and novices. The technologies are so new that there are very few people with in-depth experience. Most understand just the sim-plest concepts and try to steer firms toward the "tried and true" pro-jects—that is, projects which utilize techniques that have been around over a decade. While the novices try to figure it out, the spread of new technologies is inevitably slowed down. Ultimately, this destructive behavior ends up costing the firm. It is a totally ineffectual way to motivate people to work for the good of the com-pany.

The Greeks had another way for people to challenge each other without the carnage of dog-eat-dog confrontations. They called it the "polis." This was a public forum where people and groups competed with their peers in word and deed. Underlying the competition, how-ever, was an ethic of participation enforced by a continuous commu-nity with a strong social memory. This social memory and ethic counteracted any tendencies participants might have to engage in negative competitive tactics.

For those who have never worked in a polis-type community but have only known the competitive type, the distinctions are subtle.

Modern Japanese business has thoroughly enforced and promoted this polis form of community within each work group, department, division, and company. The long memory of each of these communities insures aboveboard competitive tactics. In turn, each of these positive tactics increases the firm's store of technique and effort. By the simple addition of a few minor social components, vicious fights are transformed into edifying struggles. The polis requires a special management style. Essential to managing the polis is the creation of "spaces of appearance." These are the arenas where people gather to focus group attention on words and deeds. Different kinds of events that display both deeds and tactics must be presented to employees to capture their interest and attention. An AI group that works as a polis becomes a proud society striving to achieve excellence. Work groups that are managed to this level furnish each member with resources to perform well, and each member's pride and desire for perfection dominate group planning sessions.

When U.S. firms implemented quality circles programs, they immediately eliminated the polis component. The conferences of blue-collar workers, the regional and national awards conferences, the company technology update meetings—were all watered down or eliminated. Without spaces of appearance, circles were reduced to nothing more than technical discussions and soon died from lack of interest. Similarly, when AI groups embed themselves in a competitive environment and ignore the polis concept, they have no opportunity to display their deeds to the corporation.

A Japanese Alternative for Computer-Integrated-Manufacturing

CIM, as performed in Japan, bears only a passing resemblance to the American version. There are four readily apparent differences in the two: technical, social, automative, and competitive.

Around the world, the emerging hardware architecture is a two tier structure and not the six tier structure that AI vendors keep hoping to sell. That is, instead of six different sizes and kinds of computers ranging from the supercomputer to the workstation, only two kinds of computers will be necessary. They are the supercomputers, each one based on fundamentally different principles, and workstations, each one with uniform interface and access characteristics across the whole corporation. The mainframes which are so popular today will gradually fade into the background and act as data repositories instead of being used for computation. This emerging architecture derives its power from two main principles: the "single point of access" principle and the "computer customized around function" principle. The workstation is merely a tool for gaining access to the company's computing resources. The procedures used to gain access are identical for all workstations. With the various operating system and networking connections and commands hidden from the user by a universal interface, everyone in the company learns only one interface in order to access all applications software in the firm.

Supercomputer capabilities—neural net, connectionist and massively parallel—are the power behind the supercomputer layer. Each capability completes types of tasks more rapidly than the fastest mainframes or ordinary supercomputers. Because a uniform layer of workstations (numbering in the thousands) can gain access to any of these supercomputer resources, the same funding for supercomputing will allow a much greater number of terminals to use the supercomputers than today. This system of workstation access does not exist today in American firms. For one example, a new Connection Machine may be used by only a dozen people because the other employees in the company do not have universal access workstations. The resources of this expensive system are inefficiently used at best. But this will change in the near future. Firms wishing to have the competitive advantage will have hundreds of workstations which can be charged access fees to support the acquisition of world class supercomputer resources. Upon receipt of this system (for example, a Connection Machine), all workstations can immediately draw upon its resources. In time, the workstations will become more uniform while the supercomputers will be characterized by increasing diversity.

The Cognitive Technologies envision entire jobs, companies, and even industries becoming computerized. Today, factory work and office work alike depend on computers for top performance. Tasks that had been accomplished on a social, person-to-person basis are now done electronically. Recently, the technical capability to network all these terminals has joined people thousands of miles apart. Computers not only perform the work but are also evolving into a type of alternative electronic society. Companies and software vendors have yet to explore seriously the implications of this new kind of social arrangement.

There are several new emerging cognitive sciences: ergonomics, man-machine studies, interface science, cognitive science, artificial intelligence, and mental modeling. We can expect these new sciences to come into play as the transition from face-to-face encounters to electronic mediation takes place. And there are even more new sciences on the horizon.

1. Electronic Sociatrics—The principles of conduct of electronic social encounters.
2. Job Pluralization—The kinds of work that people design together electronically across their networks to replace traditional forms of work hindered by space and time.
3. Profit and Credit Economics—Ways to calculate patent and authorship when hundreds of people contributed to the innovative process through electronic workshops.

AI will take on an alter ego role as the persona of any user on an electronic network. It will act as a kind of electronic secretary that accepts task descriptions, does the work, and then organizes the results at the direction of the human user. The Automation of Software is a gradual program of indexing all software techniques and possible combinations by the tasks they can perform. This will allow humans to type in the tasks they want to perform, and the system will automatically construct code for performing them. This is primarily an indexing task, and the current efforts to study expert programming techniques is irrelevant to long-term software automation. Instead of expert techniques, we need simple indexing of techniques, expert or not. Intelligent software libraries are an intermediate step toward software automation wherein the user types in a description of the task to be performed. The intelligence built into the library dialogs with the user to clarify intent. It then accesses a program application that can do the task. The library begins its teaching function at this point. The user learns just that part of the application that pertains to the task at hand rather than the entire application. AI has already offered key components for software automation. AI objects are, in essence, reuseable code modules. As AI object libraries become standardized and published for various functional areas, an automatic programming system will emerge.

The Educative Workplace has almost completely transformed the content of ordinary jobs. The pace of technical, market and product change has quickened to the point that the learning characteristics of certain jobs and organizational units are the primary constraints on how well the company and its technology performs. More and more technology, management study, and social system design attention will be focused on the learning properties of people and the way they are employed in organizations. General Motors' Hantramck plant is a good example of what happens when manufacturers ignore this learning property. The factory installed a well-designed automation system that, unfortunately, neither the workers nor management was able to understand. This new direction will have repercussions for the old order. In the future, the success of a manager will be measured by the ability to enable other workers to learn. Also, jobs will be viewed as curricula where every job is broken down into elemental cognitive components, each of which is analyzed for its relationship to the work task.

Meta-Polity is an organizing principle used by some large corporations. Instead of only one polity system for the entire firm, multiple parallel polity systems prevail. These different polities effect the decision making process. Most companies in the United States consider each decision on a "what shall we do" basis. Before Meta-Polity arrives at an answer, it splits all decisions into two parts. The correct polity must be found to make an effective decision and then it must be implemented. Companies will find that there is no one "right" polity that will handle all decision-making responsibilities. Instead, through experimentation and observation, they will discover which polities are best suited to certain issue types. With this diversification of polity, workplace intensity will heighten, and the degree of employee commitment and concentrated effort will increase. In Japan, this is achieved by a body of techniques called Monastic Management. This theory considers the complete and undivided attention of the human work force on customer need to be the single most critical company resource. The firm, its work, and each job are designed so that workers face no distraction from customer impact. Monastic Management strives to create an atmosphere of contentment where job insecurity, labor strife, and career building are non-issues. Because the workers do not waste time and energy trying to resolve controversial issues, they can devote their full attention to optimizing the company's competitive position.

The Meta-Cognitive Organization puts the mental protocols used by all its people under the participatory control of the work force. All forms of expertise within the organization are captured and managed. Combined with the Educative Workplace Theory, this allows generation and invention of expertise to proliferate far beyond present levels. Some Japanese firms have already accomplished simple tactics like these by employing the meta-functions necessary to achieve the Meta-Cognitive Organization. In a Meta-training function, one Japanese company instituted a roving patent team that visited every work group in the firm once a year and demanded a patent application from each of them. The patent team worked along side these work groups and "hounded" them until they had made an application. The roving team performed the actual clerical chores of filling out the forms. It also researched key technical solutions to invention problems and made drawings and wrote captions. Several weeks later, it took the completed forms back to the work group for signatures and finally submitted the application to the government. In this way, the entire clerical burden of applying for a patent had been removed from the technical workers freeing them free to pursue their work. In the years that followed, the firm observed a tripling of patents received annually.

The scaling-down of automation will be one of the most influential trends in manufacturing. It will determine the future direction of American industry. At present, the SIM structures that lead to the lean automation format found in Japan are not being copied by American firms. Instead of doing the hard work and learning the methods and theories, American firms copy the products of the Japanese SIM system. Unfortunately, as soon as they duplicate the products, the Japanese SIM system invents new ones.

The United States has a tendency to do things in an "all or nothing" fashion. This is true of the way it delivers its technologies to the workplace. Firms in this country do not implement technologies in small, easily absorbed increments. Rather an elaborate piece of hardware is installed as a company showpiece and very few know what to do with it. The PhD's who are entrusted to deliver new technologies are another example of this "all or nothing" policy. They have all the knowledge of the technology and will share nothing with anyone else. For a new technology to be viable, it must be delivered smoothly and evenly across the company and not in huge, concentrated chunks. Ideally, the technology should go directly from the R&D labs to self-training work forces. In this way, smaller increments of new knowledge will be quickly commercialized by the circles programs which have the additional responsibility of keeping a close eye on scientific developments in the international community. Company R&D laboratories will find themselves more closely linked to product development.

When implemented, the Platform as Unit of Automation will have an immediate effect on methods of automation. As companies attempt CIM, a standard set of platforms will emerge to accomplish integration. Already, leading American and Japanese firms have devised some possible standard sets. Each of these platforms combines several key pieces of software and hardware that must work together as a foundation of profound AI and ordinary software capabilities shared companywide with other systems. These platforms are then implemented and moved strategically (something in the manner of men on a chessboard) when a particular market or competitive condition requires dramatic leaps in performance. Companies lacking these units of automation will have a hard time developing the skills necessary to master automation. They will have no unifying building blocks to serve as a basis of comparison. They will not know if they have implemented something well because they will not have established any norms. Also, the platforms leading to successful automation must be designed as a set. They cannot be implemented on a random "as needed" basis, otherwise key functionality and integration components will be omitted and will have to be added on later—usually unsatisfactorily and at great expense. Even worse, more foresighted competitors will have accomplished platform implementation correctly the first time.

In Japan, the Automation of Automation refers to a consistent system for delivering successive new technologies to the workplace with increasing mastery. The organization learns from each experience and improves its performance. Since the firm has a consistent delivery vehicle, the work force compares implementations and learns. This involves creation of a Social Delivery Vehicle and Cognitive Delivery Vehicle which together determine investment and successful use of new technologies. This organizational system for new technology delivery is a more profound concept than CIM. This system is not a special department of the company that is in charge of new technologies. All workers in the firms are part of it; they are all in charge of helping to disseminate new technologies. The United States is barely aware of this system's existence and is wholly unprepared to implement it.

The Strategic Transfer of Technology depends on entire societies to motivate their people to attain mental and conceptual greatness. What lies behind this motivation determines the direction the society takes. For example, when achievements are rewarded with privilege, as in the United States, people guard their ideas jealously and don't let their expertise go beyond a certain trusted group. But, on the other hand, societies that minimize individual reward and recognition, as in Japan, face the problem of constant dependence on other overseas sources for ideas. Both the U.S. and the Japanese see the inherent dangers built into their motivational systems and seek some kind of middle ground. Americans are questioning the wisdom of having all their new technologies packaged and delivered by a few high-salaried experts. They are taking a closer look at self-training work forces. In Japan, the school system, which has long promoted conformity and disavowal of personal achievements, now encourages more innovative thinking.

Social scientists are now discovering the role that "nationalized" personalities play in competition. The Japanese "personality" justifies voluntary unpaid overtime labor for the reason that Japan, as a small island nation, has only its human resources with which to compete. The patriotic aspect of this nationalized personality directly supports economic competition goals. Countries without this kind of "nationalized" mentality will have a much harder time competing. In addition, Japanese people who work under Monastic Management are oriented to a more selfless set of goals than their American counterparts. Workers in the U.S. have the "what's in it for me" attitude and see their jobs as the road leading to material success. These motivational differences, products of the culture, have compelling consequences for national industries, and it may not be possible for firms to fully overcome these deeply ingrained attitudes. The Japanese give an almost spiritual property to international competition. The whole organization focuses a trance-like attention to market changes, attuned to each subtle nuance. It is paradoxical that Japan, as aggressive and competitive as any other nation, relies on these spiritual attitudes and techniques to shape its people and its business.

The Society of Industry as a Unit of Competition is not yet a reality in America. While all the components for it are in place, it receives no attention from those in industry or those in the media. For example, an American chemical company does not compete on a one-to-one basis with another Japanese chemical company; it competes with all its corporate allies as well. The Japanese chemical company belongs to a cross-industry group, whose members subsidize each other's competitive struggles. The chemical company may have won concessionary rates from a transport company, a real estate firm, or an insurance subsidiary. The American company is faced with competing against the economic power of the whole group. Because the Japanese keep these arrangements informal (most deals are made through personal relationships), the American government cannot prove that this "ally" system exists. The Americans have no choice but to respond in kind. They will have to retaliate with their own cross-industry links and build competitive resource networks. The American semi-conductor industry provides the best example. Whereas Japanese semi-conductor companies are embedded members of industrial groups, American companies must stand on their own. Americans erroneously believe they can ignore overall industry structure considerations when competing with the Japanese. The U.S. firm, Intel, competes with Japanese firms whose various alliances give them a war chest of over $150 billion in annual sales to draw upon. Information, joint purchase agreements, concessionary rates, and subsidies to group members all flow through this partnership. Intel has only IBM—$50 billion in annual sales—to fall back on. IBM's resources amount to just one-third of what is available to the Japanese companies.

American firms face more than these Societies of Industry. Every major Japanese manufacturer is surrounded by hundreds of venture businesses established and managed by its own employees. Within these venture businesses and these industrial groups resides a social memory which enforces serial equity. All members compile a list of other firms that were either helpful or uncooperative in the past. The group remembers both the bad and good deeds of all its members. This coerces member firms to cooperate and not exploit other members in the group for short-term goals. Rather than face the certainty of censure, firms behave. American firms, unburdened by these social obligations, go their own way. They betray relationships, double-cross other companies, and hope to get away with it. By acting that way, they lose a lot of good will and future cooperation.

Finally, there is the three currency system. Japanese firms pay employees and each other in three forms of currency. First, they pay people with money to buy life's necessities. Second, they reward outstanding performers by letting an employee choose those he wants to work with on certain projects. In some companies, these key performers are given gold medals which they can then give to any other person in the firm. The second recipient of the medal immediately transfers to work on projects with the person who gave him the medal. This type of currency blends recognition and access to resources. Third, the firm pays the highest achievers with honor. Notice that the second and third forms of currency cost the company nothing and do not increase production costs. Companies that have learned the usefulness of these higher level currencies perform better and at lower cost than the companies that reward all good deeds with dollars. In the United States, no one believes in the permanency of the company—it may be in a totally different line of business five years hence. In this case, it makes sense for the employee to want to be rewarded in cash.

American factories are attempting to make themselves paper-free, and they are trying to accomplish this with computers. The Japanese have long had paper-free factories and they did not use computers to achieve this. Instead, they simplified and built relations of trust that allowed face-to-face promises to supplant legalistic paper forms. This belief that people have in one another enormously speeds up many types of transactions within the firm. It depends on the social memory feature detailed above.

The Meiji Restoration of America has meaning only for those with some background in Japanese history. The transformation of Japan from a feudalistic enclave in the mid-1800s to the industrial giant of today required an immense national effort. A change of government, called the Meiji Restoration, launched the massive undertaking. Today, the situation is the opposite. Western competitors are playing "catch up" with Japan. Manufacturers who are serious about taking on their Japanese rivals will have to dedicate themselves to changing their methods and philosophies. Halfhearted responses to the Japanese will serve no purpose other than prolonging the agony. Before a company can compete effectively, it must have well-defined goals. In particular, it must understand that the concept of profits goes far beyond the dollars the company receives for sales. A firm is truly profitable if and only if it generates the expertise, the social systems, the societies of industry, and the financial resources to defeat rivals. Monetary profit alone is meaningless. The Japanese know those funds must be actively employed to meet the challenges of market share, quality, and advertising. All three figure into long-term campaigns conducted by Japanese companies and the industrial societies in which they are embedded. By and large, the restricted definition that U.S. companies have for profits assures future defeat.

For companies to compete successfully with Japanese societies of industry, international competition must also be redefined. A metalevel of law and innovation is needed. The laws and business practices of competing nations must be brought more into line with the Japanese system. Companies will need new laws permitting faster ways to conduct legal transactions. Only by doing so will they be competing with Japanese societies of industry on equal footing. The popular business press takes a totally different view of the future than what has been outlined on the preceding pages. Most U.S. firms have adopted an entirely different approach to automation than what is shown here. This is in part due to the cultural differences that exist between Japanese and Americans. This country has no shortage of data to indicate that the methods we are using—and plan to use—are not working. It is time for the U.S. to make some hard decisions. Which aspects of our business culture should be preserved because they help us to compete effectively, and which aspects should be eliminated? Any new technology, including AI, will be pushed and pulled in various directions while businesses change their methods. The United States faces a formidable challenge.

How CIM and CASTS Reshape Artificial Intelligence

The following outline illustrates the progression of AI programs.

1. DEFENSE ADVANCED RESEARCH PROJECTS AGENCY STYLE AI
   Characteristics
   a. $150,000 allotted per single user workstation.
   b. Special AI languages and hardware.
   c. Expensive, elite knowledge engineers.
   Needs
   a. Lower cost.
   b. Easier to learn tools.
   c. Greater access to the technology by other workers.

2. EMBEDDED STYLE AI
   Characteristics
   a. AI features embedded in ordinary languages.
   b. AI running on engineering workstations.
   c. Self-compiling experts.
   Needs
   a. Matching software to hardware network capability.
   b. Common interface shared among all applications programs.
   c. Common data exchange format shared among all applications programs.
   d. Software platforms that blend AI with key applications.

3. INTEGRATED STYLE AI
   Characteristics
   a. Shared knowledgebase networks—many departments building, updating and using one expert system population in real time.
   b. Society of Experts—reverse-engineering population of expert system components and already built expert systems.
   c. Published AI rulebases and object sets for standards enforcement and feature update
   d. Self-tutoring systems and all documentation AI tutors.
   Needs
   a. Automate the building of AI tutorials.
   b. Automatic collection of cognitive use statistics.
   c. Society of Protocols—meta-cognitive management of protocols across the network, done participatorily.

4. EXPERT ELECTRONIC SOCIAL SYSTEM
   Characteristics
   a. Trust-level network i.d.s.
   b. Promise, request, and overseer type managers.
   c. Expert relationship simulator secretaries.
   d. Expert persona simulator assistants.
   Needs
   a. Replacement and augmentation strategies.
   b. Computer supported cooperative work tools: intelligent blackboard, intelligent session manager, and cognitive furniture.
   c. Expert view arrangers.

This outline gives a brief idea of AI's beginnings, how it has progressed, and directions it may assume in the future. These are not natural or easy transitions. In America, firms are likely to keep their older systems rather than invest for the long-term. Right now, Expert Electronic Social Systems represent edge-of-field AI, but American firms are nowhere close to attempting this advanced program. At present, no American firm has even seriously pursued integrated AI. On the other hand, Japanese research groups are conducting in-depth experiments with both Integrated AI and Expert Electronic Social Systems.

We can project a fifth generation AI program by analyzing the trends present in the first four. It can be seen that AI is headed toward generalization. Each successive program more fully integrates software and hardware. Also, there is a trend toward increasing socialization. The programs progressively embed more social ways of operating in the AI system's shape, functions, and form. Finally, AI is becoming less expensive, and its features are beginning to resemble those of ordinary software.

The level of AI programs that a company chooses to implement will depend on who is in charge of the implementation. In the United States, implementation honors generally go to the elite AI professionals. They isolate the technology and prevent it from joining the company mainstream. When the entire work force is involved, as in Japan, the system will reflect this democratic implementation effort. The level of AI programs implemented now will have profound implications in the following years. Companies still investing large amounts of money in DARPA-style AI will find to their utter dismay that their non-integrated systems will not talk to each other. They run the wrong software on the wrong hardware and use non-standardized AI system constructs and components. In the race for international competition, these firms will be left at the starting gate. Those companies who are casting their lot with embedded-style AI will not fare much better. They will suffer from the unwitting isolation of their AI systems. Too late they will discover that major data and interface incompatibilities were built into their systems. The biggest losers of all will be the firms who thought they were ahead of the game when they "wisely" standardized on out-of-date DARPA-style AI languages and platforms. Not even those firms investing millions in integrated-style AI will be exempt from problems later on. Their work force will have no choice but to utilize electronic media in the same manner as they now use social media. This amounts to nothing more than putting the same, obsolete system on newer, faster hardware.

AI and CIM can mutually assist each other. For this to happen, however, there must be real interplay and formal measurable co-designing from both ends. This interaction of AI and CIM is a complex issue and requires careful deliberation. Few firms have middle managers with the right style or willingness to undertake this kind of project. However, those who choose to maintain the status quo will be at the mercy of their more adventurous rivals. AI can do a lot to help a company compete, but it cannot help with problems of commitment and faintheartedness.

6

Intelligent Platforms

*"Consumer trust, brand image, control of distribution, corporate culture
and management skill are all informational resources. I call these
information-based resources invisible assets....They are the most
important resources for long-term success....The important features of
invisible assets—they are unattainable with money alone, are
time-consuming to develop, are capable of multiple simultaneous use, and
yield multiple simultaneous benefits—make it crucial to carefully
consider strategies for documenting them."*

Itami, Hiroyuki, "Mobilizing Invisible Assets,"
Harvard, 1987, pp. 12 and 13.

Unplanned automation has unforeseen consequences. To the detriment of the firm, it can take on a life of its own. A poorly designed automation program can actually benefit rivals, because everything in the firm is thrown out of sync. Momentum is lost, sequential tactics are in disarray, and marketing and production are out of touch with each other. The firm is distracted from competitor activities as it channels all its energy into disciplining its delinquent automation program. Only well-conceived automation will deliver the coup de grâce to competitors.

Before companies can adopt automation as a competitive weapon, they must break it down into small, easily implemented building blocks that can be put into play when conditions are right. This market strategy does not center on automation as a whole but rather on the increments by which automation as a whole is to be attained. An automation program, then, is the sum of these building blocks. Too many companies are confused and default to particular technologies as the unit of automation. For example, AI is a technology. But it is not an increment of automation nor is it a unit of automation called into play when the marketplace heats up. Again, the technology is not a unit of automation. The unit of automation is something else entirely. It is something integrated, self-explanatory, self-tutoring, and self-documenting. It must amplify and dramatically boost particular areas of functionality important to the business. The unit of automation must be used for an offensive thrust that includes all facets of manufacturing strategy. It is not one relatively weak, isolated component.

This section of the book describes Intelligent Platforms, the units for automating companies. The technical, social, and competitive aspects of these platforms will be dealt with in detail. To some extent, the platforms used as examples can be generalized to other industries. The basic principles of these platforms can be applied to any manufacturing situation. Japan has focused its attention on standards rather than platforms and only a few of that country's leading firms understand the difference between standards and platforms. Americans, behind the Japanese, are now just grasping the strategic uses of standards. They have yet to explore platforms which lead to the implementation of automation in manageable-sized increments. The ideas presented in the following chapters will be new to Americans and many Japanese as well—and beneficial to both.

15

Establishing Platforms

Types of Platforms

The following lists the different platform types.

Dealers:
The expert dealer sale platform.
The expert dealer service platform.

Customers:
The expert customer product design platform.

Head Office:
The expert business intelligence platform.
The expert system corporate specifications publisher platform.
The expert finance platform.

Offices Everywhere:
The intelligent document platform.
The intelligent text platform.
The expert electronic social system platform.

System Development:
The intelligent graphics platform.
The intelligent software development platform.
The intelligent facilities simulation platform.

Production:
The expert real time process control platform.
The expert product simulation platform.
The expert production process simulation platform.

Temporary Platforms:
The expert training platform.
The expert interface platform.

The Temporary Platforms are not really platforms as much as they are acknowledgments that all other platforms should have facilities to build in AI tutoring and a universal interface generating capability. Even though they are listed as temporary platforms, they are difficult to implement and most companies will not start off with them. Each of the platforms previously described has a particular competitive thrust.

The Expert Dealer Sale Platform

This platform speeds up transaction time and allows more customers to be served more accurately, more personally, and with the latest information.

The Expert Dealer Service Platform

This platform accelerates diagnosis of product faults or service, significantly reduces customer uncertainty, and permits faster part re-order and more accurate skill inventory application to problem areas.

The Expert Customer Product Design Platform

This platform enables the customer to design product configuration or service features. By doing so, each customer becomes part of the company's market research. It also allows the products themselves to gather data from customers on how the products get used.

The Expert Business Intelligence Platform

This platform enables many in the work force to interpret data collected on competitors which helps increase the firm's competitive responsiveness and sharpen tactical focus.

The Expert System Corporate "Spec" Publisher Platform

This platform allows specs for product, process and office procedure to be published in the form of AI tutoring expert systems so that all workers can learn the the meaning of the specifications.

The Expert Finance Platform

This platform automates dozens of possible financial strategy and classification alternatives from the best people in the firm and allows each body of expertise to compete in simulation for best performance in particular financial situations. It turns tens of thousands of spreadsheets into aggregates of issues at every level of the organization, automatically spotted and solved by software.

The Intelligent Document Platform

This platform creates self-managing documents across electronic networks so that scheduling, data collecting, and similar functions are automated. It prevents data from delaying transactions either from customers or other constituencies in the firm.

The Intelligent Text Platform

This platform automates structured subsets of natural language across networks and allows easy input and output as well as input and output to have robust cognitive qualities like memory and cogency. It permits fine-tuning the cognitive intensity of interactions, designed to outwit competitors, throughout the firm.

The Expert Electronic Social System Platform

With this platform, the firm takes on a new form in electronic guise. There is a proliferation of patents, joint projects between employees and new customer-supplier tie-ins. It accelerates innovation and companywide involvement in implementation issues.

The Intelligent Graphics Platform

This platform allows one model of a part or product to drive all functions in the firm, eliminating redundant data formats and interfaces.

It ultimately allows the customer to design his own complex products, and the shorter design to manufacture time makes the firm more responsive to its market.

The Intelligent Software Development Platform

This platform automates software generation by utilizing reuseable code and standard AI libraries. It means faster response to the market and much more rapid design of overall systems.

The Intelligent Facilities Simulation Platform

This platform automates plant design, plant expansion, and production line design and expansion. It allows for the discovery of the Japanese principles that scale down and optimize systems.

The Expert Real Time Process Control Platform

This platform manages systems in real time. It permits the unmanned operation of major systems combined with the automation of equipment maintenance. In Japan, inventory is a real time entity only, so materials management and distribution are included in this platform.

The Expert Product Simulation Platform

This platform allows a product still in the design stage to be tested in simulated conditions: simulated flaw response, simulated wear conditions or simulated ease of use. It allows "spec flex" to be designed into the products. (The Japanese are skilled at designing so as to allow variations in key product features after production so that input from customers can fine-tune the product after first sales.)

The Expert Production Process Simulation Platform

This platform allows simulation of all production equipment and processes. This means fully optimized human and technical systems.

The Expert Training Platform

This platform allows some automation of the building of AI tutoring systems and completely automates the transformation of systems specs and simulations into training material for the firm. This means that mistakes like Hamtramck, where work forces fail to master their systems, will be less likely.

The Intelligent Interface Platform

This platform puts one universal interface on all applications in the firm. It allows all workers easy access to all applications, and it allows all software vendors to deliver functionality instead of clumsy, added-on interfaces.

The Minimal Criteria of Platform Performance

The previous section defined platforms as building blocks of automation that can be selectively implemented or "moved" as needed. That is, a specific platform is implemented at an appropriate time in response to a particular opportunity or competitive threat. As mentioned earlier, each platform has eight levels—four social levels and four technical levels. With the assistance of AI, the technical components are combined with several ordinary software systems functioning together in the workplace, but still unintegrated.

There are four steps to be followed when creating a platform:

1. Strip the separate interfaces off each existing application program and then substitute a universal interface across different functional domains.
2. Remove the various incompatible data exchange formats used by each application and substitute a common universal data exchange format that all applications read to and write from.
3. Add AI to the remaining elements: the functional cores of each application, the universal interface, and the universal data exchange format.
4. Add an AI tutor generator assist facility and compile all system and application documentation into AI assisted tutorials.

Figure 15-1 illustrates the required capability for any intelligent or expert platform. Each platform must have three main capabilities. First, there must be the power to do the assigned job. Second, there must exist several ways for users to view inputs, results and processes. Third, there must be features that make it easy to use accurately. (This may not be the same as easy to use personally.) All three of these capabilities have two subdivisions. There are two kinds of power function. The platform must have the power to compute over its domain and, more importantly, it must give users the ability to make use of that compute power. When the first power is present without the second, it leads to frustration. Many applications today suffer from the absence of this second "accessibility" power.

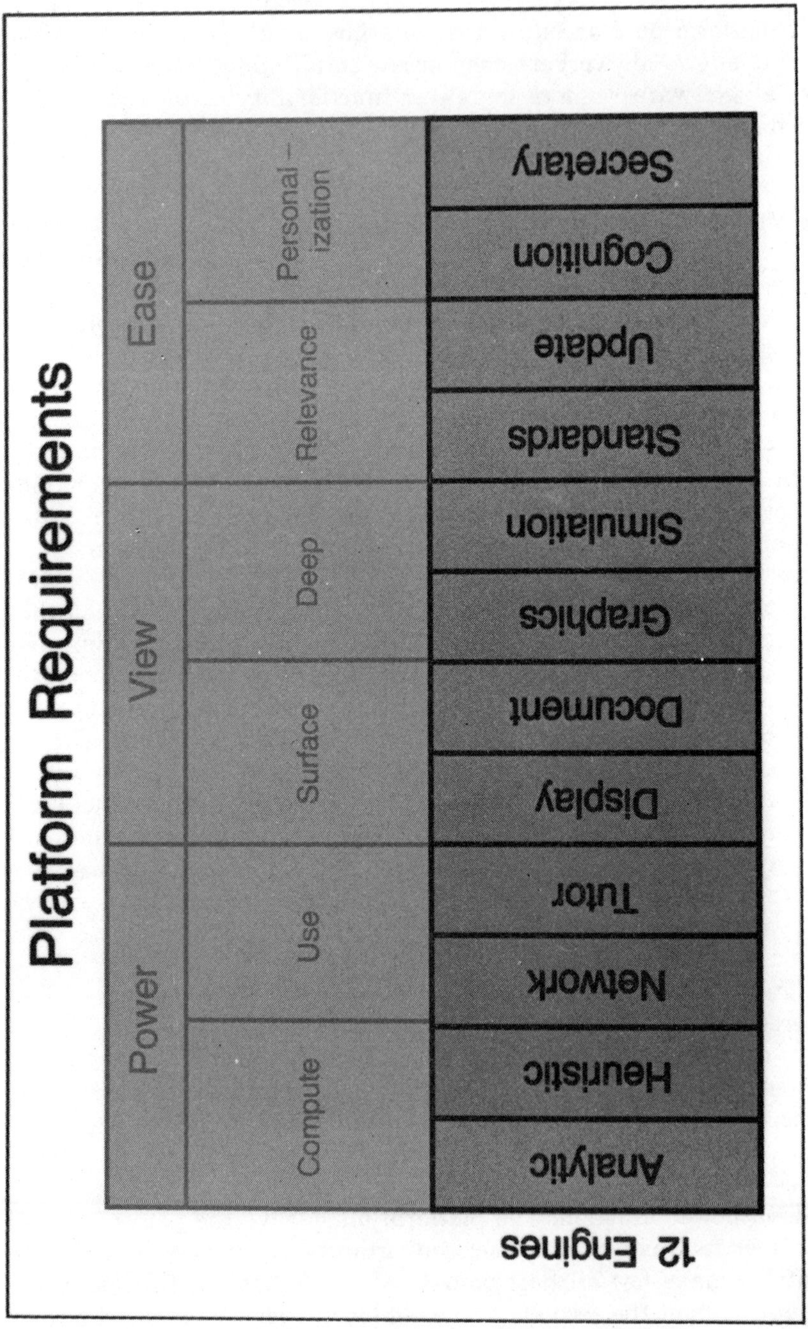

Figure 15-1 AI Platform Requirements.

Systems have a cornucopia of features that are so difficult to access and understand that the confused work force ignores them.

There are two levels of viewing systems. The surface level tracks and documents data. The other level is deeper. It observes the system as it goes through its paces to analyze its performance. The first level of viewing, then, offers a summary of the second's observations.

The third capability, ease of use, is essential. An easy to use system has relevance and can be personalized to the task at hand (as well as to the user at hand). But for some reason, this relevance is often omitted in software systems, and the consequences soon become apparent. If the system is the slightest bit out-of-date, users will have to spend time and effort to compensate. In companies everywhere, there are little "band-aid" programs or paper calculation systems that have been added on to existing programs. Truly useful programs are those that are conveniently updated by the user.

To achieve these three main capabilities (power, view, and relevancy), each intelligent platform needs twelve software engines. The first four engines—analytic, heuristic, network and tutoring—represent the power dimension of platforms.

First, an analytic engine is the heart of any ordinary software application today. It includes the algorithms, the determinate mathematical calculations, and the fixed data look-ups that comprise the traditional world of computing. Every platform has these analytic engines. When older programs are rethought and redesigned, they are made into parametric models. These models then become the analytic engines of platforms.

Second, a heuristic engine, a facility that captures expertise, must be included. All platforms capture domain expertise in various domains of analytic engines. Also captured is the expertise of workers as they use the platform. Through experience, they learn ways to make the platform really work well. Third, each platform has a network engine. Included in the network engine are the universal interface and the universal data exchange format. These integrate platforms with other platforms and items within the platforms themselves. Fourth, each platform has a tutoring engine. This acts as both an AI tutor facility and its inverse, an AI learning facility. The tutoring facility is the documentation of the platform itself. All details of the platform operation are taught to the user either in the learning session mode (such as electronic classes) or in the coach mode (taking the user through particular operations to accomplish a specific user goal). The inverse facility, AI learning, is applied to automatic machine learning of human operator efficiencies and characteristics. This optimizes the system for each user. AI learning is also applied to automatic machine learning of the rules of a particular analytic engine's knowledge domain. When technology permits, this facility ultimately grows into the automatic driving of intelligent dialogs with the user for automatic construction of expert systems by each platform.

The next four engines outlined—display, document, graphics, and simulation—represent the "view" dimension of platforms.

Every platform has a fifth engine, the display engine. This intelligently arranges displays for each user. It remembers each user's preferences and, with the help of the tutor engine, enforces them over similar domains—even if these domains have not been seen before. It works closely with the sixth engine, the document engine, which implements an intelligent self-managing document system. Seventh is the graphics engine which handles solid modeling, three (and higher) dimensional displays, intelligent spreadsheeting, and data views. It interacts closely with the display engine. The latter manages the actual representations on the screen while the former manages the simulated world or object itself. The eighth engine is the simulation engine. It adds a time dimension and a function-over-time dimension to everything already in the display or graphics engines.

The remaining four engines—standards, update, cognition, and secretary—belong to the "relevance" capability of platforms.

The ninth engine, the standards engine, automatically makes all additions to the platform conform to the standards upon which the platform is based. It has a combination prompting and policing function. It prevents the user community from altering standards for the sake of short-term function. The tenth engine, the update engine, is the converse. It allows alteration of the system in ways that do not harm the integrity of its basic standards. Indeed, the update engine is a network manager that automatically calls around the world to get updates for particular subsystems of the platform. It publishes and reminds the platform users of these changes and, with the tutor engine, generates new system tutorial documentation on all updates. The eleventh engine, the cognition engine, automatically generates cognitive statistics on platform operators usage patterns. This body of knowledge allows the platform to be fine-tuned. The cognition engine collects such things as error rates and types of error for each user; type and frequency of tutorial session usage per user; times-to-learn for key system functions; and optimal and suboptimal command sets used for key system functions. Every platform has a twelfth engine, the secretary engine, which carries out tasks assigned it by users. It knows the location of everything in the platform and, with the help of the tutoring engine, it knows how to get everything done. The tutoring engine also helps it learn new methods that human users have invented to do things. It can be customized for each user into a personal advisor over various subdomains of the platform. It acts as a combination tour guide, watch dog, and prompter for users on the platform.

These descriptions of the twelve engines of platforms outline only the minimal functions of expert or intelligent platforms. At present, only a few of these functions truly test present AI capability. It must be remembered that our knowledge of machine learning is still in its infancy. And yet, today's state of the art functionality, no matter how primitive it may be, must be embodied in platforms being created now. This functionality must not be delivered to platforms by itself. Instead, it must be welded together with the rest of software.

Detailed Components Lists of Some Key Platforms

Intelligent platforms and their twelve essential engines have been examined from the perspective of competitive value. Three of these expert platforms will be analyzed in greater detail. The Intelligent Text and Intelligent Document platforms will serve as examples for the service industries. The Intelligent Geometry platform will be illustrated for manufacturing.

These three expert platforms build on each other. The Intelligent Text platform is one of several components of the Intelligent Document platform, and the Intelligent Document platform is one of several components of the Intelligent Geometry platform. We will begin with the least complicated.

The Intelligent Text platform has too many components for any kind of detailed explanation. Briefly, it manages English text and structured subsets of English text. It is a key component of Expert Electronic Social Systems and is also essential to more modest document and display systems. This platform manipulates texts by content and not just by surface structure. Yet it is not a full natural language processor. Usually it is implemented to scan natural English and transform it into semi-structured messages, a simpler form of formatted English that is easier for both machines and humans to process.

The Intelligent Document platform is a more inclusive version of the Intelligent Text platform. But instead of semi-structured messages or natural English, documents and forms (like any business uses) are its base content. That includes engineering drawings, 3D shaded texture surface renditions of production parts, and spreadsheets. Its components are:

1. Automatic computer system administrator.
2. Project management and work/appointments scheduler.
3. Financial management.
4. Self-managing intelligent documents.
5. Engineering drawing editor and manager.
6. Electronic publisher and document layout.
7. AI rule, object, association development environment for the "common man".
8. Framework for workstations.
   a. Word processing.
   b. Spreadsheets.
   c. Diagram creation.
   d. Telecommunications.
   e. Database manager.
9. The Intelligent Text platform.

Some of the above components may seem out of place. Computer cost administration is a key cost factor in the spread of computer networks. Often for the first couple of "shake down" years, a new installation of four or five workstations will require the services of a full-time person to allocate costs and fees, to repair simple things on the spot, to call maintenance for more difficult problems, and to train users on system features. Time and money can be saved by automating all of these functions and putting them in the hands of the end users rather than a resident on-site expert. The Intelligent Document platform system administrator function does just that. Most mid-level managers need only the functions collected in the Intelligent Document platform for virtually all their office work. With the assistance of AI, one platform across the entire corporation can handle 80% of the office work in a unified way. There is one interface and one data exchange format. A company will find this arrangement much more helpful than an unwieldy army of independently developed expert systems scattered everywhere—systems with no shared vision of the firm's overall future needs.

The Intelligent Geometry platform is the future of Computer Aided Design (CAD) systems. However, unlike the offerings of CAD vendors, its foundation is a complete data integration approach to the entire workplace. CAD vendors have vigorously fought this trend but market dictates will soon have them rethinking their position. Customer consensus these days leans toward systems integration, even at the cost of the latest features.

These are the components of the Intelligent Geometry platform:

1. Variational geometry (solid modeling version of Mathpak).
2. Parametric finite element modeler for automatic mesh generation and result interpretation.
3. AI development environment for CAD.
4. Network file system extended to allow shared computer processing time across a network of workstations.
5. A software bus providing common interface and data exchange format across applications.
6. A self-tutoring software environment where AI tutorial sessions in "teach" and "coach" mode explain all the features and uses of the applications.
7. The Intelligent Document platform.
8. Edge-of-field 2-D, 3-D and 4-D graphics libraries.
9. An automatic simulation generator and interpreter.
10. Standard AI object libraries.
11. System updates published in AI object/rule form.
12. Society of Experts reverse engineering based modularity of all system software components.
13. Automatic user model builder and monitor for collecting cognitive use statistics on users for incremental system personalization and improvement.
14. System guide and coach AI expert assistant.

The list should be compared with features of current generation CAD systems. Right now, for one example, one Digital Equipment Corporation MicroVAX workstation alone comes with a truckload of orange manuals to explain the system and its features. No one in the world has read all of them. They are so poorly indexed, so untested, and so massive that they constitute a "pretend" system of documentation. Actual MicroVAX users are condemned to operating in small subsets of what the machine actually offers. In addition, there will be a couple of dozen applications that CAD shops will run on the workstation, and each of these applications will arrive with its own "pretend" documentation. It would take several lifetimes to read and master the contents of all these manuals.

Instead, the Intelligent Geometry platform proposes on-screen system documentation in the form of AI assisted tutorials. This does not require advanced AI tutorial technology but merely state of the art technology as of the early 1980s. The AI program is there to index flexibly the interconnections between user tasks and system features. It also manages a system memory that addresses the balance between user needs and system features.

How Platforms Affect AI Delivery

So far we have looked at expert platforms as individual components of automation strategy. These platforms also can be seen from the perspective of AI involvement with ordinary software. In an earlier chapter, AI was related to software in seven stages. Expert platforms realize a number of those stages. Building an expert platform takes more time, thought, and care than doing a simple expert system project.

Because of AI's relationship to ordinary software, the minimal requirements of an expert platform are:

1. An AI development environment for use by end users.
2. Adding AI to the data and interface layers of applications software.
3. Self-tutoring AI tool for all applications to use.
4. Shared knowledgebase network features that allow many departments to update and share one knowledgebase population.
5. An AI automatic analytic software generator—an automatic code generator for particular kinds of application software needed in the platform.
6. An AI relational database generator.

The purpose of this list is to demonstrate how the expensive knowledge engineer can be eliminated from the AI process. The building of AI systems belongs in the hands of ordinary domain experts who dialog with intelligent AI text drivers. To achieve this, AI must teach itself to users on the screen, and this is not hard to do. Also, some aspects of AI need simplification. The incompatible features of the Defense Advanced Research Projects Agency (DARPA) style AI need replacing with national standard object and rule libraries in various important domains.

Expert platforms have the potential to achieve mass distribution of AI capability across all software systems in companies. But the United States is confronted with one formidable social barrier: we isolate expertise in expensive, elite, and highly educated packages called AI experts. Until these experts loosen their grip on technology, companies have no alternative but to build their systems using their help and then construct network facilities that make recourse to the experts less needed. AI needs an interconnectivity standard for creating shared knowledgebases, the truly democratic form of AI. Firms that incorporate platforms into AI systems from the beginning can achieve standards, interconnectivity, and immediate application. Firms that omit platform development will suffer in future years from incompatible AI systems that do not readily mesh in an overall hardware or software architecture.

How Platforms Should Be Used

When a division in the company needs an AI project, it is up to the AI group to determine upon which platform the project will be constructed. Once the platform is known, the AI group then proceeds to secure funding not for the project but rather for the platform. One approach is to obtain platform funding from divisional headquarters and then acquire local funding for a particular application. Many AI groups make a mistake when they seek applications funding. They artificially raise the price of the AI project to what they think the market will bear. This means that no division can afford to underwrite the project and the group must try its luck with corporate headquarters where funding is often highly political, undependable, or slow in coming. While headquarters mulls over funding decisions, AI is not being implemented in the firm.

Some AI groups, leery of going to the top for funding, commit another tactical error. They ask several divisions to invest in a particular project that will only benefit one of them. This has several unhappy results. First, since these AI groups develop projects and not platforms, they are requesting other divisions to fund something that is not generalized to everyone's needs. And second, once divisions invest money to benefit someone else, they will be counting the days until the favor can be returned. They will devise their own projects and apply some political arm-twisting to even up the funding score. It goes without saying that these new projects will be unstrategic, unrelated to the current capabilities of the technology, and a general source of frustration. This problem is easily avoided by constructing platforms which can be used unchanged in different divisions. Each division would then use these all-purpose platforms for its own specific applications.

Once funding for a platform has been obtained, an AI group's best strategy is to keep the price of the individual project as low as possible. If projects are relatively inexpensive—and useful—then all divisions will soon be sponsoring their own projects. The AI group (which has built platforms) can make itself look good by implementing virtually identical projects in several divisions and being paid for each application. The excess funding can then be used to build a cross-divisional platform for particular areas of AI.

Earlier in this book, a development rhythm for AI groups was described. As mentioned, four types of coding are involved in any one AI project. One of those four types was platform coding, the standardized, non-ideosyncratic integration type of coding. By building expert platform coding into the two week development rhythm of any AI project, the firm makes a very powerful commitment to integration of systems and integration of AI into all systems development. Additionally, the AI groups commit an AI component to all other software development projects of other groups in the firm.

The Competitive Use of Platforms

When competitors respond more quickly to the market, it is because they go from product concept to product manufacture faster. As a countermeasure, a firm can develop an Intelligent Geometry platform to shorten the time from artwork to process plans and use machine vision inspections of the part or product. When competitors manufacture products more cheaply, the Intelligent Document platform can be used to accelerate design-for-assembly across the firm and allow the manufacturing and design divisions to communicate with each other more effectively across the network. These two examples illustrate that there is no set order in which platforms are to be built. Though there is some interdependence between platforms (some platforms are components of others), a company develops first the platform that meets the competition needs of the moment. The platform concept and the standards built into it on the eight social and technical levels prevent the chosen platforms from leading to incompatible systems later.

7

Setting Up a First-Rate AI
Delivery System

"... it keeps alive the tantalizing proposition that what we have in
Japanese organization is an emergent form that represents the future, not
merely a carry-over from the Japanese 'feudal' past, and that, as Dore,
Ouchi, and others have argued, can be witnessed with growing regularity
in the structures and management styles of modern organizations in the
West."

Lincoln, J. R.; Hanada, M.; McBride, K.; "Organizational Structures in
Japanese and U.S. Manufacturing"; *Administrative Science Quarterly*,
vol. 31; no. 3/338-508; September 1968; p. 359.

We have already discussed the various components necessary for effective AI delivery systems. But lists alone don't provide much help
when it comes the the actual installation of such systems. This section of the book demonstrates, step by step, how these individual
components are put together to achieve an overall effective delivery
system. This approach to delivery systems is solidly based on practices and theories developed in Japan. It has since been modified to
suit the business and social climates of Scandinavia and the United
States. This hybrid approach is somewhat different than the Japanese version, but these deviations should not be seen as weaknesses
or faults. Although aspects of this approach may appear strange,
they have stood the test of time in Japan's and Sweden's best firms.

The chapters that follow examine not only a theory of AI delivery
but also a theory of AI itself. The firms that deliver technology most
efficiently are the ones that understand the technology itself and the

role it is to play. These firms know that each technology is distinct—just as each employee or workstation in the firm is distinct. The people working in this type of firm are driven by a different set of motivations than people working for average firms. This unique orientation alters the concept of technologies and the way every structure in the firm imagines and relates to them. New technologies are delivered most effectively only when this new motivational structure is securely in place.

16

The Social Delivery Vehicle

The Three Aspects of Delivery

Three facets of technology delivery need management: the design of the system, the mapping of the problem domain, and the delivery of systems to the problem domain. American firms place far more emphasis on design of their technologies than their "leaner" and more profitable Japanese and European competitors. That is, American firms allow the design and the technical content of systems to determine problem domain mapping and delivery system building. This policy results in second-class implementation of fascinating, edge-of-field technologies. World competition is forcing American industry to rethink its ways. U.S. firms will have to achieve an equal balance of design, domain mapping, and delivery system construction or lose out to their more aggressive rivals.

There are nine components to good delivery of artificial intelligence. AI, as a design science, is composed of cognitive science, AI coding knowledge, and some linguistics. As a problem domain map, AI requires a surveying of all possible applications, a priority list of these applications, the invention of expert platform building blocks for integrated delivery, and a study of potential applications. As delivery system building, AI includes building a Social Delivery Vehicle and a Cognitive Delivery Vehicle.

Most firms divide their resources very unequally among these nine components. Almost all money ends up with the technical AI people, and most of their expenses are for hardware and software. The mapping of problem domains and the co-designing of expert platforms

237

with the rest of the firm's software establishment is largely neglected. Almost no money or time is allotted for delivery system building. In most AI programs I encountered, there was no design of delivery system going on at all. It was simply (and mistakenly) assumed that the usual methods would be just fine.

Many employees in firms are literally begging for certain kinds of AI services. Some workers are merely curious about AI. Others know a little about the technology and would like to see the firm follow a path of structured development. Some workers in disciplines totally unrelated to AI have observed the benefits that competitors have derived from the technology and want their own company to enjoy the same advantages. But, unless a comprehensive system of advice delivery is quickly established in the firm, all these persons could make poor decisions on AI issues which could ultimately lead to bad investments in equipment, training, or vendor relationships. These people, then, create a constituency for an AI delivery system.

Japanese firms have already established delivery systems for any new technology, including AI. Simply put, they "plug" AI into these polished systems and fine tune its delivery to defeat competitors—just as they did with previous technologies. Moreover, the participatory nature of Japanese technology delivery systems entails a great amount of work in the areas of problem domain and delivery system improvement. Compared to American firms, Japanese firms maintain a better balance among the mapping of domain, the building of delivery systems, and the understanding of the technology itself. Americans, so brilliant with the technology itself, bungle its application, but not for reasons of capability. They are victims of a technology-perverted sense of business values and don't even comprehend the deep cognitive habit and cultural roots of the shortcomings of their methods.

Components of a Social Delivery Vehicle for AI

There is one final list of components that must be presented before giving the step-by-step recipe for building a first class AI group. Throughout this book, references have been made to the Social and Cognitive Delivery Vehicles for implementing new technologies. Nowhere have they been described in any detail. This is not accidental. In Japan, although each major firm has such delivery vehicles, their composition varies in each firm. Indeed, the degree to which delivery vehicles are self-conscious entities—part of the formal structures of their firms—differs between firms. By listing the components I personally used in several American and Japanese firms, I generalize across a great deal of variation. But it is a generalization with utility and practicality—and not just an empty abstraction.

The thirteen components which follow are not in any special order. This is deliberate. There is no rigid rule that dictates the sequence in which they are implemented. Later, I will outline the management theory that permits this flexible order of implementation. This unstructured order also works to prevent, in practice, top-down imposition of preordained AI delivery systems. A method using interactive dialog to deliver AI and its delivery systems works best. This is where theory becomes transformed into merely a map of where to probe and where to look for data, and practice becomes a series of exercises that raise new questions for theory modification

The AI Auxiliary

The AI auxiliary is a group of experts in domains of knowledge unique to the firm. They become the firm's knowledge engineers— paradoxically by eliminating the knowledge engineers. At first, these domain experts demonstrate that ordinary engineers and office managers can teach themselves AI. They can mine their own expert knowledge and put it into expert systems. Later, they become an expanding body of company domain experts who have taught themselves AI. In the early phase of transition when the auxiliary is being taught AI by the knowledge engineers, it is important that the domain experts do not switch sides and become higher-salaried knowledge engineers. (Poorly managed AI programs can lead to employees trying to move up the career ladder.) Rather, auxiliary members instead of the expensive knowledge engineers perform the first knowledge extraction of real AI projects in the firm. This becomes a statement to the rest of the firm that even ordinary workers can add "knowledge engineer" to their job description. Anyone can be a knowledge engineer; it is not some prestigious, overpaid occupation for the very few.

Application Qualification Tours

All during the year, AI development groups travel to every part of the company looking for possible AI projects and applications. However, they do not announce the purpose of their mission. They make it a point not to ask people in various divisions which AI projects are needed. Instead, they seek to find out what problems in general are in need of solution. The AI group listens carefully and spots particular instances where AI could make a positive contribution. In this way, the AI group does not look like a special interest group promoting its own product and strengthening its hold on the technology. Ideally, these tours should visit all parts of the company annually. New members of the AI group should be given the opportunity to interview and discover problem areas. This will serve to make AI groups more accessible and democratic. The group should impress others with their trustworthiness and their sincere interest in rooting out problems. Once this trust is established, real results can be delivered. Any accolades for the AI group will come only after positive results have been achieved. Conversely, if the tour comes across as nothing more than an advertisement for AI, then the group will have to undergo retraining.

AI Application Workshop Fairs

Visibility is key to policy change in large organizations. Without a strong public relations campaign, even the best ideas can die of corporate apathy, because no one in the power structure knows about them. Putting a new technology in the limelight may be the only way to make it part of company policy commitments. There is a second political principle of new technology delivery. Sharing or borrowing power from other groups is a losing proposition. New sources of power and visibility must be created. An AI Application Workshop Fair is the creation, from scratch, of a new political center of power, and it doesn't require borrowing funds, offices, time, or anything else.

Many AI groups make the mistake of attempting to ingratiate themselves with the existing power structure. These groups feel weak and unsure of themselves, and they will give away major control of the technology in exchange for a secure niche from which to operate. They hope that acceptance by company leaders will confer an instant respectability upon them. Typically these groups get a vice president to write a memo asking all in the firm to think of AI applications. This is the worst imaginable approach to new technology. No one has ever implemented a new technology successfully because a vice president wrote a memo. This arrogant and counterproductive tactic reveals an old-fashioned top-down image of the firm, where workers spring into action based on orders from the top.

Usually the first step after an Application Qualification Tour is getting people to organize their own AI Application Workshop Fair. At these events, AI vendors demonstrate their products on actual workstations and computers to middle-level managers. In addition, there will be speeches, presentations, endorsements, and workshops. But these fairs are more than just conventions; they are detailed workshops. Both AI development groups and managers using structured workshop procedures listen closely to each other's needs and concerns. They establish a mutual understanding in the form of a workshop results document. This document is critical to a new technology's success. Too many managers have experienced selfish groups promoting new technologies that didn't live up to all the hype. It is truly a revolutionary idea that those promoting a new technology would survey divisional needs before proposing help and solutions. These groups can determine the best directions for the AI program by asking fair participants their reactions to certain demonstrations and what applications were brought to mind.

A detailed workshop report is printed and sent to every participant of the fair. These results travel rapidly up the managerial hierarchy and become the basis of top divisional management endorsement of official experimental applications of AI. It is critical that the workshop findings be well-formatted and organized so that policy makers can make immediate use of them. In one case, within six weeks of an AI fair, the printed report led directly to five-year funding (at one million dollars a year) for AI support of Computer-Aided Design. Such a commitment is an enormous step forward for both AI and the AI group, and it can be done merely by listening carefully to those the new technology is supposed to serve. When a new technology is stripped of its remoteness and arrogance, it is far more acceptable to those who approve projects and funding.

AI Application Workshop Fairs have another beneficial consequence. Local divisional people give presentations based on initial AI applications found in Application Qualification Tours. A few weeks before the fair, these people were just anonymous entities. Now they are giving slide shows of potential AI applications uncovered in their area during a previous Application Qualification Tour. They have the opportunity to speak before a couple hundred assembled conferees in their division's management. Their own self-esteem grows, and they gain the attention of their colleagues. Suddenly, everyone wants to have this same recognition. They clamor for AI Application Qualification Tours in their area of the firm. They will be ready with well-thought-out AI applications when the tour arrives. This human characteristic, envy, can be harnessed by the firm and used to its advantage. Fairs give AI group leaders great visibility, because they have the opportunity to control the pace and content of the fair. In the speeches they make, they can set forth terms and conditions for new technology delivery in general. Key managers listening to these speeches may later on incorporate the AI group leader into the upper levels of management.

As shown in these few examples, these fairs create political limelight from nothing. In big corporations, it is this visibility (or lack of it) that makes and breaks careers. There is a human tendency, however, to copy someone else's ideas to get the same results. In time, some of the less imaginative people in the company "vulturize" the fairs. That is, they will stage an exact replica of the AI fair to promote their interests, and the freshness of the concept will be lost. It is essential for the AI groups to design a succession of different types of fairs. While the "vultures" exploit one fair format, the AI group busily unveils a novel kind of fair. A creative AI group with several types of fairs in the planning stages will eventually wear down their imitative competitors.

Pilot Projects

There are three kinds of pilot projects: elite, lateral, and everyman. In the first type, the AI core group applies edge-of-field techniques to new projects. In the second type, the homework done in an AI training session evolves into a project. Finally, the third type of pilot program includes dozens of work groups working together in AI Circles programs. They implement AI projects under different circumstances.

Elite AI programs are quickly accomplished—and that is roughly where the benefits of this type of project end. Although the project is efficiently implemented, the price is high and the technology is slow to spread to the majority of workers. It is strange that many firms insist on this expensive, sluggishly disseminated technology. This policy makes absolutely no sense from a business standpoint, but it indicates a certain peculiarity of the human animal. We are awed and impressed by our technology, but we have little faith in it. It is new and uncertain and has the potential to misbehave in dozens of unpredictable ways. Managers whose annual raises depend upon an absence of errors in their personnel folders, detach themselves from anything that might be risky. They have no knowledge of the new technology and do everything possible to disassociate themselves from it. That is why technology is given to the "geniuses." If they cannot handle the new technology, then obviously nobody can. In this way, nobody loses face, but the firm ends up strangling on its own policies. It ventures nothing, it gains nothing.

Tool Courses

Tool courses are two day on-site sessions where the AI core, the AI auxiliary, and the AI training faculty deliver seminars on various AI tools and techniques. Members of AI Circles attend these meetings to learn better ways to implement their projects. It is important that these classes be held in the local plant or division where the need exists rather than in corporate headquarters. People interested in new technologies don't want to make the trip to headquarters for training. Headquarters is a service organization for those parts of the firm that serve customers—and nothing more. No business important to the firm goes on in headquarters. Quality production and delivery of competitive products, the real business of the firm, are performed elsewhere. Companies with the "imperial headquarters" mind-set, unfortunately, treat their customers just as condescendingly as they treat they own production organizations.

Structured Group Readings in AI

The traditional methods of training people in a new technology are expensive, and firms that rely on these methods will inevitably fail competitively. As a lower-cost alternative, Japanese firms have created Self-Training Work Forces that train themselves in successive new technologies in weekly meetings. Tested methods help groups teach themselves new technical material. When a study dynamic is added to each job, it embeds part of the future in the daily routine of each employee. Recently a number of firms have used a method from Cognitive Science called Structured Reading to help work groups teach themselves new technologies. Based on research into macrostructures (the hierarchies of themes that allow two or more sentences to talk about the same "point"), these sixteen reading techniques allow work groups to turn complex texts into clearly ordered diagrams that lay out the particular lines of argument and relationships between main points. These diagrams reveal what was learned and what was not explained well in the text. Calls are made to the experts for explanation of unclear material. Other than that, the work groups study the texts without the intervention of outside lecturers.

Structured Group Readings are an open event, and anyone in the company is invited. Although they are led by AI core members, they are sessions where workers teach each other new technologies. Each person in attendance is assigned certain sections of the text to structurally read for presentation in front of the group later on. Between meetings, group members have access to experts to answer any questions or to clarify difficult points. This type of program may have difficulties in its early stages while members become accustomed to this new "teacherless" style of classroom. Americans, in particular, believe in an autocratic figure to lead learning and react with discomfort when no central authority is present to take charge. The Japanese have a long tradition of teaching themselves and feel more at home in this situation. Group Structured Readings profit the firm by instilling the habit and tradition of selfteaching. This is a revolution in work force attitude. If employees can instruct themselves in new technologies, then expensive seminars can be eliminated. The money saved promotes continued technical improvements

Group Structured Coding Sessions

Most major firms do not facilitate the transference of programming skills from expert programmers to novices. The technique called Group Structured Coding Sessions makes that transfer faster and easier. AI is a programming technology, and it can spread only as quickly as ease of code generation permits.

Japanese software factories are working on two forms of Group Structured Coding Sessions, a face-to-face form and an Expert Electronic Social System form. Basically, the apprenticeship model determines the design of this training method. The firm's best AI programmers perform part of their actual week's work (not special tutorials or simplified exercises) once a week in front of an assembly of less-advanced programmers. The newest programmers transcribe verbal protocols of the expert programmer at work. Those with more experience take on specific assignments to track down information or try out particular algorithms. The most advanced programmers solve major subproblems aloud at the direction of the (best) programmer leading the session. The results of these sessions can be impressive. In one firm, within eighteen months, sixty percent of those attending tripled the speed of their coding. They were evaluated for cogency of ruleset (number of rules and rule clauses to achieve operation), errors per line of code, lines per assigned program function, and error rate of updating a program (to measure the transparency of the code written and its self-documenting quality).

After a year of operation, spin-off subgroups can be formed where the same dynamic continues with the addition of new members. That is, when the more advanced programmers achieve certain base levels of performance, they become the experts for these new groups. This self-replicating quality allows exponential growth, and this is exactly what a firm needs to spread AI coding skill.

AI Circles

Earlier in this book, it was mentioned that U.S. firms removed the polis feature from their AI Circles almost immediately. The Japanese, however, see polis as an integral part of their circles. This discussion deals solely with the Japanese "spaces of appearance" version of AI Circles and not their anemic American counterparts.

AI Circles are formed of ordinary work groups (or else representatives from various work groups) who meet once a week to study AI and design and build AI applications. It takes a Circles group perhaps two to three times longer to complete their projects when compared to the rate of AI core groups. But this is only at first. With additional projects, they gain practice and efficiency. AI Circles generally follow a companywide curriculum which details the work to be done each week on a project. Also, a vast set of resources is made available to each circle. These resources are indeed considerable: visits from problem solving teams, quarterly project evaluation and enhancement conferences, annual awards conferences, and commissions of circle members to measure financial impact of all projects. Selected AI core experts maintain the curriculum and adjust it each week based on the feedback received from each AI Circle. This weekly feedback is absolutely critical to the success of Circles programs, and most Americans are unwilling to devote the time and effort required. Without this feedback, projects go largely unmonitored. Small errors, if not spotted and corrected quickly, can doom a project. Moreover, the errors are published so that other Circles can avoid them.

Each Circle prepares an academic paper every quarter detailing their progress with a project. These papers are presented at conferences where other Circles and outside experts examine and expand upon each circle's work. The AI core members present, evaluate, and improve Circle project code and design. This is complicated work, but it does have one important function: it unmasks core members who lack an in-depth understanding of AI. Once exposed, these experts have the option of either devoting further time to the study of AI (in preparation for the next Circles conference) or transferring to another company where they will not be asked to exhibit their "expertise" in public.

Problem Solving Events

No one likes criticism. But errors are committed all the time, so a tactful way to correct them must be found. Japanese companies have done this with the creation of Problem Solving Events. When problems arise in particular projects, teams composed of outside AI experts, local core managers, and domain experts visit the project in trouble for a two or three day stint to resolve the difficulty. This roving band of troubleshooters is key to overall motivation throughout AI applications programs.

This tactic is based on a profound insight into human nature. If AI groups implementing projects are forced to pretend they have a perfect knowledge of the technology (when in fact they know they don't), they cannot possibly succeed. They cover up gaps in knowledge by reducing the scope and aims of their project until it is more in line with their actual capabilities. This is an omnipresent insidious force present in most company AI programs. Instead, members in a new technology program must be given tacit permission not to know everything. Furthermore, it's all right to make this fallibility public. The Problem Solving Events spur groups to work on their own to their full potential by guaranteeing that major problems will receive assistance. Groups no longer have the temptation to minimize their projects to avoid being wrong. Along with this problem solution function, Problem Solving Events educate workers as well.

The Problem Solving Team visits projects in trouble, although the team may disguise this and claim that it visits all projects on a random basis. In any case, it visits projects and circles that have problems and literally lives with the project for fourteen to twenty hours a day for two or three days. This lengthy work day is necessary. This intense scrutiny indirectly stimulates the group in trouble. At the same time, it intensively engages everyone in problem solution and demonstrates real dedication to completing the project at all costs. Finally, the team brings with it an arsenal of AI resources for the battle. These visits—unpredictable, intense and spirited—serve to enliven the entire AI applications effort of the firm. Generally the team does not accept invitations; it prefers to decide on its own which projects are experiencing genuine difficulties and which projects are looking to be mollycoddled. Because the team can arrive at any time, workers are apt to keep their projects disciplined.

Even though the team visits create vast amounts of work for people, these visits are also stimulating and entertaining. In principle, no amount of work is too much. The team may assign local AI project members to phone in three days all two hundred AI vendors around the world to obtain data. These immense workloads, enforced and real, make AI groups realize how much more they are capable of doing in an eight hour day. In this way, certain robust levels of minimal intensity and hard work can be managed into the AI program.

The AI Meta-Applications Group

Most firms, lacking in imagination, create an AI applications group and an R&D group. After all, every other company has them. This lazy, commonplace approach to new technology delivery is fatal. National economies decline when there is a policy (unwritten) of avoiding the new and the different. In some Japanese companies, there is a third group that acts as a liaison between R&D and AI applications groups. This group is the meta-applications group and it considers the balance between invention of new technology and the true business needs of the firm. It serves a technology transfer function. The meta-applications group accelerates use of new technology for the sake of competitive advantage and bottom line contribution. More practically, it keeps the R&D focused on working on the real edge-of-field projects. Most R&D groups keep their own standards of work and are considerably behind their own discipline's most advanced breakthroughs. No one else in the firm has the specialized knowledge to realize that the R&D section is behind the times. The meta-applications group, however, keeps abreast of edge-of-field developments and can spot submaximal performance.

The meta-applications group polices the applications groups by compelling them to make individual projects conform to long-range platforms in the firm. AI applications groups are also encouraged to scope out and maximize all possible similar utilizations of the technology rather than just doing projects where it is politically expedient. The meta-applications group insures that the initial intent of the project is realized in the project's final form. Furthermore, years later, when completed projects are in operation, it remembers these initial expectations and forces their actual achievement.

Finally it builds an overall need map of the company that shows R&D where new technical capabilities are needed or can have major impact.

AI Application Generator Conferences

About ten years ago, the general problem solvers of AI were phased out in favor of investigating expert performance in specific domains. (Recently, SOAR, a system at the University of Michigan, has revived general solver approaches by replacing OPS83's conflict resolution set with general chunking and learning facilities.) The domains were fairly broad ten years ago. Today, with thousands of AI applications and projects underway, there is a need for another level of detail. For one example, we need to divide all of AI application to CAD into roughly twenty subareas of application within CAD. When a firm reaches this level of twenty AI projects in CAD, all project leaders should meet to discuss the common and distinct areas of their projects. First, if the firm has a responsible AI program, all projects are built on a CAD platform. At these conferences project leaders extend the definition and power of their firm's CAD platform. Second, they standardize AI rulesets and object libraries over the firm's CAD domain. Most likely, this is part of the platform definition and extension process. Third, they automate aspects of constructing AI projects on the foundation of the CAD platform. These automation efforts amount to creation of what ordinary software departments would call "application generators." These are programs that allow input to take the form of task intent, and the program itself carries out the creation of an expert system to accomplish those task intents.

Most firms have not reached this critical level of twenty AI projects in one functional area. Those few who have, held conferences in which participants shared general experiences but made no attempts to formulate an automation program. Those firms wishing to compete in the international market will have to make sure that AI application generator conferences fulfill their whole mission.

Vendor Education Seminars

Vendors and companies have had a difficult partnership throughout the years. Vendors have customarily unloaded hardware and software on companies that created as many problems as were solved. (In defense of the vendors, companies did not always articulate their needs well.) Because vendors had the technology and equipment, companies bowed and scraped to maintain their favor. When vendors realized they had the upper hand, they became less concerned with customer needs. Companies that want to break out of this routine and share in the co-design of their equipment should consider Vendor Education Seminars. At these seminars, AI vendors are exposed to the kinds of products and features the company seeks. The firm's entire AI program instructs the vendors. If the seminar is successful, the company and the vendor will have a better understanding of each other. They may reach an agreement: the vendor will supply the co-designed product if the company agrees to buy it. This puts the burden of responsibility on the firm. It must articulate its exact requirements since it has already agreed to buy.

Vendor Education Seminars give the company an opportunity to present a united front (provided all the diverse groups can cooperate) and outline exactly what services the company as a whole needs. This may not be easy, because each company has dozens of AI groups with contradictory and incompatible aims. (Traditionally vendors have exploited these situations and reaped hefty commissions.) Therefore, the company has the responsibility to create its own consensus and impose that on the vendor community. At first, it may only request that certain standards be embodied in vendor products. Later, it may ask for new features in future generations of the vendors' products. There may also be a request to follow certain protocols when making a sale.

Cognition Improvement Training

AI mines the minds, maps the expertise, and enhances the learning of companies. It discovers ways people in the company think and act. It continually uncovers mental processes all across the firm. As movement toward Expert Electronic Social Systems is made, AI locates mental process under the most mundane company decisions and activities. All this can be fed into company training programs, company career development, and company job design. This Cognition Improvement Training construct teaches the company to develop, manage and use this data on cognition by-product of AI. Metacognitive Organizations excel at this.

17

A New Outlook

AI Circles Programs

Ideally, a firm has already established a circles program tradition when artificial intelligence arrives. Like any other new technology, AI becomes part of the circles implementation program. For most of the world's firms, this is an impossibility, because they have no circles programs.

The quality circles mentioned in this chapter are the type found in Japan where each work group implements solutions it designed itself. Should the work group lack particular skills, the members teach themselves what they need to know under the supervision of a local expert. American circles programs suffer from a classic (and terminal) case of all talk and no action. I examined several American company circles programs, and some had lists of over seventy-five designed solutions per work group. None ever got off the drawing board. Their solution designs were given over to the ordinary company work assignment system where none of the circle proposals had any priority. These circles designed hundreds of solutions, all of which were subsequently ignored. The difference between the two types of circles programs can be summed up this way: Japanese quality circles implement their own designed solutions; American quality circles implement nothing.

In an AI Circles Program, then, each work group of the company is invited to design an expert system tailored to its own needs. It may even design an application for another area of the firm where the need may have gone unrecognized.

The following paragraphs describe a number of AI delivery problems that can be solved by implementing an AI Circles Program.

First, unless there is a general coordinated effort, there will be chaotic, incompatible AI projects scattered throughout the firm. However, there is also a danger in centralized coordination. A bureaucratic structure can greatly slow down use of the technology in order to achieve compatible systems. Compatibility and quick dissemination of the new technology can be accomplished simultaneously. AI circles permit every work group to try out a uniform, companywide curriculum of AI implementation. Its uniformity insures systems compatibility; its companywide character insures technology dissemination.

Second, in the usual American-style AI programs, career aspirations wreak havoc with projects. The AI core group slows down the spread of the technology to maintain its mystique (as well as their high salaries). The most politically astute group (not the most qualified) forms overall AI policy. This generally insures a second-rate program for the firm. An AI circles program prevents the technology from stagnating in the hands of elitist experts or corporate politicos. Circles spread the technology so quickly that, in spite of themselves, AI core group members end up transferring their expertise to ordinary workers rather than hoarding it.

Third, "wildflowers" AI projects are common in undisciplined AI programs. Indeed, Mahler's Dupont approach suffers from this. Various groups start projects for various reasons. The groups do not consult or communicate with each other. For this reason, each project is unique. It becomes hard to judge a project's success (or failure), because there is no basis for comparison in the firm. With the absence of norms, bad projects are prolonged. An AI Circles Program can impose a standard discipline of AI project development across hundreds of work groups simultaneously (through part-time participation of each work group in weekly circles meetings). This discipline and development standard become a base line for comparing AI projects and for insuring quality from the start.

Fourth, most company AI programs in the United States don't really know where problem areas exist. American firms have a propensity to be driven by the technical content of technologies. They omit the mapping of the application domain and the designing of delivery vehicles. Consequently, a lot of resources are allotted to projects of marginal economic value to the firm. The AI Circles approach has a cure for this. Each week, as part of its curriculum, it maps out the problem domain for AI in each workplace.

Fifth, no one, especially the experts in the firm, has free time. No one wants to commit a large block of an expert's valuable time to what could turn out to be a very time-consuming AI project. This prevents most AI projects from even getting started. Because circles programs are part-time and have deliberately slowed down the development process, they can get by with as few as four hours a week of an expert's time. This multiplies by hundreds the number of AI projects that can be initiated. Moreover, by having each work group in the firm build an AI project, every expert can become involved with what the technology has to offer. Also, AI development ends up being done where the domain knowledge resides, not in some central AI group at headquarters.

Sixth, many managers and workers lack confidence to work in new technologies. AI Circles build confidence by demonstrating how employees all over the firm can implement a new technology on a gradual basis. The Circles establish that everyone in the firm is capable of learning the new technology.

Seventh, in many firms, those who are interested in new technologies have no auspices under which to become involved. An AI Circles program welcomes everyone who wants to find out more.

Eighth, many managers have no incentive to implement new technologies. They are rewarded only for not making errors, and a new untested technology offers fertile ground for mistakes. AI Circles increment new technologies so gradually that only small outlays of time and money will be needed. This considerably lowers the risk for any one work group.

AI Circles programs offer a number of advantages. First, they offer common AI systems, standards, and tools for use in projects across the firm. Second, they invite participation in the new technology by identifying and developing all areas that may have an interest. Third, through circle conferences, those designing superior applications and those feigning quality can be publicly exposed. This establishes a level of self-correcting quality. Fourth, circles establish a basis of comparison for projects using common training tools and project development discipline. Fifth, circles bring AI to the domain experts in the plants and offices of the company. They move AI away from elite headquarters staff offices. Sixth, AI circles demand minimal time investment by busy experts, thereby expanding the number of projects that can be undertaken. Seventh, AI circles programs follow a certain sequence of events. Each work group can experience incremental victories with the technology and gain confidence. Eighth, the AI circles program creates standards for vendor tools and eliminates vendor domination of AI strategy. This lowers costs to the firm.

There is no one set way to design an AI Circles program. The components discussed here illustrate one way to go about it. A number of factors determine the final structure of an individual company's circles program: the way AI was established before circles were started, the types of projects to be undertaken, competitive opportunities in the industry, and the window of opportunity for each of those competitive opportunities. Three kinds of people belong in every circle: a domain expert, work group members willing to learn AI and perform the coding, and others outside the work group who have no training in AI but wish to learn.

An AI circle meets every week for two and one half hours—split between company time and personal time. Informally, the members spend additional time on circles activities. The formal meeting represents nothing more than a starting point. Each week, the firm prepares a formal schedule which outlines the week's work load for all AI circles. This allows all work groups to share common insights, learning, vocabulary and issues. Conferences continue the momentum of the weekly meetings. On a quarterly basis, all AI groups assemble to evaluate projects and suggest improvements. Outside experts may be invited to analyze written code and offer help. (They are not permitted, however, to give lectures or make speeches.) Biannual conferences are held on specialized topics that benefit all circle members. And annually, those who have excelled are honored at an awards conference.

Tools courses, Problem Solving Events, auxiliary development, three-tier training systems and other background components become the library of resources for all circles. Circles have one more characteristic—they replicate themselves. That means, every eighteen months, each circle creates a new circle and trains it in techniques and applications. This establishes new generations of involvement and a training dynamic between generations. This gives first generation participants the leadership and teaching experience to deepen their understanding of AI. It is also an incentive for other workers who aspire to leadership roles to join the circles program early. A well-designed whole company circles program will demonstrate that many different types of work groups can participate in any given technology. For example, if there is a Robotics Circles program throughout the company, then employees in the finance department can design new methods of accounting that better reflect the actual cost benefits of the robotics program. It requires talented people to design ways for all work groups to participate in some kinds of new technology. AI is easier to handle in a circles format than many technologies, because it is useful in all areas of the firm where expertise and software already exist.

Setting Up an AI Program

This section summarizes and integrates previously presented material. The sixteen steps that lead to a viable AI program are put in chronological order.

1. The world's rarest commodity, a person deeply trained in AI who thinks and acts like a businessperson, must be hired.
2. This person then hires a handful of competent college graduates who have programming background but no AI training.
3. Management recommendations to build one showcase AI application to give the technology "credibility" should be ignored. That approach is needlessly conservative and indirectly insults the intelligence of ordinary managers throughout the firm.
4. All divisions should be polled for their views on firm needs and not firm needs for AI. Roles that AI can play to support existing priorities can then be spotted.
5. The first projects pay for the AI hardware and software.
6. The expert trains the college graduates in embedded-style AI using expert system-building tools running on a workstation environment.
7. AI Application Workshop Fairs are held to cultivate participants so that some key divisions generate seed funding for AI.
8. Pilot divisions must be chosen where a certain critical mass of AI projects will be reached. Pilot functions within those divisions must also be chosen where critical mass within that function will be reached. Effort must be concentrated to make these two pilots succeed. This makes the sponsoring top managers into heroes, and it creates envy in all their competitor managers. These envious managers become interested in AI.
9. Regionally located Group Structured Readings and Group Structured Coding Sessions are sponsored. These overt training activities are open to everyone and allow constituencies to be built up for AI projects throughout the firm. AI opportunities that exist in all divisions are noticed.
10. A two week code development rhythm for the AI group must be established. Initial small AI projects are then created at lower costs than competitor projects. Also, fewer hours of expert time are required.
11. Expert platform development for the pilot function in the pilot division begins.

12. Divisional sponsor supports an initial ten circle AI Circles program. Training and code development begin in each of those circles.
13. A Problem Solving Team of consultants and AI core members begin solving the first project problems.
14. Projects are started in several divisions. Some have identical AI function even though they are in different domain areas. Each project then receives low-cost divisional funding. This, in effect, achieves multiple payment for the same project. The excess funding is then used to develop a platform to be shared across all divisions.
15. At an annual AI conference, the AI circles discuss their pilot projects and the effect they had on the division's performance. The presence of the press, AI vendors, and outside experts gain recognition for these AI pioneers.
16. Intensified AI Application Tours capture new interest in AI generated by the annual conference.

These sixteen steps are not to be construed as the sole recipe for success. They are merely guidelines that represent the absolute minimum necessary to begin an AI program. It would be hard to create a program with less. To insure minimum success for a brand new AI program there must be:

1. A million dollars a year for several years allocated for AI that is applied to one function in one division. This money is budgeted within twelve months of the project's start.
2. Ten AI Circles operating in one division within one year of AI program start.
3. Two hundred fifty domain experts trained in AI techniques within one year from start.
4. Fifty AI projects under negotiation for divisional funding within one year. These monies are neither corporate nor R&D funding.
5. Two expert platforms defined, funded and under development in conjunction with AI projects being developed to run on them.

Theories of AI Delivery

The four theories presented in this section enabled the AI programs I set up to use visibility to gain needed resources for profound strategic commitments to AI expert platforms within a year of start. They combine Eastern and Western perspectives. The Western theories emphasize use of visibility and the creation of poleis around new technologies. The Eastern theories emphasize the tactics that attack historical underpinnings of company practices using Monastic Management techniques to gain undistracted employee attention.

These theories offer U.S. firms a way to set up Social Delivery Systems for new technologies. To Japanese firms, these theories offer guidance to speed up innovation and make it more responsive. They offer a greater "space of appearance" in the events and routines of the firm. There are obviously other theories that achieve similar ends, but these four are presented because they made the successful transition from abstract theory to concrete results in the real world.

The first of these theories, the "Sand, Pearl, Oyster" theory, is derived from the work of Hannah Arendt, the leading scholar in the twentieth century on poleis and democracy. Much of her work is relevant to the spread of technology in industry. She presents the concept that human beings who promise to cooperate together on certain projects can create power out of nothing. They vow to create activity where there was none and establish communication between persons who did not communicate before. She also explains the need that all new things have for "darkness" or protected privacy and the eventual emergence of "words and deeds" into a public realm of competition and limelight.

Some may be puzzled by the name Sand, Pearl, Oyster, and wonder how it applies to industry. The sand is an irritant that provokes the soft oyster into manufacturing a pearl to protect itself from the source of irritation. In the corporation, the "irritant" might take the form of a quiet buildup of impressive initial AI projects, of funding support, and of people trained to work on the projects. AI technology basks in the corporate limelight as the star of AI Application Workshop Fairs and AI Circles Conferences until the rest of the organization—the oyster—reacts. It may attempt to take over the AI program or it may copy some of its most innovative aspects. The latter is what is needed; the former (called "vulturization" in the Sand, Oyster, Pearl theory) is what is too often seen.

The second theory is called "Interest Formulation." It treats the tactics of initial AI program setup as probes into the organization that generate data about priorities, politics and so on. It creates events that heighten visibility for new technology, thereby creating a new source of power from nothing. In this respect, the Interest Formulation theory is similar to the Sand, Pearl, Oyster theory. It makes the latent interest in AI throughout the company manifest. Then it translates that newly visible interest into events and ongoing structures like Group Structured Readings and AI Application Qualification Tours.

The third theory, "Contradiction Analysis," was devised by the Chinese. It separates a firm's business concerns into two levels. Firms routinely operate at the level of the problem to be solved, avoided or delayed. Contradiction Analysis takes the firm to a level that underlies the everyday problem solving routine. This deeper level examines the historical forces operating within the firm. These forces determine which problems are generated and which of these problems are extremely resistant to contemporary solutions. This level dissolves the accidental and the incidental into the inevitable historical trend. This theory operates nearly everywhere in Japan and allows the Japanese to make strategic modifications to the techniques that they copy from others.

The fourth theory, "Monastic Management," originated in Japan over two hundred years ago. The Buddhist influence is apparent in this theory with its ideals of good management and the role workers play in the planning and the growth of the entire enterprise. Quite simply, the good managers are those people who never handle a single issue because well-trained workers are able to deal with the normal variations in the work routine. A good manager relies on his section members to handle all of the daily work and helps them to anticipate all potential issues. In modern Japanese companies, the senior managers will have spotlessly clean desks. One incident I witnessed will make clear exactly what is at stake here. At one firm the manager had the requisite uncluttered desk. And then the unthinkable happened—one morning his desk telephone rang. He was visibly upset and this show of emotion is rare in a Japanese businessman in his fifties. He retreated from the phone and ordered one of his assistants to answer it. He listened in dismay while his assistant spoke. Later at lunch I asked the assistant about the incident and his superior's reaction. He explained that if a manager is doing his job well, there is absolutely no reason for his phone to ever ring. The manager should have anticipated all problems and issues. A ringing telephone publicly announces a manager's failure to do his job well. To Americans, this may seem like a fanatical response to a common occurrence, but it is not considered an extreme incident in Japan.

The implementation of these four theories will benefit groups attempting to deliver new technological systems. In the case of AI, the fight for central resources to fund new technologies is eliminated. The price of new technologies is actually lowered. There is no struggle with established power groups for a share of the annual budget, because the power behind the new technology is newly created. Secondly, these theories create a public "space of appearance" for the early pioneers in a new technology. This enhances career prospects as new technologies are viewed as the path to success. There is no faster way to distribute a new technology than by convincing people that it will gain them the respect and attention of their superiors.

Thirdly, these theories set minimal levels of attention, discipline, and code development (every two weeks) that exceed the level of work performed in the most industrious sections of the firm. This visible intensity and discipline win the trust of clients and upper management who are pleased to see excellence overcoming mediocrity. Because those workers are free from distractions, they win the respect of managers who have tired of technical groups that have devolved into self-interest groups whining for special privileges.

Fourth, the AI group embodies, in its own internal discipline and dynamics, resolutions to major historical dislocation of corporate practice in late twentieth century America. The AI group serves as a positive example to other groups in the firm. This is one of the Eastern aspects of the four theories coming into play—a unique mood of peaceful intensity and undistracted anticipation of change. Not to be forgotten, AI itself, as one of the Cognitive Technologies, changes the social and cognitive properties of the firm after implementation becomes widespread. Firms able to digest AI rapidly join the future early and have the chance to develop profound competitive advantage over their rivals.

An Agrarian View of Industry

The Japanese will tell you that their industrial organizations share the same principles as their rural society. This perplexes Westerners to whom industry and agriculture occupy opposite ends of the spectrum. But those Westerners with enough patience to explore the relationship between Japanese industry and rural society will find similarities in structure. They will gain an understanding of how Japanese culture generates new techniques. The Japanese see new technology, skilled employees, and competitor firms from an entirely different vantage point than Americans and Europeans. The Japanese gain great competitive advantage from this different perspective. Many Japanese apply a metaphor to their own workplaces. They compare Japanese industry to farms. These industrial farms raise two kinds of crops: people and technologies. This rural perspective of "raising" new technologies has some subtle properties. Of course, you cannot deliver a complex technology by metaphor. This section describes the general background that works to create concrete delivery systems for new technologies in Japan.

The two bonuses a year employees receive in Japan correspond to the two harvests a year in village Japan. Ringi documents passed around offices correspond to ringi used 600 years ago in village Japan. The flow system of production in Japanese factories corresponds to village irrigation of hillside rice paddies. A Japanese firm views its new technologies much in the same way a farmer views his crops. The new technology is basic to the firm's financial health just the way a crop is to the farm. That is, the new technology is not a product in the same way as a crop, but it is carefully cultivated using certain principles. A crop is fertilized, rotated into different fields, weeded, monitored for growth, and managed through changes of weather. Technologies, too, are carefully nurtured. Similarly, the people of a Japanese firm, as cohorts hired together, are cultivated in the same painstaking manner.

This is an entirely new outlook for American industry. This view preaches a patient and forbearing attitude toward new technologies and company workers. Both the people and the technologies must be slowly nurtured through "diseases" and periods of "inclement weather." A firm devotes a lot of time and resources to this growing process. If these human and technological crops are poorly raised, they underperform and the firm reaps no profits. The Japanese have a tradition of patience which is evident in their handling of people and technologies. Historians have studied this rural attitude to Japanese industry and offer the following theory. Japan remained a feudal country until the early twentieth century when it rushed headlong into the postindustrial age of knowledge and business. It omitted the transitional industrial age phase that other Western countries went through. Japanese industry essentially escaped (substantial pollution notwithstanding) the by-products and scars of industrialization.

In the West, the communal world of feudalism was broken up, and for two hundred years workers endured the harsh conditions that characterized the industrial revolution. The bonds and relationships between human beings that had existed in feudal times were abruptly severed. Labor unions exist in the West, some say, to fill this communal void. Japan, by contrast, never lost her communal roots and established the same powerful social forms in the midst of advanced technical systems. High technology, then, may be the logical next step after farming.

Japanese firms are structured to emphasize these rural characteristics. Japanese firms hire a whole crop of graduating students once a year. Each crop is carefully selected to offer a necessary balance of talents and technical skills. In formal stages, the new crop of people is socialized into the life of the firm. Each employee crop arrives with the technical skills that each person embodies. In essence, the Japanese do not raise two separate crops in their firms but rather one person-technology crop. Often firms hire forty or fifty new employees at one time, all of them with the same technical background and skills. Suddenly, everyone in the firm is aware of a new technology. American firms do not show the long-term patience required to cultivate a new technology. They are too anxious for results and implement technologies poorly-conceived strategies. They expect too much or too little from a technology, and it never fulfills the company's expectations. People become bitter as careers are placed in jeopardy by recalcitrant technologies. The United States could very well benefit from a closer look at the Japanese rural approach to industry.

Structural Reading

When the Cognitive Technologies penetrate firms, they will encourage people to manage their own cognitive patterns and acts. This Meta-Cognitive Organization has been prefigured by certain social systems—some Japanese and some American—that used people as processors in a parallel array. That is, companies envisioned organizations as "compute" facilities and people as the processors. They distributed work that was usually only done by elite groups in staff offices over that array. Such vital functions as research and development, sales, and new product development were distributed so that many people performed these functions. Some scholars refer to Japanese ways of handling new technologies as social connectionism (from connectionist computers).

The advent of the Expert Electronic Social System (EESS) will expand the kinds of work any one person can do. Rigid job definitions will become blurred. Many firms, victims of their own backward thinking, will be in the awkward position of prohibiting their employees from doing as much work as they can capably do. This conflict between medieval theories of managing people and the realities of Expert Electronic Social Systems will rage on until the winners emerge. The more innovative firms will exploit the new technical alternatives to defeat their more traditional competitors. Eventual victory for EESS is assured.

Where is the Cognitive Delivery Vehicle leading us? The Cognitive Delivery Vehicle not only enables a new technology like AI to be delivered with understanding and quality, it also presages a fundamentally new form of social integration, the Expert Electronic Social System. The Cognitive Delivery Vehicle consists of the following functions which are socially embedded in the Social Delivery Vehicle. Using AI as an example, the Cognitive Delivery Vehicle:

1. Measures and manages the cognitive effectiveness of AI program tactics.
2. Measures and manages the cognitive effectiveness of AI systems when employed in the workplace.
3. Measures and manages the effect of an organization's learning properties for AI delivery and use.
4. Manages the mental protocols across EESS work tasks in the firm across the network.
5. Researches and tests competitive thrust and benefits of EESS realization of functions which are only socially realized at present.
6. Establishes an ever-increasing level of thinking skills and formal cognitive methods which are involved in doing the most routine kinds of human interactions—at first in EESS and then face-to-face.

The Cognitive Delivery Vehicle manages a kind of mental intensity to technology delivery. It sees that every AI delivery tactic is interesting enough to capture everyone's attention. Knowing how to deliver AI is not enough. The delivery tactics must attract enough attention to achieve worker commitment. The Cognitive Delivery Vehicle transforms edge-of-field research into readily learnable increments that any worker in the firm can train himself to do. It makes AI the form of system documentation for all new systems in the firm. The Cognitive Delivery Vehicle manages the effect of the Cognitive Technologies on the learning properties of the workplace as well as the learning properties of new technologies in the workplace.

Finally, the Cognitive Delivery Vehicle formally applies the results of cognitive science research to organizational improvement. Cognitive science insights are the natural by-products of the thousands of experts who have been protocol-analyzed by AI programs. Cognitive science today is a body of knowledge in research communities. It was established as a by-product of AI work that went on in universities and labs. The Cognitive Delivery Vehicle in firms is an applied cognitive science function that probes into human social forms of cognition and EESS forms of cognition and puts them under participatory redesign and improvement events. For the firm, this means a technical imagination beyond competitors, managed to perform several steps beyond the norm for any technical field. Rather than merely keeping up with the Joneses, a firm can do now what the Joneses will not be doing for another seven or eight years. Japan's best firms are probing consumers' minds using neural net computers to detect consumer preferences before consumers themselves detect their own preferences and model those in expert systems. It is not as hard as it seems to establish cognitive minimal levels of performance. Many people in organizations spend too much time in unproductive meetings and discussions. Experiments that I carried out in Japan proved that cognitive minima could be slowly established for social face-to-face encounters and be established even more rapidly for EESS activities.

My experiment uncovered a key measure of mental ability that separated top Japanese managers from middle managers. This experiment used a method of reading a hierarchy of themes that unite parts of any text. This method was developed based on research by Kintsch, Dijk and Meyer. I present it here as one example of the many cognitive science constructs that can be used to manage new cognitive minimal levels of performance across whole firms.

In Structural Reading, any one text can be broken down into sixteen different diagrams. There are specific methods of producing each diagram. They serve as a picture of the points of a text. They visually display the number of main points, the name of each point, and the principle by which the main points are ordered. This is done in a simple, two-dimensional diagram. The ability to write out such a diagram is less useful than the ability to mentally construct such a diagram while listening to a lecture, following a discussion, or reading a passage. I tested workers at all education levels in three Japanese firms using the same text passages. There was no opportunity for consultation between groups. All groups were given simple two hundred word paragraphs and asked to list the main points, the name of each main point, and the ordering principle. They were given forty minutes for the task. The results of this test indicated that no one named themes well but managers outperformed the rest. If this were a test of any randomly chosen cognitive skill, it would hardly matter. Instead, it is a test of ability to discern main points from a two hundred word passage. Needless to say, an organization where most of the workers cannot even indicate the main points has lots of room for cognition improvement.

Our technologies are transforming the workplace. In effect, they are the workplace. Right now we have reached an impasse with our technologies. Video taperecorders now have so many features people cannot operate them at all, for one example. We have to make them understandable to people so that they serve people and not themselves. Natural language is an increasingly poor medium for fundamental communication. Specialized communities develop lingos, jargon, and ritual patterns of discourse interaction that all improve the efficiency and reliability of natural language itself. Structural Reading is one technique from the cognitive sciences that elevates the minimal level of mental operation in every meeting, discussion and report. A gradual ten year Structural Reading campaign would not place strain on any one person, but its cumulative effect would lift the firm above its competitors. Computer programs have main points as do paintings, discussions, remarks, careers, and competitor moves. Each one of these topics can be diagrammed in a Structural Reading Program. Everyone tested experienced difficulty managing main points in normal company discourse. The converse of Structural Reading is Structural Writing. Geometric and image combinations of ideas are formally transformed into text using principles that ensure the number of main points, their names, and their order will be obvious to the reader.

Change of the Cognitive Technologies

The combined pressures of Japanese competition and new technologies are producing an interesting synthesis. Larry Hirshhorn at the Wharton School is researching socio-technical systems and the ways new technologies open up whole new vistas for worker participation in the design of their organizations and their work. Terry Winograd is building a theory of system design as the design of organization and work. The Japanese are learning to achieve more and more of the characteristics of the new technical world in face-to-face social forms.

In the clash and mesh of these new ideas, systems designers are switching strategy. They are abandoning the approach to technology application based on replacing people. Instead, they are working on an approach where technology augments human social encounters and functions. This more modest strategy can easily be seen in Japanese factories where little blue cardboard cards are used for scheduling alongside the technical capabilities of networks of workstations all over the firm. Let's now examine some of the edge-of-field topics in the cognitive technologies that are shaping AI's future evolution.

Computer-Supported Cooperative Work

In late 1986, the first conference on Computer-Supported Cooperative Work was held. Many of those in attendance thought this new field represented the intersection of a half dozen edge-of-field disciplines. This conference heralded the coming of a new, de-individualized form of software that will allow real time workshopping across networks of workstations. This will enhance AI shared knowledgebase networks with a real time component.

Cognitive Measurement of Work

How are we doing in terms of cognitive performance? No one knows because no instruments have been created to measure group cognitive performance and performance in social interactions. New sciences such as Meeting Science, Remark Making Science, and Act-Speaks Communication Science need to be developed.

A Neutral Cognitive Currency Across Disciplines

Cognitive Science now has a fairly well developed mental operator vocabulary with which to form common ground across disciplines. The establishment of this neutral currency will require a formal research effort. This neutral currency is needed to express different disciplines, their concerns, methods, assumptions, targets, and accomplishments. This is the heart of a fundamental restructuring of all knowledge being started by AI.

Socio-Technics of Distributed Computing

If successful, this body of research will prevent corporations from "upgrading" their computer systems by running obsolete programs on newer, faster hardware. To fully utilize networked computers, Expert Electronic Social Systems will have to be built. Each step in the implementation of an Expert Electronic Social System will be supported by a business case. Electronic sociality, new work coordination software, electronic patent systems, and whole workforce authorship are some of the social/technical inventions being generated by this work.

Cognitive Augmentation of Work

Meeting Science, Remark-Making Science, Error Science, and the other Cognitive Sciences that will be developed over the next ten years are breathtakingly trite and mundane on one level and therefore offer immense productivity improvement on another level. The

Cognitive Sciences are transforming the most mundane aspects of doing business and thereby allowing quality and competitiveness to depend more and more on the general capabilities of whole work forces. Like the Saint says, look to the lowest of God's children for your revolutions.

Technology Transfer

This is where a lean new form of automation is being born—a form that is competitive from the start. It is easily learned and implemented by work forces. This area of research distinguishes human ways of doing things and the computer ways of doing things. It used to be that corporations justified complex computer systems for no other reason than they offered the latest scientific achievements. Now the Japanese are streamlining and simplifying their production systems and are replacing the machines with people. Simplified human social systems accomplish more than complex computer systems. Moreover, they do it more reliably and less expensively. Swedes are researching these six edge-of-field disciplines. They represent a modest start on a whole new set of technical fronts needing research and application. They are a real opportunity for the United States to push ahead of the Japanese—an opportunity that the United States cannot afford to lose.